D0875403

**Multinational Corporations,
Environment, and the Third World**

# Multinational Corporations,

# Environment, and the Third World

Business Matters

Edited by Charles S. Pearson

A WORLD RESOURCES INSTITUTE BOOK

Published by Duke University Press
Duke Press Policy Studies
Durham 1987

© 1987 Duke University Press

All rights reserved

Printed in the United States of America on
acid-free paper ∞

Library of Congress Cataloging-in-Publication Data

Multinational corporations, environment, and the Third
World: business matters.

(Duke Press policy studies)

Based on an international meeting held in 1984 and
sponsored by the World Resources Institute.

Bibliography: p.

Includes index.

1. Environmental policy—Developing countries.
2. Natural resources—Developing countries—Management.
3. International business enterprises—Management—
Environmental aspects—Developing countries.
I. Pearson, Charles S.  II. World Resources Institute.
III. Series.

HC59.72.E5M85 1987   363.7′009172′4   86-19810

ISBN 0-8223-0707-3

ISBN 0-8223-0761-8 (pbk.)

# Contents

Tables and Figures

Foreword

Without fanfare or adversarial tension, a new consensus has formed in the 1980s on priority resource and environmental issues of international concern. Worldwide, the losses of agricultural land and soil, the depletion of tropical forests, the extinction of critical genetic resources, climate change as "greenhouse gases" accumulate in the atmosphere, rapid population growth, air pollution, freshwater mismanagement and shortages, overfishing and marine pollution, improper handling of toxic substances, and mismanagement of energy resources make up the list scientists and others now believe should provide the environmental agenda for the rest of this century. Collectively, these threats bode more harm for the poor countries than for the rich. But their effects cannot be isolated. And industrialized countries —especially the private sector—possess much of the know-how, technology, and capital needed to tackle these problems before they become irreversible or forbiddingly expensive to treat.

In *Multinational Corporations, Environment, and the Third World: Business Matters*, the obligation of the rich to the poor or of the technologically advanced to the not so advanced is not the issue. Instead, the *convergence* of political, economic, and humanitarian reasons for multinational corporations to help take on the environmental agenda is. The course of action urged by conscience or diplomacy makes practical business sense as it never has before. It is now plainer than ever that self-interest bids multinational business to help protect and enhance economically important resources no matter how far from headquarters they may lie. Equally clear is that if multinational businesses do not set high standards of conduct for themselves, they could face increasingly rigid or inconsistent regulation and restraints. Multinational corporations also need assured access to resources and stable markets abroad. An underlying issue here is international business's operating latitude. As former World Bank president Robert S. McNamara put it to a group of business leaders in late 1984, "There is not going to be corporate freedom to deal with markets in the kind of world we'll be facing in the year 2000 and certainly in the first quarter of the next century unless we are more farsighted [about population and environmental problems] today."

Since 1983, World Resources Institute has worked closely with multinational corporations to put the emerging international environmental agenda into terms that make sense to business and to sustain a dialogue on the respective roles of multinational corporations and developing-country governments in Third World environmental management. Several WRI studies—which culminate in this book—have explored key relationships between natural resource management and business's long-term economic interests in developing countries. In addition, WRI's Private Sector Initiatives Project has many times brought business leaders together, most recently in Bangkok, to consider such issues as the need to control pollution from small and mid-sized firms and the need to strengthen national environmental protection agencies in developing countries.

Nowhere is WRI's approach to multinational corporations' stake in the international environmental agenda clearer than in *Multinational Corporations, Environment, and the Third World*. Charles Pearson and his colleagues separate fact from myth, put questions of corporate and government responsibility into economic and political perspective, test theories about the newly industrialized countries' changing resource-management practices and mores against detailed case studies, and draw the generalizations and recommendations that documented research permits. Their informed and pragmatic approach to the resource-management challenge now before the international business community and both industrial- and developing-country governments represents the best hope for finding common ground over what is, after all, common ground—the land and other natural resources on which economies and civilizations ultimately depend.

James Gustave Speth
President, World Resources Institute

## Acknowledgments

Editing a volume of research studies with multinational authorship can be a fine balance of pleasure and pain. In this instance, however, the pain was minimal because of the superb cooperation of the authors, whom I collectively thank. I also wish to thank Gus Speth and Jessica Mathews for their intellectual contributions and for the full support of the World Resources Institute in the project and publication. Kathleen Courrier and Linda Starke provided invaluable editorial assistance, helping me and the book in equal measure, and I thank them also. Frances Meehan has done an outstanding job of typing, retyping, and typing once again the many drafts of the papers, all with unfailing speed, accuracy, and good humor, and I am greatly in her debt.

C.S.P.

Editor's Introduction

Environmental and natural resource degradation, increasingly serious problems in the Third World, threaten long-term development in some countries. The problems arise from two sources—a vicious cycle of poverty, natural resource abuse, and greater poverty, and in some countries or regions, pollution and environmental degradation incidental to rapid industrialization and economic growth.

Multinational corporations play an important economic role in many developing countries. The recent trend toward greater reliance on the private sector and the desire to substitute foreign direct investment for international commercial bank lending may strengthen that role. Relatively little is known about the relationships between MNC's, environment, and development. What is the environmental performance of foreign-owned firms in the Third World? Is it better or worse than that of domestic firms? Are MNC's part of the problem or part of the solution? How are MNC's adapting to the more stringent environmental regulations in host countries, and what problems arise for the regulators? How can environmental disputes between MNC's and host countries be avoided and how can the generally superior technical and managerial expertise in international business be harnessed to improve environmental management? What are the interests, responsibilities, and policies of *home* country governments in regulating the overseas activities of their MNC's?

Analyzing these issues is difficult. Discussions of environment and development, and of MNC's and development, are as often emotional as factual. In industrial countries, the need for government to regulate private-sector behavior and reverse environmental deterioration has only quite recently been recognized. The problem is compounded in poor developing countries, which struggle with a Hobbesian choice, perhaps more apparent than real, between economic growth and environmental quality. The presence of foreign direct investment by MNC's further complicates the debate. MNC's, if profitable, produce a surplus. The distribution of this surplus between the firm and the host country is highly contentious, and is at the root of most investment disputes. In short, the nexus of MNC's, environment, and development generates two controversial issues—how to protect the public interest from private environmental abuse while maintaining economic growth and how to secure the host country's national objectives in its relations with MNC's.

The common theme of multinational corporations, environment, and development has many facets, and research on a variety of economic sectors, issues, and countries is needed for a rounded picture. World Resources Institute, as part of its Private Sector Initiatives project, commissioned the eleven studies that form this volume. The topics and authors were selected to reflect a diversity of approaches. Thomas Gladwin, in a comprehensive overview chapter, traces how our understanding of the apparent trade-off between environment and economic development has evolved. The earlier view of a sharp conflict between environment and growth has softened, and the concept of sustainable development as the spline joining the two has emerged. Gladwin also traces the parallel evolution of environmental policies and practices within corporations and within developing countries. Gladwin analyzes the need for international governmental cooperation in regulating the environmental behavior of MNC's and concludes with an agenda for further research.

Developing countries depend heavily on natural resources—agriculture, forestry, fishing, and mining. While pollution problems are not absent in these sectors, the rational long-term management of the resource base is an additional environmental concern. The three case studies in section II, by William Pintz, Malcolm Gillis, and Louis Goodman, consider the environmental role of MNC's in the Ok Tedi copper mining project in Papua New Guinea, in tropical forestry in Indonesia, and in the agricultural pesticide industry in Mexico. One common theme in these natural resource studies is conflicting interests between development and environment-oriented agencies *within* the host country.

Section III examines three contentious issues involving international trade and investment, and the policies and responsibilities of *home* governments in industrial countries. I analyze the relocation of "dirty" industry, through trade and direct investment to so-called "pollution havens" and conclude that the problem has been exaggerated. Jacob Scherr looks at policies toward the export of hazardous products, an issue of sharp national and international debate. Finally, Barry Castleman investigates evidence of MNCs' "double standard" on environmental health and safety in their industrial versus their developing-country locations and argues for mobilizing public pressure on MNC's.

In section IV two authors from the Third World, Engin Ural and João Carlos Pimenta, present country case studies for Turkey and Brazil. Both countries have achieved great success in industrialization, but pollution is exacting a high price. Environmental legislation is in its infancy in Turkey; in some respects, control at the state level in São Paulo has outdistanced federal control in Brazil. Neither author finds that MNC's are viewed within the countries as the principal culprits in industrial pollution.

The Bhopal tragedy raises complex questions. By its nature an industrial accident is not deliberate, although it is possibly foreseeable. This contrasts with effluent and emission standards and the regulation of natural resource exploitation, in which calculated decisions are often made to tolerate some pollution or resource degradation. The two chapters in section V, one by Thomas Gladwin and one by Wil Lepkowski, use the Bhopal experience to return us to this book's central theme—MNC environmental performance in the Third World and how it can be improved.

The book concludes with the Conference Statement and Guidelines for Multinational Corporations and Host Countries, both of which grew out of an international meeting of business, government, and private environmental experts held in 1984 and sponsored by World Resources Institute. The guidelines summarize steps that corporations, governments, and private organizations might take to improve environmental management in developing countries.

Drawing general conclusions from these differing studies is difficult, and each author provides his own. Still, a few common features emerge. Developing countries are changing their views toward both MNC's (becoming more pragmatic) and environmental protection (now seen more as a necessity, less a luxury). The results, however, are distressingly modest, not least because the position of new environmental agencies is weak vis à vis powerful domestic development ministries and because excessive attention has been paid to legislation at the expense of monitoring and enforcement.

The available evidence suggests that multinational corporations and domestic firms receive similar legal treatment with respect to environmental regulations. But because MNC's are large, visible, foreign, and guests they may be held to higher implicit standards than local firms. Their superior financial, technical, and management expertise suggests they can play an important and constructive role in improving environmental management in the Third World, but they must be motivated or induced to do so.

MNC environmental performance itself is probably better, on average, than that of local firms, and some evidence indicates that environmental concerns are being slowly built into corporate policies and procedures. Enlightened long-term self-interest by corporations will relieve some problems, but a need to protect the public interest from what economists call external costs, along with tension over the distribution of the surplus, suggests that improved regulation of MNC's by the environmental authorities of developing countries remains an important task.

Finally, although widespread industrial relocation for environmental reasons through MNC trade and investment does not appear to be a critical problem for either industrial or developing countries, the control of hazardous exports and the improvement of the workplace environment will continue to be subject to spirited public debate.

C.S.P.

Contributors

**Charles S. Pearson** is an Adjunct Senior Associate at the World Resources Institute and Professor of International Economics at the Johns Hopkins University School of Advanced International Studies in Washington, D.C.

**Barry I. Castleman** is an Environmental Consultant in Baltimore, Maryland.

**Malcolm Gillis** is Dean of the Graduate School and Professor of Public Policy Studies and Economics at Duke University in Durham, North Carolina.

**Thomas N. Gladwin** is Associate Professor of Management and International Business at New York University.

**Louis W. Goodman** is Professor and Dean of the School of International Service at American University in Washington, D.C.

**Wil Lepkowski** is a Senior Editor at *Chemical and Engineering News* in Washington, D.C.

**João Carlos P. Pimenta** is an Environmental Engineer and Consultant in São Paulo, Brazil.

**William Pintz** is a Research Associate at the East-West Center in Honolulu, Hawaii.

**S. Jacob Scherr** is Senior Staff Attorney at the Natural Resources Defense Council in Washington, D.C.

**Engin Ural** is Secretary General of the Environmental Problems Foundation of Turkey in Ankara, Turkey.

# I  Background and Overview

# CHAPTER ONE  Environment, Development, and

## Multinational Enterprise

Thomas N. Gladwin

This chapter provides a general overview as to how corporate, national, and international views and practices have been evolving with regard to the interactions of environment, development, and multinational enterprise. The first section surveys the evolution of the environment-development debate and hypothesizes about the comparative role of multinational versus local enterprises in the process of sustainable development. This is followed by an examination of developing-nation environmental policy which emphasizes key factors constraining effective environmental management in the Third World, including possible limitations due to the very nature of multinational firms.

With this as background, a third section examines what is known about multinational corporate environmental management policies and practices, and attempts to explain the major patterns which have been observed. The next section highlights the need for international governmental cooperation regarding the environmental behavior of multinationals and surveys emerging forms of cooperation such as environmental codes of conduct. The final section suggests an agenda for further research regarding multinationals and the environment.

The macro-level analysis of this chapter is complemented by a micro-level case study of environmental management failure in the Bhopal tragedy, which is examined in chapter 10.

## Multinational Corporations and Sustainable Development

The Environment-Development Debate. The perceived relationship between environment and development has undergone a remarkable transformation.[1] In the early 1970s these two concerns were seen as being largely incompatible, with societies forced to choose between them. Since then our understanding of the environment-development nexus has broadened and deepened, with the result that today one finds in international circles a much "increased acceptance of the view that environmental considerations are an essential and integral part of sustainable national, and even global, economic development."[2]

The preoccupation of some industrial nations with the environmental issue in the early 1970s was greeted with considerable skepticism on the part of many Third World leaders, who feared that industrial-country environmental concerns could affect them adversely in the fields of trade, aid, growth, and the transfer of technology. Planning ministers of developing nations generally saw the development imperative as overriding all else; Brazil's planning minister even observed that he hoped it was the Third World's "turn to pollute."[3]

It became apparent to the planners of the 1972 UN Conference on the Human Environment in Stockholm that the relationship of environment and development would be a sensitive issue in the international debate. At the initiative of the Conference Secretariat, a panel was convened in 1971 to grapple with this fundamental problem, and out of this came the "Founex Report," considered to be the first comprehensive document on the development-environment issue. Its primary contribution was to broaden the definition of environmental concerns to include a variety of development-related problems.[4] At the Stockholm Conference that followed, 113 nations agreed on a sweeping action plan consisting of 109 separate recommendations designed "to safeguard and enhance the environment for present and future generations of man."

A further broadening of the debate occurred at the Symposium on Resource Use, Environment, and Development Strategies, which was held in Cocoyoc, Mexico, in 1974 in the midst of calls in the UN General Assembly for a new international economic order. The Cocoyoc Declaration redefined the whole purpose of development, noting that "this should not be to develop things but to develop man. Human beings have basic needs: food, shelter, clothing, health, education. Any process of growth that does not lead to their fulfillment—or even worse, disrupts them—is a travesty of the idea of development."[5]

During the mid-1970s, the concept of "ecodevelopment" emerged, a shorthand phrase for ecologically sound development strategy.[6] The normative character of this concept made it controversial and its complexity made the derivation of practical guidelines difficult. As a result, what evolved in the late 1970s and early 1980s were more general concepts such as "development without destruction,"[7] "rational use of resources," and, in general, "sustainable development." These elusive phrases have also proved difficult to define operationally, but as overarching concepts they have begun to gain some acceptance. This receptiveness can be traced to the impact of the consciousness-raising series of world conferences on food, population, human settlements, water, desertification, and environmental education held since the Stockholm Conference. It can also be ascribed to the growing realization, especially in the industrial world, that poverty itself exacerbates environmental problems and that the destruction or deterioration of the environment in many developing countries is, in turn, in danger of destroying the very basis for their economic growth. Moreover, it is the result of considerable evidence that environmental protection measures yield significant economic and social benefits, such as improvements in mortality and morbidity rates, improvements in working conditions, increased amenities, higher productivity and profitability of investment, technological innovation, etc.

Many leaders in government, industry, and international organizations now realize that the dramatic dilemma of environment versus development is a false issue — the real problem for countries is how to redefine the objectives, forms, and ways of development.[8] Despite much lip service to the concept of sustainable development, however, there is still often a continued emphasis on "short-term ad hoc gains that may not be sustainable over a longer period of time,"[9] along with too little awareness and understanding of the concept at the operational level, as case studies of Bhopal illustrate (see chapters 10 and 11).[10]

Multinational Versus Local Enterprises in Sustainable Development. The question at hand is what role multinational enterprises do and can play in sustainable development. Unfortunately, there is very little systematic evidence available bearing upon this central question. It is possible, however, to offer some tentative hypotheses that contrast multinational with local enterprises.

Consider first the ways in which the activities of multinational corporations (MNC's) may have relatively greater adverse impacts on natural systems and environmental quality, or be less in compliance with governmental environmental management measures, as compared with local enterprises. The production processes of local enterprises tend to be less capital-intensive, with the result that locals may rely less on production processes that are energy- and synthetic-intensive, and thus pollution-intensive. The technologies and products of local enterprises may also be more appropriate to local conditions with regard to climate, diet, and culture and thus less likely to cause adverse environmental consequences than alien technologies and products developed under different conditions. If the local enterprises are state-owned, they may not need to earn profits, may not have to pay dividends or worry about bankruptcy, may have preferential access to state financing, and may enjoy monopoly power, protected markets, and hidden subsidies. It may thus be easier for them than for privately owned multinational corporations to incur environmental control expenses. And perhaps most importantly, local enterprises are likely to enjoy fewer options and less flexibility in resource allocation.

Dunning has proposed, in this regard, that the multinational (or its affiliate) is more return- (response-) elastic than its indigenous competitors: "Within a marginal costing framework, any measure taken by the government that alters the relationship between marginal cost and revenue will provoke a compensating response on the part of a profit-maximizing firm. Its response or reaction to changes in costs or risk changes, reflected by a change in its return on investment, will be greater in terms of its investment and/or output behavior than that of an indigenous producer because it deploys more alternatives for investing its resources (managerial, financial and technical)."[11]

For other reasons MNC's may have relatively fewer adverse impacts on natural systems and environmental quality or be more in compliance with governmental environmental regulations than local firms. Multinationals operating in a host country may, for example, be under greater scrutiny and be more vulnerable to adverse publicity and punitive action. Local firms may enjoy greater influence with governmental regulators and may be granted preference with respect to the stringency and timing of environmental performance standards. As Leonard and Duerksen have hypothesized, "a host government under public pressure to do something about industrial pollution is likely to clamp down first on foreign industry."[12]

The MNC may also represent a channel for transfer of productive and environmentally sound technology and may be more in touch with environmental developments and innovations abroad. As such, the MNC can play, and many believe should play, a demonstration and leadership role, and be an agent for change. The MNC's role is facilitated by the fact that the multinational corporate subsidiaries are typically larger firms than their local rivals and also tend to be more profitable.[13] They may be better able to absorb the costs of environmental controls. In addition, the technologies and equipment employed by transnational affiliates tend to be more modern, more recently constructed, better maintained, and more efficient in terms of waste control management.[14] The affiliates typically also employ more professionally qualified managers on average than local enterprises do, and may also employ better skilled workers, given their generally higher wages. Finally, MNC affiliates, unlike their domestic rivals, tend to be more vulnerable to demands and pressures emanating from home and host countries with respect to social responsibility.[15]

### Environmental Policy in the Developing World

Although the normative vision of sustainable development now dominates the agendas of international organization meetings and academic conferences, in reality a perception of conflict between short-term needs for economic growth and long-term protection of the environment is still very prevalent and powerful in policy and management circles throughout much of the world. This is supported by findings that show that the demand for environmental quality—particularly amenity services—is income-sensitive.[16] Both the prerequisites to effective environmental management and the stringency of actual environmental policies empirically have been found to correlate closely with per capita income.[17]

Trends in Developing-Nation Environmental Policy. Multinational corporations operate in a heterogeneous world of environmental problems and policies—sovereign nations have been going about the business of environmental and health protection at different speeds, with different degrees of rigor, using different techniques. A great deal of environmental policy is in place in some of the highly industrialized nations. It is just beginning to emerge in others. In still others—particularly in the least developed—it will probably be some time in coming. As of 1986, a ballpark estimate would be that 95 percent of all environmental laws, environmental agency personnel, environmental group memberships, and environmental protection spending around the world was concentrated in the Western industrial nations.

But things have been changing. At the Stockholm Conference in 1972 only twenty-six countries had national agencies that dealt, in some way, with environmental issues. A survey ten years later showed that 144 countries had established such institutions.[18] (Mere creation of an institution, of course—especially if it is staffed with only a few people, as is the case in numerous nations—implies little about the ability to implement effective environmental policy.) That growth was accompanied by an increase of more than 5,000 in the number of nongovernmental organizations concerned with environmental and resource issues, many based in developing nations.[19] There are other signs of an increasing awareness of environmental issues in many developing countries. A recent survey of people involved in environmental protection issues in seventy-two developing nations showed that a large proportion (88 percent) believed that present environmental protection efforts in their nations were inadequate (the figure for respondents from industrial nations was 55 percent).[20]

A sampling of developments in various developing nations, as reported in a recent survey by the Organization for Economic Cooperation and Development (OECD) provides a flavor of the direction of change.[21] Separate ministries for the environment have been established, for example, in Morocco, Singapore, and Indonesia, while joint ministries combining environment with housing or natural resources have been created in nations such as Nigeria and Venezuela. Environmental divisions have been established within existing ministries and government agencies in Nepal, Kuwait, Zambia, Argentina, Brazil, and Ecuador, while environmental protection agencies have been established in countries such as Hong Kong, Saudi Arabia, and Mexico. Other countries, like Swaziland, India, Jordan, the Philippines, and Ghana, have set up interministerial councils for environmental matters to coordinate the activities of various government departments.

A number of countries (for example, Venezuela and Indonesia) have embarked upon environmental management plans, while environmental considerations have been explicitly included in the development plans of countries such as Honduras, India, and Malaysia. Environmental quality standards have been elaborated in a number of countries, including Kenya, Ghana, and the Philippines. Procedures for environmental impact assessment have been established in various ways in countries such as Thailand, the Philippines, Malaysia, Indonesia, Sri Lanka, and Singapore.

Remote sensing, soil surveys, water-quality monitoring, and other scientific information-gathering efforts are under way in nations such as Somalia, Jordan, Malaysia, Indonesia, the Sudan, and Rwanda. Public campaigns for environmental awareness have been launched in various countries (for example, Indonesia and the Sudan), while training courses in environmental and resource management and pollution-control techniques have been established in the Republic of Korea, Sri Lanka, the Philippines, Thailand, Ivory Coast, and elsewhere. India and Indonesia have developed environmentally oriented research centers at major universities, while environmental courses are taught at universities in a number of countries, including Egypt, India, Indonesia, Papua New Guinea, the Philippines, Singapore, and Thailand. Environmental matters are even being integrated into primary and secondary education programs in countries such as Ecuador, Somalia, Indonesia, and the Philippines.

Constraints and Shortcomings in Developing-Nation Environmental Policy. Despite this scattered evidence of progress, it is important to recognize—as the Bhopal case studies demonstrate—that most developing countries face severe problems in the planning and management of natural systems and environmental quality and remain poorly equipped to protect and manage their environments.[22] Hufschmidt and his colleagues have identified ten critical environmental management problems confronted by most developing nations:

1. Inadequacies in monitoring and enforcement of existing environmental protection laws and regulations.
2. Extensive poverty that puts a premium on current income producing activities to the detriment of long-term protection of natural systems.
3. Scarcity of financial resources in relation to current needs, which constrains the willingness to protect natural systems.
4. The often perverse distributional effects of environmental quality plans and programs, which may worsen the existing inequitable distribution of income.
5. Difficulty in controlling the environmental effects of private-sector and public-sector development activities, which limits the effectiveness of public programs for environmental quality management.
6. Inadequacies in the technical, economic, and administrative exper-

tise available for the planning and implementation of environmental management programs.

7. Widespread market failures, which require extensive use of shadow prices to replace market prices.

8. Minimal participation in environmental quality planning, either by the general public or by many affected governmental agencies, which reduces the effectiveness of implementation.

9. Inadequacies in environmental, economic, and social data, including difficulties in data collection and processing and lack of knowledge of past trends and baselines, which limit the quality of analysis.

10. Wide diversity of cultural values, which increases the difficulty of social evaluation of environmental quality effects.[23]

The consequences of such shortcomings are serious. A recent cataloging includes rapid degradation of agricultural land via desertification; pesticide-related deaths estimated at 10,000 per year in developing countries, with persons suffering acute pesticide poisoning estimated at 1.5 million to 2 million; rapid deforestation with severe environmental effects; accelerating habitat destruction and rates of species loss; air pollution from major urban centers exceeding commonly accepted standards set to protect human health; widespread water contamination; and a staggering incidence of environmentally related disease—afflicting over one billion people.[24]

Possible Limitations in Environmental Controls Due to the Nature of Multinational Enterprise. On top of this sobering set of constraints, a number of factors related to multinational corporations may further conspire to make purely national control systems either evadable, inefficient, incomplete, unenforceable, exploitable, or negotiable (at the expense of desired environmental quality or occupational safety).[25]

One factor to consider is the flexibility, mobility, and leverage of multinationals. The global production, logistics, and marketing systems of many pollution-intensive multinationals provide them with a wide "options space." The natural consequence of this, in the view of one observer, is that "their autonomy concerning public policies has increased and, conversely, their accountability to the institutions of public policy has decreased. This is especially the case for host countries, but increasingly also for home countries."[26] It is fair to assume that the typical MNC as a global profit maximizer tends to react to host-government environmental policies so as to minimize any impairment of expected profits. As such, if it maintains capacity to produce the same good in different national markets, output curtailed or made more expensive due to environmental restrictions in one market can be replaced from another subsidiary's plant. Faced with the prospect of onerous environmental regulations, a multinational can credibly threaten to close down a given plant, or to shelve expansion or investment plans there, and choose another national market for any additions to output. This bargaining leverage is offset, of course, by the capacity of host countries to influence the environment or health-affecting actions of foreign investors, which is a function of (1) the country's ability to monitor investor behavior, (2) the cost of duplicating, or forgoing, what the foreign investor offers, (3) competition within the industry, (4) the vulnerability of the foreigner's assets and earnings to adverse treatment by the host government, (5) the ability of the host country to discount the international political tension caused by investment disputes, and (6) the dissipation of uncertainty over the course of an investment project, which attenuates the foreign investor's bargaining strength.[27]

A second limiting factor relates to communication and control gaps within multinational corporations. Their management systems vary from "closed" to "open" depending on the intensity of the parent's supervision of the subsidiaries and the density of communication and information links between them.[28] Control tends to be closer and supervision more centralized over standards, procedures, and the major decisions of subsidiaries where the parent and subsidiaries enjoy similarity in plant size and product lines, where technology is more complex, where they are bound by greater transactional interdependence, and where the market situation is more predictable.[29] In short, MNC's "lavish extensive resources on internal coordination when close coordination pays, as when the profits of different affiliates are strongly interdependent and inconsistent policies would be very costly. Fewer resources are devoted to control when it is costly (e.g., for a remote location) or when the affiliate's local environment is unstable or highly distinctive (i.e., making coordination ineffectual)."[30]

A third factor that can limit the effectiveness of national environmental control is MNC corporate secrecy. A significant portion of multinational corporate environmental behavior, particularly with regard to export-import operations, appears to occur in the absence of full public disclosure. The lack of transparency can be traced to the lack of appropriate information and consultation procedures between nations, to the paucity of disclosure requirements within many nations, and to widespread concerns regarding the protection of trade secrets. In many nations, governments lack the resources to monitor properly the environmental impacts of exports, imports, product sales, investments, and waste-disposal activities. Such conditions explain the lack of solid information with regard to the export and import of hazardous products and the near absence of policy concerning international movements of hazardous wastes. Few countries have a good handle on what is going where and why. The lack of information adds an air of mystery to the environmental image of multinationals, but, more importantly, makes it difficult for governments, workers, and consumers to exercise informed choice.

The fourth complication is limits on transnational corporate accountability and responsibility. There does not yet exist a uniform or global concept of what a parent company's responsibilities for their subsidiaries should be in the environmental area (although the Bhopal litigation may change this).[31] Questions of liability for accidents and environmental or occupational health damage become very ambiguous and troublesome (from the victim's perspective) when the enterprise causing the harm is only partially owned by an MNC (when it is, for example, a joint venture), is owned by the transnational only indirectly (for example, an affiliate of a transnational corporate affiliate), or is a subcontractor (for example, a "fly-by-night" waste-disposal company with one employee) of the multinational corporation. Other factors that diffuse or limit MNC responsibility for environmental damage include monetary ceilings or limits on liability (such as with oil tanker accidents), temporal limits on liability (which impedes or prevents recovery in cases involving long-abandoned waste landfills or long latency periods in the manifestation of occupational disease), institutional and legal barriers to cross-border adjudication of disputes (which is often cumbersome, time consuming, and expensive), and variations in the basic concept of liability from nation to nation (for example, negligence standards versus strict liability). The consequences of these ambiguities, limits, and barriers is that many victims may either go uncompensated or inadequately compensated for losses and injuries due to multinational corporate environmental or occupational damage.[32]

### Multinational Corporate Environmental Policies and Practices

A summary description of the current approach of most developing nations to environmental policy would include such words as embryonic, short-term, narrow, fragmented, exclusionist, discontinuous, ad hoc, reactive, superficial, under-resourced, and negotiable. How have the world's multinational corporations responded to such a state of affairs? This section surveys prototypical patterns of environmental management policy and practice associated with pollution-intensive MNC's, although it must be noted that the volume, quality, representativeness, and timeliness of the evidence available leaves much to be desired.

Performance Objectives and Measurement. Surveys of multinational corporations during the 1970s found that many of them, particularly the larger and North American-based ones, had developed formal written statements of objectives and policies concerning pollution control.[33] Their contents varied widely; most set only the broadest kinds of behavioral constraints, left open the scope for discretionary action, said little about going beyond the legal requirements imposed upon them locally, and seldom specified the means to be used in complying with them. The policy statements also appeared to be in a continual state of evolution, being the subject of frequent modification and revision. The policies, in addition, were mainly intended for home-country operations; few multinationals had attempted to develop a set of global environmental management policies applicable to worldwide operations. The prevailing idea in the 1970s was that of "separability"—environmental management was viewed as a separable task among individual affiliates on the one hand, and between these affiliates and the corporate headquarters on the other.[34] This appeared to be particularly true for joint ventures.

Surveys in the 1970s also discovered that most multinationals had not yet been successful in adapting their performance measurement, evaluation, and reward systems to handle the issue of environmental protection.[35] Corporate headquarters were not furnishing or enforcing system-wide norms of pollution-control performance on a global basis. Affiliate reporting to headquarters tended to be ad hoc—the affiliates themselves generally decided what to report, since only a few of the multinational corporations had identified system-wide data requirements. And although some firms were measuring environmental management performance at the plant level, few had attempted to inject such considerations formally into managerial performance evaluations.

Organizational Staffing. Most multinational corporations in industries with significant environmental impact employ headquarters and regional-level environmental affairs directors, advisers, or coordinators.[36] These executives, in many cases, head small staff units mostly created during the early

1970s in response to increasing citizen and governmental concern. The "boundary spanning units" were established to deal with external pressures, with functions extending both outward to the external environment and inward into the firm. The functions include the scanning, filtering, coding, interpretation, and dissemination of task-relevant environmental information, coordination of activities, external relations, and so on. Environmental management staff units in multinationals typically educate and advise, but do not decide on environmental questions. Most MNC's view environmental management as a line-management responsibility and, as such, have not chosen to create large centralized problem-solving groups.

A large number of multinationals also have corporate-level, top management environmental committees that are charged with policy formulation and progress review and that serve as a catalyst in this area. The dominant orientation of such committees, however, has tended to be toward home-country operations, and they are typically composed only of home-country executives.[37] A number of horizontally diversified MNC's have installed environmental management advisers in their major product divisions.[38] Likewise, a number of vertically integrated multinationals have assigned environmental professionals to their corporate-level engineering, research, product development, legal, and public relations departments. These professionals handle specialized tasks, initiate search procedures for more efficient techniques, and perform a monitoring function. Such specialized roles appear to be more permanent than the aforementioned generalized coordinating and committee roles, which, in a few multinational corporations, have already been phased out.[39]

At the foreign affiliate level, multinational environmental staffing seems to follow a pattern similar to the setting of performance objectives, as a matter of local accommodation. Environmental protection staffing in a given affiliate appears to depend on the size and nature of the operation, equity ownership, local organizational structure, stringency of existing regulations, intensity of citizen agitation, and extent of governmental reporting requirements.[40]

Project and Product Planning. A detailed study of the role of environmental considerations in the project planning processes of American- and European-based multinational corporations in the petroleum, chemicals, and metals industries in the mid-1970s revealed a broad range of planning behavior.[41] At one end were a few multinationals that appeared to be taking ecological considerations comprehensively into account. At the other end were many that appeared to be indifferent to ecological concerns and were considering little beyond the immediate economic and technical aspects of their projects.

The central conclusion of this research was that environmentally-oriented industrial project planning on the part of multinational corporations was still in its infancy.[42] In most of the multinationals surveyed, project design was taking place in the absence of detailed ecological and social data. Most site-location baseline surveys, for example, were typically undertaken (if at all) only after approval had been received, preliminary construction work had already begun, and the range of choice narrowed to a single favored project design. Environmental science professionals were involved in some corporate planning processes, but in others they appeared to be brought in only at the eleventh hour for purposes of "credibility." Few corporations conducted formal post-startup environmental impact monitoring. Planning attention in most of the firms was typically focussed on issues of process-related residuals discharge, with minimal attention paid to potential environmental consequences associated with other project actions such as construction and transportation. Finally, most planning processes were found to be exclusionist, low-profile, and "official-channels-only" in character. The participation of potentially affected public bodies or interests was rarely solicited.

In explaining the variation in the extent to which MNC's incorporated environmental factors in their planning, it was found that greater environmental sensitivity was predominantly explained by various public policy variables. Anticipated or immediate public pressures in the region—from government environment agencies, citizen groups, and the media—appeared to induce environmental preplanning. The extent to which institutional arrangements were available in the area of the proposed plant for public examination of the project also appeared to be a powerful motivator.[43]

During the 1970s a new emphasis on product safety emerged within many MNC's in response to the growing attention that governments and courts began according to toxic-substances control, product liability, and worker exposure to hazardous materials. New positions, advisory offices, and top-level management committees concerned with product and occupational safety were accordingly established in numerous firms. Some of the larger chemical and petroleum MNC's greatly expanded their toxicological research facilities; created new programs for the identification, monitoring, and elimination of potential hazards in the work environment; and developed new pre-market testing techniques that incorporated screening for carcinogenic properties. Some multinationals, such as Dow Chemical, put together relatively formalized and comprehensive environmental product safety programs.[44] Along with company programs, new industry associations were established in the 1970s in an attempt to ease the burdens on existing scientific laboratories and testing facilities, and to share the costs of product-related health and ecological safety.

The one issue that has perhaps generated the greatest emotion and controversy in the 1980s regarding MNC's and the environment is the exportation of hazardous products (see chapter 6). Concerns have focussed on the exportation of hundreds of different pesticides, pharmaceuticals, contraceptive devices, toxic chemicals, food products, and various consumer products that have either been banned, severely restricted, or unregistered for use in their country of origin.[45] Some observers have gone so far as to label this practice "an export trade in death" and "the corporate crime of the century."[46] Much attention has been placed on pesticides sold to customers in developing nations where safety restrictions are nonexistent or not enforced, and countries where the pesticides are used for cash crops exported to the industrial world.[47]

Much of the criticism has centered on multinational corporate practices or local conditions that either prevent or impede customers and authorities in importing nations from making informed risk assessments and proper judgments about using given products, for example: (1) withholding from the importing government or not volunteering information on the prohibitions or use restrictions placed on the product in the country of origin, or in other countries; (2) exporting/importing a product banned or severely restricted in one country into another without the knowledge and consent of appropriate authorities in the country; (3) labeling products and providing other consumer information in a way that fails to note safety precautions, use instructions, and ingredients, or that does so, but not in the language of the country of destination; (4) skirting home-government regulations (including export notification, registration, and outright bans) by shipping through subsidiaries in third countries or by changing the product name or formula; and (5) knowingly exporting a product that might be safe at home to a nation where conditions combine to make use of the product predictably hazardous.[48] Along with hazardous products, similar concerns have dominated the debate regarding the international movement of hazardous wastes.[49]

Technology Transfer. Observers have noted that it is important to separate the availability of advanced environmental management technology within multinational corporations from the application of that technology. Potentially, affiliates can draw upon the environmental science know-how and technology of the entire multinational system of which they are part. In practice, full and instantaneous intra-firm transfers of such resources usually does not take place, as witnessed in the case of Bhopal. Individual processes and techniques may not be suitable for use by the affiliates. More important, given the local accommodation policies adopted by most multinationals, advanced pollution-control technologies may not be desired by affiliates, and they rarely appear to be forced on them by corporate headquarters.[50]

Systematic evidence regarding any differences in the "cleanliness" of manufacturing technologies employed by multinational corporations in their different countries of operation, and differences between multinational affiliates and local firms, is almost nonexistent. Some observers have alleged that many multinationals employ "dirtier" or more hazardous technologies in their developing-nation operations, particularly in industries such as asbestos, copper and lead smelting, vinyl chloride, pesticides, etc.[51] Other observers, however, have reached different conclusions. Royston, for example, has stated that the "technical standards of the plants operated by multinationals in different countries tend to be similar, just because it is managerially simpler to standardize. As a result, the pollution control features of plants operated by the multinationals in developing countries are likely to be closer to those operating in the industrialized countries than to those of plants operated by local companies in the same host country."[52] After examining the technologies employed by numerous multinationals in a range of developing nations, Royston concludes that "as regards direct environmental impact, there is no evidence to suggest that they [i.e., multinational corporates] are worse than some national companies, and a good deal of evidence to suggest that they can be better."[53] Royston has also reported that a number of multinationals, such as the 3M Company, are at the forefront of the movement toward "low-waste" or "no-waste" technologies.[54] A number of multinational corporations have also added divisions to provide environmental products and services, for example, Boeing, FMC, Exxon, Dow Chemical, 3M, Caterpillar Tractor, Shell, BP, Ciba-Geigy, Krupp, ICI, and Philips.[55]

Occupational Health and Safety. Relatively little research has been directed to the health and safety policies and practices of multinational corporations. In a few industries using or producing toxic chemicals, protecting workers from environmental hazards has proved costly, with the result that some industrial relocation to less-regulated sites may have occurred.[56] But there is as yet no evidence that strict regulations protecting workers' health have caused a mass exodus of hazardous industries to developing nations. There is also no evidence that multinational corporations operating in developing countries are less responsible than local firms. But as the work of Castleman demonstrates (and see his chapter in this volume), there are numerous examples of a "double standard" in which worker and community health protection measures by multinational corporations are far weaker in their Third World operations than in those in their home nations. Examples include industries that manufacture vinyl chloride, pesticides, chromates, steel, chlorine, and asbestos.[57]

One of the few systematic research projects regarding the occupational health and safety standards and practices of multinational enterprises in home and host countries was undertaken in 1982–83 by the International Labour Office (ILO).[58] Some of the principal findings of this in-depth interview study of twelve "leading edge" multinationals were:

1. The organizational structure varied widely from highly centralized control (for example, BASF and Xerox) to no central direction from the headquarters unit (for example, Brown Boveri), and was a function of the type of industrial activity, home and host country of the enterprises, type of control or financial participation of the parent company in the subsidiary operation, and individual approach of the company concerned.

2. The safety and health legislation and practices in the home countries (Switzerland, Federal Republic of Germany, Netherlands, United States, and United Kingdom) of the MNC's constituted the basic framework throughout their global operations. In some cases, policies were established in the headquarters country and included detailed instructions applicable in each national operation throughout the group. In other cases, only the main principles of the company's safety and health policy were established at headquarters and the translation of these principles into practice was left to the discretion of the group's different plants around the world.

3. "Without exception, the participating MNC's appeared to comply fully with the safety and health standards required by the national authorities in the home and host countries studied. In nearly all cases, the representatives of the national authorities stated that MNCs' health and safety

standards went beyond these requirements."[59] National authorities in Mexico and Nigeria viewed the safety and health performance of MNC's as being superior to those of most of the entirely domestically owned enterprises.[60]

4. The home-based operations of the MNC's were generally found to have a better health and safety performance as compared to their foreign subsidiaries, particularly those in developing nations. "In particular, the lack of general safety and risk training consciousness and awareness was found to constitute a particular risk factor in certain developing country operations."[61]

5. The safety and health performance of local contractors and subcontractors was a concern for some MNC managements (for example, for Shell in Nigeria), as "very few of these contractors have developed a safety and health program and, in some cases, safety awareness is non-existent."[62]

Summary and Explanation. The available evidence (primarily from the 1970s) on the environmental policies and practices of MNC's in these five areas generally indicates a dominant pattern of "local accommodation" (that is, a fragmented, differentiated, and decentralized approach to environmental management). How might this pattern be explained? Gladwin and Walter have provided a framework for predicting whether a multinational corporation's global pattern of behavior on a given social issue is likely to be characterized by "unification" (headquarters' intervention, system-wide interchange, and uniformity in policy or practice), or by its opposite, "fragmentation."[63] The framework (see figure 1.1) suggests that dynamism, instability, heterogeneity, and independence associated with the collection of various policy climates (say, with regard to environmental protection) in which the corporation operates represent "fragmenting forces" that tend to limit the potential for system-wide unification and push the corporation toward custom tailoring or adaptation to local policy climates:

> Confronted with dynamic policy climates, the ability to perceive quickly and efficiently and adjust to rapid changes will tend to be inhibited by centralization. When the change in the various climates is erratic and unstable, the viability of headquarters-devised or executed policies will be constrained by high levels of unpredictability. Given heterogeneous climates, the feasibility of centrally-determined and standardized corporate policies will tend to be burdened by the large amount of critically important information necessary for decision-making. And

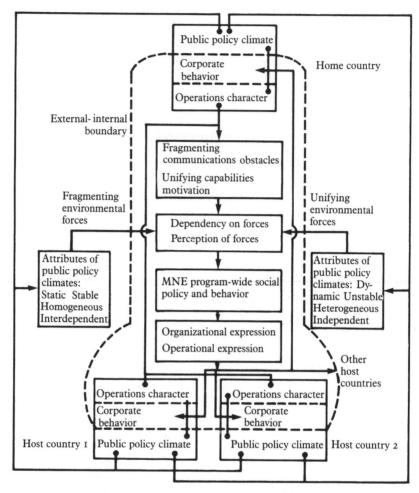

**Figure 1.1** Framework for Analyzing Unification vs. Fragmentation in Transnational Corporate Social Behavior. *Source*: Thomas N. Gladwin and Ingo Walter, *Multinationals Under Fire* (New York: John Wiley, 1980), p. 567.

the absence of international interest-linkages and demands, by virtue of policy-climate independence, implies that decision-makers need not fear repercussions of their actions elsewhere around the world. All of these elements permit organizational and operational differentiation in corporate approaches to managing the issue in question.[64]

Along with the fragmenting forces arising out of public policy conditions, the framework also suggests that multinationals must also contend with a variety of fragmenting communications gaps that arise from the absence of common values, norms, and expectations among managers in different nations, from tendencies toward ethnocentric attitudes, from psychological impediments to cross-cultural understanding, and from obstructions and deficiencies in the flow of information within the transnational system attributable to distance and conditions of shared ownership.

It is important to emphasize the contingency logic incorporated in the foregoing analytical framework. The model is enterprise-specific—a given multinational corporation's global policy and behavior on an issue such as environmental protection will depend on a unique set of internal and external situational factors. It is tempting to suggest that most pollution-intensive multinational corporations, particularly during the 1970s, in essence simply "mapped" perceived characteristics of the environmental policy world around them (a world, that is, for the most part heterogeneous, dynamic, unstable, independent) into their organizational structures, policies, and routines. These fragmenting policy forces, perhaps along with obstacles to system-wide skill and technology transfer, are thus what may be responsible for the highly diversified pattern of policy and practice observed in the environmental management field.

In looking ahead it is important to note that since the mid-1970s a number of forces have been working in favor of less fragmentation and more standardization in global environmental policy and practice.[65] The stimulation and coordination efforts of regional, global, and supranational organizations discussed in the next section, the internationalization of environmental interest groups, the creation of bilateral and multilateral environmental protection cooperation agreements, the policy harmonization programs in various regional areas, the sustained growth in international communications and contact among environmental professionals, a growing awareness of global interdependencies of many environmental problems, and the increased attention of some home governments to the environmental behavior of their multinational corporations abroad (especially after the Bhopal tragedy), have all served to bring about an increasing similarity in the environmental policy frameworks and instruments in different nations.

Multinational corporations have begun to respond by moving toward a somewhat more unified approach to environmental management, that is, creating environmental coordinator positions with international or regional responsibilities, publishing global internal environmental newsletters, holding annual meetings of environmental staff from all over the world, creating top-level environmental committees at headquarters with international representation, computerizing global environmental information dissemination systems, institutionalizing regular international visits and inspection tours by senior management staff, and so on. But the movement toward globally unified environmental management on the part of MNC's is still incomplete. At this time the balance between fragmentation and unification for most multinational corporations still seems to favor fragmentation. Full-fledged efforts at unification appear to be happening primarily at the regional level (for example, within Western Europe), with fragmentation still generally the rule at the global and interregional levels.

### Multinationals and International Environmental Management

The need for international cooperation in relation to the environmental practices of multinational corporations has already been noted. The effectiveness of national control systems is limited due to multinational corporate mobility, leverage, communication and control gaps, secrecy, nontransparency, limited accountability, and so on. And as just stressed, more unified approaches are likely to be induced by stimulation and coordination efforts on the part of international governmental organizations. All of this suggests a useful role and need for coordination and harmonization at the international level.

The Limits of Unilateral Action. Much of the concern about MNC environmental behavior would of course be alleviated if multinationals themselves engaged in appropriate setting of objectives, assignment of roles, measurement of performance, transmission of information, development and transfer of environmental control technology, and communication with relevant external groups. Although some have begun to recognize that environmental protection is good business, probably not too much should be expected from purely altruistic behavior given the short time horizons, competitive realities, and financial pressures under which they operate. Environmentally oriented behavior, as emphasized above, is often motivated by external (that is, public policy) rather than internal pressures. Also, a multinational firm's acting responsibly in one regulatory setting does not guarantee that it will do so in another; limits on cross-border responsibility, communication and control gaps, and local accommodation philosophies may account for such differences, as witnessed in the case of Bhopal.

Many observers contend that the home governments of multinational corporations bear a responsibility to ensure that their corporations do not cause environmental harm abroad.[66] Home governments have been urged to control, or even prohibit, the foreign sale of environmentally hazardous substances banned at home, and to require environmental impact statements for overseas MNC projects requiring prior approval or facilitation by the home government. But the likelihood of significant unilateral actions on the part of home countries to extend extraterritorially their environmental regulation is rather low given concerns of competitive dislocation and diplomatic sensitivity. And even if home-country control systems were introduced they would still be evadable given multinational corporate mobility and flexibility.

Host countries are thus likely to remain the primary locus of real power over the environmental behavior of multinational corporations into the indefinite future. Import restrictions, customs inspections, impact assessment requirements, disclosure rules, land-use controls, tough air and water pollution standards, serious enforcement efforts, painful sanctions for violations, and the establishment in law of substantial liability for criminal prosecution to be incurred for damages to human health and the environment all represent powerful levers for motivating multinationals to find ways of minimizing or avoiding damage to health and the environment. But, as with home governments, the forces working against the creation and use of such levers in host nations must be kept in mind. Many nations, particularly smaller developing ones, are and will remain poorly equipped for effective environmental protection. And even when they are well equipped, they will still remain vulnerable to a bargaining process in which MNC's often have greater leverage given their advantages of mobility, scale, and information.

Given such constraints, it is unlikely that existing or prospective unilateral action alone will be sufficient to bring about the degree of control thought by many to be necessary. The competitive incentive systems that guide much of MNC and governmental environmental policy formulation have a "foot-dragging" bias—that is, they avoid pain until that pain is at least shared equitably. Unilateral action, furthermore, offers little promise in dealing with the divided loyalties inherent in multinational corporations or with the transfrontier or even global nature of many MNC-induced environmental hazards (for example, oil tanker accidents and tropical forest destruction). Unilateral action also raises the prospect of overlapping or conflicting expectations being placed on multinationals. Coordination and harmonization at the international level, especially in regard to issues involving the "global commons," is thus essential.

Forms of International Environmental Cooperation. Many different forms of international cooperation have been emerging since the early 1970s that directly or indirectly bear upon the environmental behavior of multinational corporations. Those listed here represent examples of cooperation that have begun or may begin to shape multinational corporate environmental practices, and much has been written about them.[67]

1.  Government- or industry-initiated mandatory or voluntary codes of environmental behavior for multinational corporations (for example, either proposed or actually promulgated by OECD, ILO, the UN, the UN Conference on Trade and Development, the International Chamber of Commerce, the International Group of National Associations of Agrochemical Manufacturers).
2.  International information-exchange and consensus-seeking conferences on general environmental issues (for example, UN Conference on the Human Environment or 1984 World Industry Conference on Environmental Management sponsored by industry and UNEP).
3.  Multilateral environmental conventions, treaties, and protocols, of which 113 covering many issues are currently listed in the UNEP register of international treaties and other agreements in the field of environment.
4.  International information exchange schemes (for example, one being created in the UN on hazardous chemicals and unsafe pharmaceuticals).
5.  Cross-border consultation and notification systems (for example, on frontier siting of hazardous plants or transfrontier movements of hazardous wastes).
6.  Creation of international registries (for example, UNEP's International Register of Potentially Toxic Chemicals).
7.  Foreign assistance and training programs in the environmental management area (for example, the World Environment Center's "International Environment and Development Service," funded by the U.S. Agency for International Development and U.S. industry, which makes the technical skills of the private sector available to developing countries to solve their environmental problems).

8. Declarations of policy (for example, declarations by OECD ministers of the environment in 1974 and 1979).

9. Legally binding decisions and conventions as well as the promulgation of principles (for example, OECD on transfrontier pollution or UNEP on trade in agricultural chemicals, particularly pesticides).

10. Binding or nonbinding recommendations or resolutions (for example, of UN General Assembly on the subject of hazardous exports, of which there have been four since 1979).

11. Use of environmental review procedures by international development institutions (for example, Declaration of Environmental Policies and Procedures Relating to Economic Development of 1980, monitored by the Committee on International Development Institutions on the Environment [CIDIE], the secretariat for which is provided by UNEP).

12. Joint industry environmental research programs (for example, the oil companies' CONCAWE group or the West European chemical industry's toxicological research center).

13. Cooperative efforts between environmental groups and the corporate community on international environment issues (for example, the Talloires Program on International Environmental Issues, coordinated by the Sierra Club International Earthcare Center, and the Agricultural Chemicals Dialogue Group, sponsored by the U.S.-based Conservation Foundation).

14. Social action campaigns against what are seen to be environmentally hazardous MNC practices (for example, by Friends of the Earth International, Health Action International, Pesticide Action Network, Consumer Interpol, European Environment Bureau, Interfaith Center on Corporate Responsibility, International Organization of Consumers Unions).

These forms of international cooperation vary considerably in regard to breadth of coverage, timeliness of action, flexibility of approach, directness of manner, pragmatism of idea, and productivity of approach. It is hard to gauge what the real impact on MNC environmental practices has actually been, mainly because many of the efforts have not been directly targeted at multinationals and because there is often a long lag between any cooperative effort at the international level and its translation into effective national or local action. It is obvious, however, that the cumulative impact of growing international environmental cooperation will be to reduce fragmentation and increase unification in the approach of multinationals to environmental management.

Environmental Codes of Conduct. One form of international cooperation that has received considerable attention is a code of conduct or set of guidelines for MNC environmental behavior to be promulgated by international organizations such as the OECD and United Nations. The Environment Committee of the OECD, for example, began studying multinational enterprises and the environment in the early 1980s with the aim of determining how best to encourage environmentally sound investment and trade practices by multinationals.[68] The committee drafted an environmental management chapter that it hoped would be added to the existing OECD "Guidelines for Multinational Enterprises."[69]

This effort to institutionalize a comprehensive set of environmental expectations for multinationals was strongly supported by most OECD member nations. But on the grounds that promulgation of such guidelines might have discriminatory implications (with multinationals being held to higher standards than purely domestic enterprises), the effort was strongly opposed by the OECD's Business and Industry Advisory Committee (BIAC), along with the British delegation, and received only lukewarm support from the United States delegation.[70] After two years of negotiation, the OECD Council in November of 1985 formally decided not to add an environmental protection chapter to the existing "Guidelines on Multinational Enterprises." It did, however, issue a compromise "clarification" to the phrase "environmental protection" that already existed in one sentence of the existing guidelines.

Prospective transformation of this "clarification" into a full-fledged chapter of the OECD guidelines sometime in the future, completion and adoption of the proposed United Nations Code of Conduct on Transnational Corporations (which includes sections on consumer and environmental protection),[71] and creation of other sectoral-level, industry-sponsored codes —and endorsement of their provisions by multinational corporations and their industry associations—could be of great benefit, both to environmental protection and to multinationals themselves, especially if they are accompanied by improvements in national regulatory capacities. Appropriate guidelines would improve the economic and political climate for MNC's, help to codify sound industry practice, plug gaps in national legislation and control, and help to harmonize competition among nations that are reluctant to restrict the environmental behavior of multinationals out of fear of subjecting them to higher environmental costs than elsewhere. The adoption and observance of such guidelines could also do much to restore public confidence in multinationals engaged in pollution- or hazard-intensive activities—confidence that was severely eroded by the Bhopal affair. Finally, the codes would assist nations in meeting their responsibility, as pledged at the Stockholm Conference on the Human Environment, "to ensure that activities within their jurisdiction or control do not cause damage to the environment of other States or of areas beyond the limits of national jurisdiction." As indicated by the stalled efforts at both the UN and OECD, however, it may be some time before the above logic is accepted unanimously by all nations.

### Directions for Further Research

This chapter has emphasized the paucity of timely, rigorous, comprehensive, detailed, and representative information regarding the interactions of environment, development, and multinational enterprise. Considerable additional research and policy analysis is necessary in order to minimize adverse environmental impacts, mobilize managerial and technical resources, avoid disputes, and encourage multinationals to contribute more fully and effectively to sustainable development over the next few decades. Topics for research fall into four categories.[72]

Multinational Corporations and Sustainable Development. The search for sustainable development strategies, both for countries and corporations, has to be made a high priority. The concept must be elaborated, precisely defined, tested, and translated into operational criteria if it is to become truly a meaningful and widely accepted guide to action. In particular, little is as yet known about the comparative role of multinational versus local enterprises (or the roles of transnational corporations based in different industries and home countries or of different forms of transnational corporate involvement) in environmental management and sustainable development. Many hypotheses can be offered, and systematic examination of them is necessary if policy makers are to be fully informed in making industrial and environmental policy decisions.

A better understanding and realization of the constructive role multinationals can play in critical global environmental interdependencies, particularly those deemed to be of the highest management priority, is urgently needed. Also needed is a fuller illumination of how the international debt crisis, instability of commodity markets, protectionism, and other global economic problems affecting environmental quality, natural resource exploitation, and the readiness and capacity of governments to deal with the challenge of environmental improvements, can all be brought closer to resolution by enlightened MNC practices. The real challenge lies in translating "sustainable interdependent development" into policy guidance for governments and multinational corporations.

Multinational Corporations and Environmental Policy. A more comprehensive, detailed survey of how national environmental and resource management regulations have evolved and of how multinational corporations have adjusted in response to them would be of value. Issues include: what the role of such regulations is in national entry control systems; whether the same regulations are applied and enforced for foreign versus local firms; whether host-country trade, investment, and technology policies inadvertently impede environmental progress and discourage the importation of advanced pollution-abatement technology; how multinational corporations deal with the lack of enforcement, or sporadic enforcement, of environmental laws in various nations; whether notions of "environmental slack" (that is, unexploited supplies of environmental assimilative capacity) are playing a role in industrial siting policies; and whether multinational corporations are encountering difficulties with extraterritorial environmental regulation. A regional rather than a global focus may be a better approach to a survey of such issues.

An interesting question that has so far received very little attention is how environmental issues are dealt with in MNC-government negotiations and how the process might be improved for the benefit of all parties: whether developing nations lack the technical and administrative expertise needed to negotiate environment and resource management issues on an equal footing with MNC's and, if so, how that deficiency may be corrected; whether environmental conditions are being made an explicit part of investment agreements and how this may be promoted in practice; what trends can be observed in contractual arrangements with regard to environmental protection in various sectors and whether a model set of agreements may be developed so as to clearly embody various dimensions of mutual rights and responsibilities in regard to environmental management; and in what way the UN system might play a useful role in providing advisory and information support to host governments for environmental negotiations with multinational corporations, including analysis and review of environmental elements of draft agreements.

Multinational Corporations and Environmental Practices. Our knowledge of the environmental management practices of MNC's is too heavily based on research from the 1970s that was anecdotal or small-sample in nature, heavily biased toward large size and high-profile firms, concentrated in a few industries, and largely focussed on North American and European-based enterprises. There is thus a need for a more comprehensive, systematic, and current examination of transnational corporate environmental policies and behavior. The chemicals, petroleum, and minerals industries have received most of the research attention in the past. There is a need for analyses of the environmental impacts of multinational investments in forestry and agriculture in developing countries. Attention should also be given to industries producing polluting products, for example, motor vehicles, tobacco, pharmaceuticals, food, etc. The potential role of MNC's in pollution control and environmental management industries in fostering sustainable development worldwide also needs to be examined.

The general decline in developing countries of foreign exploration and direct investment in the natural resource industries, along with the trend toward reduced or nonequity forms of investment in manufacturing industries has meant that environmental protection in such pollution-intensive industries is becoming more of a shared responsibility between transnational and local enterprises. This shift in the burden of environmental responsibility may have important environmental impacts and policy implications and should be investigated. This could take the form of an examination of the relative effectiveness of environmental management in joint ventures, licensing agreements, management contracts, turnkey operations, coproduction agreements, production sharing, wholly owned ventures, etc.

The litmus test of whether multinationals are accepting the challenge of environmental responsibility and sustainable development is whether they are truly injecting environmental considerations into the planning of their strategies, projects, and products. An investigation of the extent to which environmental impact assessment is currently being effectively utilized in the design, planning, and implementation of major projects is thus warranted. Some new concerns to explore are whether social and cultural impacts are being considered and whether attention is being given to managing unexpected or emergency pollution hazards. More generally, the role of environmental criteria in the selection of appropriate technologies should also be examined.

Resource recovery and recycling on a comprehensive basis has been identified as a cornerstone of sustainable development. It may be important to examine closely how various multinational industries have responded to the challenge of materials recycling, especially when they have been collaborating with governmental programs in this regard. There is also an urgent need for a broad and representative study of MNC policies and practices with regard to occupational health and safety in their global operations. This study could assess the extent to which antiquated or dangerous technologies are being utilized by multinationals, the uniformity or differentiation of workplace standards for similar plants in different locations, the extent to which trained personnel have been appointed to monitor workplace hazards, the role of medical examinations, effectiveness of worker compensation, corporate disclosure to workers and health authorities of data on hazards, exposure levels, control measures and standards in force in various countries, and so on.

Multinational Corporations and International Environmental Protection. Lending by multinational banks has a profound impact on sustainable development through loans to companies and government agencies involved in developing infrastructure, natural resource projects, and industry in the Third World. Yet little is known about the extent to which, or the manner in which, commercial banks concern themselves with the environmental and natural resource consequences of their borrowers' activities. Building on the experience of the multilateral development financing institutions, a useful contribution could be made by a survey of the role of environmental considerations in providing lending. Likewise, more attention needs to be given to the role of home government export credit and insurance agencies in this regard.

Very little is known about the effectiveness of different forms of international cooperation vis-à-vis environmental issues involving MNC activities, that is, ways in which both nations and multinationals respond to codes of conduct, environmental conventions, information exchange schemes, policy declarations, social action campaigns, and so on, along with the ways in which these different forms interrelate. A better understanding of the costs and benefits, at the practical level, of different forms of international cooperation would seem to be needed if efforts are to be allocated wisely.

Finally, a key question regarding international cooperation is what new initiatives and institutional arrangements are needed in order to tap more fully the talent, resources, and expertise of multinational corporations so as to assist developing nations in achieving sustainable development. In this regard, major informational, cultural, financial, competitive, and organizational barriers to the transfer of environmental management technologies, products, and services from industrial to developing nations need to be identified.

# II Case Studies of Multinational Corporations in Natural Resource Sectors

Environmental concerns in natural resource-based industries (and the role of MNC's therein) can be distinguished from industrial pollution issues in at least three ways. First, there is a direct concern for the productivity of the resource base—maintaining optimal economic yield for renewable resources and securing technically efficient exploitation of nonrenewable resources. Second, environmental damages from unregulated activities are more likely to involve difficult valuation judgments concerning loss of wildlife, wilderness areas, genetic resources, recreational opportunities, and disruption of traditional rural societies. Third, developing countries are reasserting national ownership over most natural resources, and contractual relations between MNC's and host governments are changing rapidly.

The chapter by William Pintz provides a detailed analysis of environmental negotiations in the Ok Tedi mining project. Pintz demonstrates that the host-country government must acquire the best possible environmental expertise if it is to negotiate successfully with the foreign investors. The environmental provisions of the investment agreement are shown to be intimately connected with the project's financial arrangements and with the efficient utilization of the ore deposit. Moreover, the project will have major social effects on remote and traditional cultures, and anticipating these effects becomes part of the overall analysis.

Tropical deforestation for commercial log and lumber export is highly controversial. In the space of ten years, Indonesia became the world's largest exporter of tropical hardwood logs, with 89 percent of its nonprotected or reserved forest area committed under logging concessions. Malcolm Gillis explores the subtle questions of divergent interests between Indonesia and its foreign investors, and among Indonesian government agencies. He shows that, initially, most disputes with foreign investors centered on downstream processing, taxation, and use of expatriate labor, while environmental disputes were minimal. But peripheral conflicts among Indonesian government agencies with differing objectives (jobs, foreign exchange, taxes, resource protection) have had significant environmental content. Ironically, although large MNC's have the technical and managerial capacity to improve forest resource management significantly, most have now withdrawn from Indonesian forestry operations.

Another issue of international concern is the use and abuse of pesticides in developing countries, and the role of MNC's therein. Louis Goodman demonstrates that in Mexico, despite a large and long-established domestic industry, MNC's still play a key role in the import, production, formulation, and use of pesticides. The author emphasizes that the MNC-pesticide link is but one element of a matrix of pesticide issues, ranging from the safety of farm workers and consumers to pesticide resistance. Despite good legislation, fragmentation of responsibilities among government agencies and a lack of attention to implementation, monitoring, and enforcement mean that Mexican pesticide problems are far from being controlled. Yet, Goodman suggests, MNC's are well placed to take a more active role in curbing pesticide abuse, in part through technology transfer.

**CHAPTER TWO**  Environmental Negotiations

in the Ok Tedi Mine in Papua New Guinea

William Pintz

In mid-1984 the world's newest copper mine commenced operation in Papua New Guinea (PNG). Called Ok Tedi after the local river, this $1.5 billion project is being constructed in one of the world's most remote and inhospitable regions. When it is in full production, Ok Tedi will bring about profound changes both within the mining region and generally for the young nation of Papua New Guinea. These changes will range from expanded employment and small business opportunities for the local residents to important political and development changes in the general economy. One of the most interesting aspects of this project is the way mining investors and the government ultimately reconciled their differing perceptions of the environmental impact of the mine. The process of reconciliation—basically a negotiating process, rather than a legislative one—may have implications for other developing nations dealing with the problems of environmental regulation.

### The Legal and Institutional Framework

The history of environmental policy in PNG is closely related to the growing worldwide environmental awareness that emerged in the 1960s and 1970s. It is important to keep the nation's legislative and policy concerns within a global (and particularly the Australian) historical context.

As an objective of public policy, environmental responsibilities were spelled out when the PNG constitution was established in 1975 and given particular importance as one of the nation's five constitutional goals. The constitution states:

> We declare our fourth goal to be for Papua New Guinea's natural resources and environment to be conserved and used for the collective benefit of us all, and be replenished for the benefit of future generations.
>
> We accordingly call for:
>
> (1) wise use to be made of our natural resources and the environments in and on the land or seabed, in the sea, under the land, and in the air, in the interests of our development and in trust for future generations; and
>
> (2) the conservation and replenishment, for the benefit of ourselves and posterity of the environment and its scenic and historical qualities; and
>
> (3) all necessary steps to be taken to give adequate protection to our valued birds, animals, fish, insects, plants and trees.

In 1974 an Office of Environment and Conservation was established within the Department of Natural Resources. Placing this office in a department primarily concerned with resource *development* reflected a failure to recognize the distinction between regulation and investment promotion. The fledgling Office of Environment proceeded to produce a white paper on environmental policy, adopted by the PNG parliament in 1976, that sets out basic environmental principles. Whether the constitutional provisions or the white paper principles were widely understood or reflective of the attitudes of a majority of PNG citizens has never been ascertained. Nevertheless, environmental concerns are unquestionably part of the attachment of rural people to the land.

By 1978 three far-reaching pieces of legislation had been prepared and passed by the PNG parliament: the Environmental Planning Act, the Environmental Contaminants Act, and the Conservation Areas Act. These formed an integrated environmental regulatory framework for the nation. Although the acts were passed in 1978, their actual implementation was delayed until March 1980, when implementing guidelines were eventually published.

At an administrative level, the Office of Environment has been faced with chronic funding and staffing problems and has never been equipped to service the regulatory functions outlined in its legislative mandate. Thus far, the office's major accomplishment has been translating the lofty ideals of the constitution into legislation rather than serving as a regulatory watchdog. In carrying out its mandate, the relatively weak Office of Environment has come into direct conflict with other agencies of the government, particularly the powerful Finance, Planning, and Minerals and Energy departments which have been preoccupied with mineral developments.

The history of modern large-scale mining in PNG began in the 1970s with the discovery and ultimate development of the giant Panguna mine on the island of Bougainville. The discovery of the Bougainville mine led other multinational mining companies to base exploration on geological concepts that related major mineral occurrences to theories of plate tectonics. An early entrant into this Pacific rim exploration strategy was the American copper producer, Kennecott. By late 1968 Kennecott had discovered the Ok Tedi deposit at Mt. Fubilan in the Star Mountains of Western PNG, about twelve miles from the Indonesian border. Following an intense exploration program on Mt. Fubilan, Kennecott approached the Australian administration in 1972 regarding development terms and conditions. Over the next eighteen months, negotiations continued sporadically against a growing background of PNG nationalism and pressure for independence. By mid-1973 it was clear to all parties that an agreement would be possible only through direct negotiations with representatives of the emerging PNG state. For a number of reasons (including a violent resident reaction and a secession movement at Bougainville, which was partially related to environmental issues), the Kennecott negotiations collapsed in late 1974. New investors were sought and eventually attracted to the project.

Given the history of the aborted Kennecott negotiations, prospective new investors sought a comprehensive development agreement with the government as a precondition for entry. Such an agreement was, in fact, concluded with the Australian mining company, Broken Hill Proprietory (BHP), on the eve of independence in 1975; following BHP's formation of a project consortium, it was enacted as the Ok Tedi (Mining) Act of 1976. The Ok Tedi agreement is a long and complicated document that encompasses a wide range of feasibility and developmental questions. Environmental conditions are prominently featured in clause 29 and schedule II of the agreement, which set out an elaborate environmental studies problem. The pragmatic character of the environmental provision of the agreement is embodied in clause 29.13, which recognizes that mining is inevitably an environmentally disruptive development activity:

Without in any way limiting the Company's obligation to implement the Approved Proposals relating to environmental management and protection and the disposal of overburden tailings and other waste in accordance with Clause 29.2, regard in determining the extent and limits of the Company's obligations under this Clause 29 shall be had to the limited present use of the area, to the need for its development, to the State's desire for the Project to proceed and be economically viable, and to the effect the Project must necessarily have on the Environment. The Company's obligation will be to act reasonably to mitigate damage to the Environment in these acknowledged circumstances.

Several points need to be made regarding the overlapping histories of the Ok Tedi and Bougainville mines with the evolving environmental, legal, and institutional framework. First, the Bougainville mine was developed against a background of regulatory laissez-faire toward environmental issues in Australia. That such an attitude permeated mining development in Australia's colony—PNG—was natural and hardly surprising. As a result the mine was developed in a manner that would clearly be unacceptable today. Of Bougainville's many adverse environmental effects, the two that were subsequently most significant for Ok Tedi were the effects of mine sediment and tailings on the adjacent river system and the social impact of mine development.

Second, the negotiation of the Ok Tedi accords took place in 1975, after the constitutional declaration but before the promulgation of the government white paper of 1976 and the enactment of specific legislation in 1978. An interesting commentary on BHP's perceptions of the status of environmental protection at this juncture is reflected in the single mention of environment in its project appraisal document (designed to solicit consortium partners), which states, "It also covers the necessary environmental studies to ensure that no damage is done to the life of the people or the river system" (page 67). Although BHP undoubtedly took its environmental obligations under the Ok Tedi agreement seriously, its relegation of environment to a single sentence in a seventy-page document shows that establishing the mine's economic and technical viability definitely had priority in the feasibility evaluations.

Third, the eventual passage of environmental legislation in 1978—when the BHP consortium was well along with its feasibility study—presented the government with a policy dilemma and prompted a short but intense power struggle within the bureaucracy that seriously eroded the institutional power of the Office of Environment. In 1979, the Office of Environment insisted that all mining projects should come under the ambit of its legislation. It proposed drafting guidelines for both Bougainville and Ok Tedi—even though both projects had existing environmental provisions in their agreements. The Minerals and Energy Department, together with those of Planning and Finance, countered this proposal by pointing out that the imposition of retroactive environmental requirements would be tantamount to bad faith on the government's part. Further, they argued that the clauses on environmental protection of the Ok Tedi agreement, together with the regulatory backing of an administratively strong department, would be preferable to the weak administrative capacity and still-to-be-defined environmental guidelines of the Office of Environment. In the end, the Minerals and Energy Department prevailed, and both Bougainville and Ok Tedi were exempted from the environmental legislation. Since the guidelines under the environmental legislation were not finally promulgated until mid-1980, there is little doubt that imposition of the general law over the provisions of the Ok Tedi Agreement would have delayed the implementation of the project.

### The Ok Tedi Project

Early Environmental Understandings. By mid-1976 BHP had successfully formed a consortium consisting of the Standard Oil Company of Indiana (AMOCO) and a group of German companies[1] operating under the name Kupferexplorations-gesellschaft MGH (KE). The consortium immediately embarked on an ambitious feasibility study to verify and expand on the geological and design concepts studies by Kennecott and the PNG government.[2]

The environmental obligations of the Ok Tedi consortium were defined by the basic agreement. However, in an attempt to limit their environmental expenditures, the consortium successfully negotiated a budgetary ceiling of 150,000 kina (U.S. $180,000). This limitation (which the consortium saw as an expenditure ceiling) meant that only limited environmental fieldwork could be undertaken. Consequently, the environmental data presented in the ten-volume feasibility study drew heavily on secondary sources and was subject to direct challenge by the government. Furthermore, the willingness of the government to spend several times the consortium's commitment on its own environmental investigations meant that in the ensuing negotiations, the tactical advantage on environmental issues was with the PNG government.

A second interesting feature of the basic Ok Tedi Agreement was the public nature of all environmental information. Although the agreement contains a far-reaching confidentiality clause (clause 5.8), the environmental studies are specifically exempted. Furthermore, since the agreement was enacted as an act of the PNG parliament, the extensive description of the Environmental Impact Study (EIS) in schedule II meant that basic environmental concerns were public knowledge. Thus, both the Environmental Impact Study blueprint (schedule II) and the EIS studies (exempted by clause 5.8) were open to public review.

Several points from the feasibility experience are worth highlighting. First, the consortium, because of an understandable desire to limit its budgetary commitments to an unproven project, was unwilling to carry out primary fieldwork and thus was not in a position to present hard data on environmental impact during the negotiations. This may have resulted in unnecessarily onerous—and costly—environmental requirements being placed on the consortium. Second, the imposition of an unreasonably low budget on an environment obligation indicates something about the people who normally negotiate Less Developed Country (LDC) mining agreements. Certainly there is nothing to suggest that the lawyers, financial analysts, and planners normally involved in negotiations of this sort are equipped to anticipate the cost of a scientific environmental study program. This provides a strong argument for involving project implementors and environmental specialists in at least some aspects of the agreement negotiations. Third, at Ok Tedi—and other similar projects where one of the tasks of a feasibility study is to define an environmental baseline—it is probably inappropriate to expect that process design or infrastructure planning will be environmentally sensitive, since environmental information is rarely available early in the feasibility period when the designers most need it.

The Natural and Socioeconomic Setting of the Ok Tedi Mine. The physical environment of the Star Mountains is inherently unstable. The mining region is characterized by extremely heavy rainfall, infrequent but intense seismic activity, unstable geology, and volatile hydrology. Massive landslides are common, and overnight river fluctuations of up to twenty-five feet alternate with periodic drought conditions.

Rainfall at the mine township varies between 450 and 550 inches per year. Residents refer to the dry season as a period when it rains all night and the wet season as a period when it rains all night *and* all day. The topography of the mountains is extremely rugged, and the geology largely comprises porous, discontinuous limestone structures of varying strengths. Between 1900 and 1976, twenty-seven seismic events were recorded within 112 miles of the mine site, with ten in excess of 6.0 on the modified Mercalli earthquake scale.[3] The combination of seismic activity, heavy rainfall, and relatively weak geology account for the size and frequency of major landslides and erosion patterns in the area. In addition to the substantial engineering challenges presented by such conditions, the unstable nature of the physical environment also makes it extremely difficult to determine baseline conditions and to monitor mine-induced effects.

The estimated population of the Kiunga subprovince in which Mt. Fubilan is located is probably less than 25,000, divided between five culture groups. The people of the region have a simple way of life, and their development prospects are very limited. The smallest of these groups —the *Min* people—subsist in the inhospitable Star Mountains. Other groups live in the nearby foothills and lowland regions. Mosquito-borne diseases are pandemic throughout the district, and malnutrition is widespread.

A simplified profile of the various ecological zones and their subsistence uses is presented in figure 2.1. Basically, the *Min* people are hunter-gatherers who practice a shifting subsistence agriculture based on taro. Hunting is widely practiced by the men, but due to cultural taboos many types of meat protein are not eaten by women or girls. Instead, females tend to depend on fish and certain reptiles as a primary protein source. Thus, any interference in the aquatic ecology of the watercourses could affect dramatically the already marginal protein intake of women.

In the foothills the *Ningerum* people practice a slightly more sophisticated subsistence agriculture using riverbank gardens. Since the foothills region is transitional in the topography of the area, river flow drops significantly from that in the mountains. This abrupt drop in river velocity has important implications for the deposition of river sediment in the *Ningerum* area: sediment deposits could cause flooding of the riverbank gardens. Maintaining a significant fish protein dietary source and sustaining the viability of the *Ningerum*'s gardening practices were the primary objectives of the government's environmental policy toward Ok Tedi. Late in the feasibility period, however, a question was raised about the possibility that heavy metals in the mine sediments might be deposited in the middle reaches of the Fly River, where water flow rates dropped significantly.

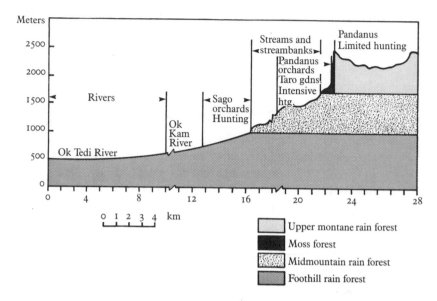

**Figure 2.1** Star Mountains Ecological Zones. *Source:* David Hyndman, "Wopkaimin Subsistence: Cultural Ecology in the New Guinea Highland Fringe," Ph.D. dissertation, University of Queensland, 1976.

In the area of concern the Fly River forms the international border between Papua New Guinea and Indonesia.

Since the mining activities themselves, together with the supporting infrastructure, were to be spread over a broad region of the Star Mountains, it was inevitable that changing land-use patterns would conflict with the traditional way of life in the *Min* and *Ningerum* areas. In addition, since residents who wanted to get jobs or start businesses would be given preference over outsiders under the Ok Tedi Agreement, it was thought that the transformation of their economic prospects might threaten their traditional culture. Finally, the rapid influx of outsiders seeking mine employment was seen as a challenge to the social environment of the region.

### The Ok Tedi Mine—A Short Technical Description

The Mineral Deposit and Technical Strategy. The geology of Mt. Fubilan is most easily thought of as a heavily weathered, gold-mineralized blanket overlying a copper ore body. Over time, the surface of the porphyry intrusion underwent extensive weathering and structural deterioration. This weathering, combined with percolating rainwater, tended to concentrate the copper minerals within the mountain at the water table. Two aspects of this mineralization had direct environmental importance to mine development: the weak character of the weathered capping rocks and the spatial and technological implications of the capping-enriched zone interface. A simplified scheme of the Mt. Fubilan mineralization is presented in figure 2.2.

The Ok Tedi consortium proposed developing the mine in three stages. In stage one the gold-bearing capping material would be mined at a 15,000 tpd (metric tons per day) rate. In stage two a copper processing plant would be developed and operated (in parallel) with the gold plant. With the depletion of the capping material, in stage three the gold plant would be converted to a second copper processing plant with a total daily throughput of 45,000 tpd.

**Figure 2.2**   The Ok Tedi Project Mt. Fubilan Ore Body. *Source:* Adapted from *Information Brochure Ok Tedi Copper Project* (1980).

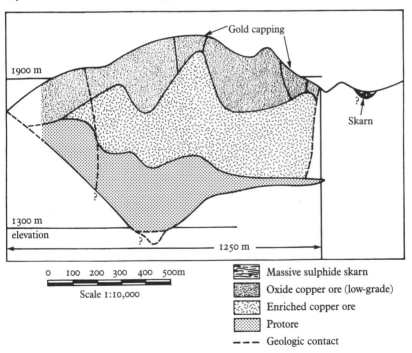

Associated with actual development of the ore body, the Ok Tedi consortium proposed to construct supporting road, township, and hydroelectric infrastructures. Cost estimates for the completed three-stage project, including infrastructure, are about $1.5 billion. The results of the feasibility study were extremely promising and suggested a profitable but high-risk investment opportunity. The financial analysis of the proposed project suggested that overall economics were more sensitive to operating costs than to changes in capital expenditures. This fact had a significant bearing on the ultimate environmental agreements.

Emerging Environmental Issues. The main environmental issues under dispute at the conclusion of the feasibility period principally involved the physical impacts of the mine on the region.[4] Since these issues were actively debated and argued within the broader context of mine development proposals, it is difficult to judge whether the PNG government would, in fact, have stopped the project purely for environmental reasons. Without question, however, environment was an important political issue[5] as suggested by its inclusion as one of five overriding principles established by the PNG cabinet to guide the government negotiators:

> Council directed the negotiating team to negotiate with the Ok Tedi Consortium on the following principles. . . .
>
> (e) The Consortium should follow a policy of optimal resource utilization consistent with economic viability and adequate protection of the environment especially in relation to the gold in the leached capping rock of Mt. Fubilan;
>
> (f) The Consortium should be advised of the Government's concern with the social and ecological consequences of the soft waste rock proposals and of the Government's view that these proposals cannot be approved on the evidence currently before the Government.

As set out in the cabinet directive, primary concern focussed not only on the effects that the leached capping material (that is, "soft waste rock") would have on the river system but also on the social consequences of ecological disruption (such as to fishing and riverbank gardens). There was concern about the impact of possible turbidity and sedimentation, of processing chemicals (cyanide), and of heavy metals (leached copper) from the waste rocks. It was felt that provision should be made for maintenance of environmental control structures, like tailings or waste dumps, after mine closure.

Post-feasibility discussions focussed on the effect of mine-induced deposition in the river systems. Studies of the effects of waste rock from the mine were conducted by both government and company scientists and involved fieldwork and laboratory tests. The sedimentation scientists seemed to agree that the most important physical parameters were the quantity and size distribution of waste rock: the greater the mean size of the mine waste rock and the greater the volume of waste rock, the greater were the anticipated depositional effects of mine waste on the river system. Greater deposition implied flooding of the *Ningerum* riverbank gardens and villages.

The consortium collected and analyzed several samples of riverbed material from various places in the Ok Tedi and Fly River systems and concluded that the Ok Tedi waste rock would simply wash through the river system and be deposited at sea in the Papuan Gulf. In contrast, government-sponsored studies, conducted by scientists from the Australian National University (ANU), focussed on applying hydraulic equations in conjunction with river profiles and cross sections of the Ok Tedi-Fly system.[6] The ANU studies reached considerably less optimistic conclusions than the consortium's. They concluded that the deposition could raise river levels by up to ten meters in areas adjacent to important *Ningerum* settlements. Thus, the consortium and the government studies used different and equally imperfect depositional analogies and came to opposing conclusions about the downstream effects of the mine.

Laboratory studies aimed at simulating the size distribution that would result from the natural aggrading effects of the river system were also conducted. Several techniques were employed, including grinding the ore in a conventional ore grinding mill, manual crushing using mortar and pestle, and running the weak waste rock in a food blender. None of the techniques was convincing nor was there any correlation in the resulting size distribution information.

The estimation of waste rock quantities should have followed from the mathematics of the basic open pit mining plan, but here again major estimating uncertainties seemed to be the rule rather than the exception. The waste quantity estimates were complicated as a result of geological differentiation in the rock strengths of the capping rocks. At first, all size and volume estimates were made on the premise that the capping material was homogeneous and that waste rock and ore rock had the same essential characteristics. However, some months after the feasibility study was completed, this assumption was challenged by the chief project geologist. He concluded that the waste rock (although still relatively weak) was at least twice as strong (competent) as the ore rocks. The combination of changing mining plans and different rock strengths made estimation of waste rock volumes extremely problematic, with estimates ranging from 170 million metric tons (weak waste) to 720 million metric tons (all waste).

The converse of the deposition problem was the turbidity problem. Concern was voiced that the volume of finely suspended sediment in the river might adversely affect aquatic ecology and eventually disrupt subsistence fishing. Anthropologists noted the devastating effects of previous natural landslides on subsistence fishing in the Ok Tedi region. Although deposition attracted more attention than turbidity in the negotiations, it was clear that suspended sediment was an urgent problem. Since both a large and small waste rock size distribution would have adverse (but different) ecological consequences, the obvious conclusion was that the waste rock must be kept out of the river if environmental objectives were to be achieved.

The mining consortium planned to develop the leached (gold) capping of Mt. Fubilan using a sophisticated carbon-in-pulp (CIP) cyanide process. The toxicity of cyanide raised public health and ecological concerns connected with the chemical's transportation and eventual release in the mine tailings. Although cyanide processing of gold ore has a long history in the mining industry, there is a surprising vacuum in the professional literature about permissible release standards and ecological effects at tropical sites. This situation is complicated because cyanide is released there both chemically "free" and combined with other minerals in mine tailings. Free cyanide is known to undergo a rapid natural decomposition, but complexed cyanide, which is considerably less toxic, is environmentally more persistent. In August 1980 AMOCO's environmental department modeled the hypothetical cyanide release and reviewed the professional literature on the subject.[7] AMOCO concluded that "the cyanide effluents anticipated to result from the Ok Tedi Project pose no threat to either public health or aquatic life."

The various technology decisions behind the three-stage strategy of project development meant that the facilities available for processing the gold ore were economically suboptimal. This suboptimization arose as a result of a design constraint imposed by the Bechtel Corporation, which acted as engineering advisor and technical auditor. Bechtel argued that early processing capacities should not exceed twice the processing capacity of the largest operating CIP cyanide plant. The consequence of this processing constraint was that a significant volume of material above the ore cutoff grade of one gram per metric ton could not be processed and had to be rejected into the river system as waste rock. This rejected material amounted to about 17 million metric tons over the first five years of operation and had a value of $290 million. As discussed below, additional substantial tonnages of economic ore were also classified as waste and scheduled for river dumping. Needless to say, this rejection of economic ore substantially accentuated the sedimentation/turbidity consequences of the mine.

### Relationship of Environment to Other Negotiating Issues

To appreciate the context of the Ok Tedi negotiations, the interplay of environment with two other major issues—financial structure and resource utilization—must be examined. The interaction of these issues, like the strong political mandate resulting from the ecological consequences of the Bougainville mine, was an important policy factor that determined the government's approach to individual environmental questions. That the interrelation of such tangential issues had a bearing on the environmental strategy of the basic negotiating process is testimony to the growing sophistication of developing-country governments in understanding and negotiating natural resource agreements.

Taxes, Finance, and Environment. As plans for Ok Tedi were being made, a series of questions related to fiscal policy and to the project's financial structure were addressed:

1. Should environmental expenditures be considered as investment or operating costs?
2. How can uncertainties in the costs of environmental facilities be dealt with?
3. What implications do legal questions relating to the environment as an undefined contingent liability have for lenders who are assessing the project's financial soundness?

Environmental expenditures were related to the way the project's annual tax liability would be defined. Should the cost of environmental facilities be counted as a depreciable capital investment or as an immediately deductible operating expense? The environmental expenditures most affected by this distinction were the waste rock retention structures (about $25 million) and the tailings dam (about $40 million). Within design limits, there was scope for constructing these facilities either as part of the initial construction program (and therefore as an initial capital investment) or incrementally over a significant period (as an operating expenditure). At first glance, the incremental approach would appear to be preferable for the consortium.[8] Within a traditional business-tax system, it would certainly be preferable. Under the PNG mineral-tax scheme, however, an additional profits tax (APT) is levied when project profitability exceeds an agreed-upon discounted cash-flow return on investment. Without going into the complexities of the APT system, it is sufficient to note that for a sufficiently profitable project the greater the investment base the longer the APT will be deferred.

Although this tax structure is not uniquely related to expenditures on environmental facilities, the technical nature of the Ok Tedi tailings and waste rock facilities, together with the sizable sums involved, meant that tax considerations could be important to the selection of design and construction strategies. Since such facilities and technical options are relatively common to mining projects worldwide, the Ok Tedi example may well have many parallels elsewhere. Similarly, although the APT system is uniquely Papua New Guinean, the generic notion of a resource rent tax based on project cash flow is rapidly gaining favor throughout the developing world, as well as in developed nations, such as Australia. At Ok Tedi, the incremental (operating cost) approach to environmental facilities expenditures was taken.

Given the inherent uncertainties of environmental impacts as well as remedial costs, the estimation of the financial consequences of environmental regulation is, at best, a hazardous task. At Ok Tedi, two potential environmental costs were particularly problematic: the neutralization of residual cyanide in the mine tailings and the costs of establishing and maintaining the waste rock dumps in the unstable Star Mountains. Under such uncertainty, overzealous environmental regulation is both illogical and probably contrary to the long-term interests of both parties.

During the Ok Tedi feasibility study, provision for chemical destruction of residual cyanide in the mine tailings was periodically considered by the project engineers. However, there were genuine technical uncertainties associated with the cyanide destruction question and it was not squarely faced until after the feasibility financial evaluations had been completed. This gave the government the impression that the company was insensitive to one of the government's primary concerns. In commenting on the consortium's cyanide submission, the government's technical consultants reached the following conclusions: "We consider the Consortium documents, in present form, to be inadequate as the basis for deletion of the cyanide destruction facilities from the project plans and believe it would be prudent of the Government to require the inclusion of such destruction facilities in the project estimates, at least for the purposes of the Feasibility Study and Proposals."[9] Similarly, uncertainty about the disposal of weak waste rock worked to undermine the government's confidence in the consortium's commitment to environmental protection. Uncertainty worked three ways that were contrary to the investor's interests:

1. The consortium's commitment to a major policy concern of the government was brought into doubt.
2. In the consortium's attempt to establish an attractive financial evaluation of the project, environment was implicitly treated as an unnecessary "extra."
3. A direct adversarial relationship based on stereotypes of environmentally abusive multinational corporations was reinforced.

In short, the tactical handling of what both sides understood to be legitimate uncertainty was corrosive to the immediate negotiating framework and to the long-term relationship between the consortium and the government. The resolution of these environmental interests was remarkably rational, but the long-term psychological legacy of the suspicions they engendered are proving costly to the project.

Two other financial-environmental factors are of some importance at Ok Tedi: compensation for environmental damage and the perception of financial institutions that environmental obligations can form contingent liabilities and financial risks.

Clause 29.12 of the original Ok Tedi agreement contains provisions for compensation for injuries or damages arising from the environmental consequences of the project. Blanket clauses such as 29.12 are deceptive, however, since they imply an obligation that, given the unstable natural conditions of the Star Mountains, would be virtually impossible to establish legally. The burden of proof lies with the party bringing suit, and since environmental monitoring for Ok Tedi is in the hands of the company, it is difficult to imagine how legal redress could ever be successful. On the other hand, it is naive to believe that the absence of effective legal or administrative remedies would release the mining consortium from compensatory liability. There is ample evidence from PNG and elsewhere that where Western legal systems fail to meet customary notions of justice or compensation, social disruption (such as riots, strikes, or the destruction of property) may result.

Environmental liability raises another question related to debt finance. In their assessment of project loan documents, lenders are interested primarily in risks that the project will not be as successful financially as anticipated. Typical loan agreements provide for investor obligations that range from direct loan guarantees to performance, marketing, and completion undertakings. Clearly, an open-ended environmental liability, such as offered in clause 29.12, poses a substantial financial risk that lenders may well take into consideration in their overall loan assessment.[10]

Environment and Resource Utilization. The term "resource utilization" was used to describe the extent to which the in-situ mineral resources at Mt. Fubilan (such as gold, copper, silver, and molybdenum) would be converted into direct project revenues. Thus, resource utilization covered a wide range of techno-economic questions including ore cutoff grade, metallurgical recovery, and process design capacity. Although such technical matters are normally within the management prerogatives of the mining company, the increasing participation of host governments as equity partners in new mining ventures implies legitimate—but nonregulatory—rights to review such decisions. Furthermore, the almost universal claim of developing-country governments to public ownership of in-situ resources implies a derivative policy concern with how those national resources are being developed.

At Ok Tedi, the chief relationships between environment and resource policy involved the definition and disposal of mine waste. Here, the government faced major problems in defining "the public interest." The dilemma related to assessing and weighing the adverse environmental consequences associated with *all* technical resource development options. It has already been pointed out that the choice between turbidity and depositionally induced riverbank flooding was a Hobson's choice. A parallel problem existed on the resource utilization issue. The government wanted to increase production to the point where marginal revenues equaled marginal costs. This led to arguments about the ore cutoff grade that defined ore versus waste. If the cutoff criterion was set below that proposed in the feasibility study, the volume of waste rock entering the river system would have been dramatically reduced. Conversely, the increased production volume resulting from the lower grade ore would have aggravated the cyanide and mine tailings problems.

The situation for the copper ore was further complicated by the water-soluble nature of the copper sulfide minerals. The waste rock contained significant, but subeconomic, quantities of soluble copper that, under the heavy rainfall conditions of the Star Mountains, were expected to leach into the river even if the mine waste itself never entered the drainage system. In a careful review of the geochemical processes and chemical pollution from the mine, a government consultant concluded: "The toxicity of heavy metals removed into the aquatic environment of the Ok Tedi River drainage system from the waste rock dump areas of Mt. Fubilan and the Ok Ma tailings basin is an issue of principal concern in evaluation of the possible effects of the proposed mining project."[11] Since the waste-dump copper leachate had direct economic value, there existed a financial as well as environmental incentive for leachate control. In contrast to the controversy that surrounded the cutoff grade debate, leachate control was readily accepted by both sides. The lesson here is two-fold: the interplay between enhanced resource recovery and environmental concerns cannot automatically be assumed to have been factored into the feasibility evaluation, and the *net* benefits and costs of enhanced recovery options are not easily estimated.

### The Environmental Negotiations—Contractual Understandings and Implementation

Setting and Atmosphere of the Negotiations. Environmental, resource utilization, and financial issues were taken up in February 1980 in conjunction with consideration of the feasibility study. At this point the economic evaluation of the project had moved from marginal to attractive amid soaring gold prices.[12] Thus the negotiations took place in a psychological climate that saw Ok Tedi as a highly profitable, if risky, investment opportunity.

To permit consideration of the feasibility study by the various boards of directors, the original schedule had to be delayed by six months. The postfeasibility study negotiations thus overlapped with provincial elections in the Fly River Province where Ok Tedi is located. To avoid the possibility of having the project become a political football, an extensive public consultation program jointly planned by the consortium and the national government had to be abandoned. Given the technical nature of the environmental debate during 1979–80, it is probably fortunate that public anxieties were not raised over environmental solutions that were still evolving.

In practice the public nature of the Ok Tedi environmental studies had little direct, but enormous indirect, consequences for public perceptions of the environmental impact of the project. By their nature the studies were highly technical, and it is doubtful whether laypersons could have directly grasped either their methodological nuances or their ecological implications without an extended tutorial. Moreover, the "open-for-public-review" character of the environmental studies legally pertained only to work undertaken by the consortium. The government, on the other hand, had no such sunshine requirement on its own environmental work. Indeed at various times the government's environmental reports were among the most closely guarded negotiating documents.

This information gap was partially, but indirectly, bridged with the publication in 1981 of Richard Jackson's highly readable and popular book, *Ok Tedi: Pot of Gold*. Jackson, as government consultant and impact analyst, had a long association with the project and had spent innumerable hours as a member of the government management team plowing through the environmental reports. *Ok Tedi: Pot of Gold* presented an almost painless exposition of the Ok Tedi environmental and social anthropology and popularized the project far better than any formal publicity campaign.

Resolution of Environmental Questions. Four weeks before the negotiations convened, the government received the final report of the ANU sedimentation studies. Although it was slightly ambiguous on some questions and cautious on others, the report suggested that the river disposal of the weak leached capping rock was environmentally risky. In preparing for the negotiations the government team had to reach a decision about what course to follow on the waste rock issue. Outright rejection of at least some river disposal was impractical since construction activities and preproduction stripping of the ore body would inevitably create waste rock volumes in advance of the construction of any containment structure. On the other hand, the government could not accept the environmental risks of unlimited river disposal. In the end the government decided that, given the uncertain impact of river dumping, a maximum limit should be set and provisions should be made to reevaluate the impact of the waste rock. This solution, although hardly elegant, was pragmatically based and politically defensible. Obviously the key was to find an appropriate maximum dumping limit that would not constrain the project timetable but that would force an early review of the environmental impact.

After considerable discussion the government negotiators concluded that a limit of 60 million metric tons of weak waste rock would form a suitable limit. Continued river dumping beyond this level would require a specific variance from the government that would be granted only on the basis of convincing empirical evidence that the river system was not being affected. Two things are important about the government's waste rock negotiating strategy: the dumping limit had little or no scientific basis and was chosen for negotiating, not ecological, reasons; and the strategy was tied to one of the government's other major negotiating issues—resource utilization.

Although the 60-million-ton limitation initially slipped quietly into the negotiations, it subsequently became the focus of heated debate. At one point the government actually invited the consortium to justify some other limit. In the final analysis the limitation was accepted simply because both sides feared the delay and potential inconclusiveness of attempting to scientifically set a less arbitrary limit more than they feared the increased costs and environmental risks of a completely arbitrary one.

Although less contentious, the cyanide question was equally difficult. Predictably, the debate centered on the release, breakdown, and toxicity of free and complexed cyanide. In discussions it emerged that the consortium's real worry about the neutralization of cyanide stemmed from the high operating costs of neutralization facilities. Once this was recognized, the pragmatic solution similar to the waste rock agreement was structured. The consortium agreed to construct facilities for chemical destruction of cyanide as part of the initial construction program on the understanding that if it could empirically be demonstrated that cyanide toxicity was not an environmental threat, the facilities might not need to be operated.[13] Although the burden of proof in the waste rock and cyanide provisions is clearly on the mining consortium, implicit recognition by the government of environmental uncertainties enabled the negotiators to reach an understanding.

Since the waste-dump copper leachates had potential commercial value, and control measures were not expected to be costly, negotiations on this issue were not contentious. The governing clause states simply that the escape of leached minerals into the Ok Tedi and Fly River systems or to groundwater aquifers will be minimized. Since the ultimate generation of waste rocks containing potential copper leachates (and, in particular, subeconomic oxide ores) would not occur until stages two and three of the project, the government was satisfied with such a general agreement on this issue.

Of all the environmental issues, the questions of environmental monitoring and compensation were the most intractable. The government proposed that an independent agency should be set up under a jointly appointed supervising scientist to defuse both the problem of monitoring naturally unstable situations and the liability-compensation questions. In addition to its field monitoring functions the agency would be empowered to adjudicate compensation claims and arrange payment from an environmental compensation fund set up by the consortium.

In its rejoinder the consortium argued that it would want total control over any such field program, since it would be paying for the monitoring. The consortium also believed that the mere existence of a compensation fund would tend to encourage claims. In any event those seeking compensation would still have access to the PNG courts.

For negotiating reasons the government did not press the proposed monitoring and compensation scheme, and the issue was dropped. This failure to deal with the compensation issue was probably not in the long-term interest of the project. Monitoring and compensation problems had already arisen at the Bougainville mine. In particular the consortium's desire to have compensation claims handled under general PNG law meant that settlements will be decided in "warden courts" by mining wardens who are untrained in environmental, scientific, or compensation evaluation techniques. Furthermore, to leave such a key public relations aspect in limbo in the face of the widespread political support for a strong environmental policy would seem to be a dubious step.

With environmental monitoring totally in the hands of the mining consortium it is hard to see how the environmental intent of the Ok Tedi master agreement can ever be routinely enforced. Although such a statement may seem at odds with the intense effort and substantial sums that the government committed to the environmental negotiation, such an approach is entirely consistent with PNG's philosophy toward mining. On numerous policy questions the PNG government has consistently chosen to leave day-to-day management with investors and to regulate through periodic audit or general legal means. Such a system has inherent risks and is open to potential abuse. But as multinational corporations have learned through bitter experience with developing country governments, compliance costs and good government relations are often a small price to pay —considering the alternatives.

If such a "self-interest" approach to environmental regulation succeeds, the question of ex post revision of agreement provisions becomes less pressing. In this regard, the Ok Tedi agreement is at odds with current contractual trends in developing countries, which set out schedules or conditions for the mutual reconsideration of basic provisions. Renegotiation clauses would no doubt have been easily accepted at Ok Tedi had they been sought by either party.[14] However, the fact of life of foreign investment agreements is that the real balance of power is essentially extralegal, and such clauses do little to alter this reality.

The environmental agreements for Ok Tedi stipulated that a massive tailings dam to retain mining residues would be constructed. Over the period of mine operation this dam would be progressively raised to accommodate several hundred million tons of fine-grained material. The environmental threat posed by this impounded material would grow as the mine aged and would logically reach its maximum at mine closure. To insure that the costs for maintenance of the impoundment dam would not become a public liability at mine closure, the supplemental agreement specified "the Company shall make provision to the reasonable satisfaction of the State for the maintenance of the tailings dam after the mine is closed."[15] Such a postclosure trust fund is relatively uncommon in the mining industry of either developed or developing nations. Including it in the Ok Tedi agreement reflects the broad negotiating strategy of the PNG government, which sought to quantify overall project costs and benefits as precisely as possible as part of the general understanding with the investment consortium.

Implementation Experience. During project construction two additional environmental studies were completed: an in-depth Environmental Impact Study (by the consortium) and a Social Impact Study (by the government). These reports shed a great deal more light on the environmental consequences of the project. It is unfortunate that they emerged only after the major contractual negotiations had been concluded. A further environmental controversy arose during this implementation period over development of the mine tailings dam.

*The Environmental Impact Study (EIS).* After the postfeasibility negotiations, the mining consortium commissioned an extensive environmental study by the consulting group of Maunsell and Partners at a cost of nearly $1 million. This study drew on work previously undertaken by the consortium and tapped virtually every environmental expert who had ever been associated with the project region. On the major negotiating issues the consortium consultants reached the following conclusions:

1. *Tailing effluents.* "Under most conditions of flow both free and complex cyanides should decay naturally to below suggested allowable

limits [free 5 micrograms/liter; complexed cyanide 100 micrograms/liter] but the cyanide destruction plant will need to be operated during periods of high flow."[16]

2. *Sedimentation.* "About 64 percent of waste rock reaching the river system is expected to pass through to the Fly River during the mine life; 85 percent of this as suspended soils which will largely continue through to the Fly Delta. . . . [F]luctuating deposition in the Ok Tedi is likely in the reaches of Manga/Birim (1 to 2 meters average from slug transport) and Mart/Fly (.1 to .5 meters)."[17]

From these conclusions it would appear that the estimates of environmental consequences that were debated during postfeasibility negotiations were essentially extreme positions. The refined methodologies and field study of the Maunsell EIS predicted a moderate environmental impact and supported the need for the environmental precautions (for example, cyanide destruction and waste rock retention) that had been negotiated. Although still to be empirically determined, the economic consequences of acceptable environmental facilities at Ok Tedi should not be a significant consideration in the profitability or operation of the project.

*The social impact study.*[18] The social impact study, sponsored by the government, was conducted by a team of researchers who had never before worked together. The report that emerged was confrontational in its advocacy of the interests of local residents and became a benchmark against which future social programs would be judged. Overall, it was an unqualified success that both challenged the conventional wisdom and advanced constructive suggestions for promoting the interests of local residents. A few of its conclusions are:

1. *National impact.* "Very little impetus is likely to be given by the project to the economic expansion of the Papua New Guinean controlled sectors or sub-sectors of the economy as compared to the impetus it will give to resident foreign business activities. . . . Ok Tedi will, under all circumstances, tend to function as an enclave with only weak links to the rest of the economy."

2. *Provincial impact.* "The project will lead to migration within the Province being directed northwards and will also attract migrants from other parts of the country."

3. *Local impact.* "Landowners are still not in a position to appreciate the long-term implications of the project nor of the agreements they will shortly be asked to consider. . . . We would urge both the Govern-

ment and Consortium to exercise the greatest diplomacy and caution on even the slightest land issue."

4. *Work force.* "Thus, we can expect that even under conditions of good training, over 30 percent of the work force will be outsiders . . . and that 85 percent of the local work force will not be employed in the project either in the mine or in urban activities which will be generated by the mine."

5. *Rural migration.* "On the whole, despite urban growth, we expect the rural populations of the two districts other than in the area immediately around Tabubil [the mine site] not to decline."

6. *Social inequality.* "We list what we feel to be the most damaging social impacts of the mine which are primarily the generation of different forms of inequality in the area; these would include expatriates/nationals, landowners receiving royalties/landowners receiving occupation fees only, skilled employees from outside the region/local employees, etc."

In response to the social impact study, the government and consortium embarked on what, for want of a better term, might be called a "participation strategy." The basic premise was that further minimization of impact costs (beyond the quite considerable measures agreed in the postfeasibility documents) were likely to be expensive and of questionable effectiveness given the uncertainties and unstable natural environment of the area. However, there seemed to be significant scope for increasing the direct participation of the local people in the project's benefits through promotion of small business and agricultural projects. The "participation strategy" has been one of the outstanding successes of the implementation period due mostly to the efforts of the mining consortium (see below).

*The tailings dam controversy.* A final and unusual twist in Ok Tedi's environmental history occurred between November 1983 and February 1984. The design criteria for the tailings dam had long concerned government policy makers. Midway through the feasibility period, government planners recognized the formidable engineering challenges involved in developing a tailings dam to retain several hundred million tons of fine-grained material in an area of pronounced seismic events and heavy rainfall.

During construction of the mine, several tailings dam schemes were considered. Eventually a design that involved a complex diversion and retainment structure on the Ok Ma River was adopted. Due to numerous delays, however, the tailings disposal system fell behind the overall construction schedule for stage one of the project. In November 1983 the consortium approached the government and proposed that an alternative retention system be adopted that would permit production to start nine months earlier than under the approved scheme. The alternative proposal involved a new technical concept developed by the KE partners for the steel industry in Germany; it had never been tried for the retention of base metal mine tailings. The consortium estimated that this method would accelerate nearly $150 million of project revenues, whereas adhering to the originally agreed scheme and timetable was expected to cause both additional direct costs and problems with debt service. In December the PNG cabinet considered the alternative retention system. In an affirmation of its strong environmental attitudes, the cabinet rejected it as unproven and environmentally less certain than the approved scheme. Rejection by the cabinet of an option that would enable production to begin sooner came as a major shock to consortium management.

On January 7, 1984, the tailings dam controversy became a moot issue when a massive landslide dumped an estimated 50 million tons of material into the center of the dam site. The landslide left the PNG cabinet with no option but to accept the alternative scheme—at least as an interim measure. However, the landslide clearly suggested that the geo-technical basis for the original (approved) proposal was inadequate. This recognition increased the government's distrust of the consortium's tailings dam proposal, a distrust reflected in the following newspaper account of the government reaction to the landslide: "We might have to call in specialists to check out why it occurred. It is possible it was done with a little bit of help."[19]

The ironic conclusion of the tailings dam saga occurred in early February, when the government's own regulatory agency, the Water Resources Board, threatened to bring a public-interest lawsuit against the government and the consortium for breaching discharge standards of the Water Resources Act. Although nothing came of this suit, the threat suggests how divisive the interim tailings dam decision had been within the government bureaucracy.[20]

**Summary and Conclusions**

In summarizing the Ok Tedi experience, it is tempting to generalize to similar projects elsewhere. Whether such generalization is warranted is beyond the scope of an individual case study. However, it is worthwhile to briefly review the major environmental lessons from Ok Tedi.

Lessons Learned.

1. The institutional, legal, and bureaucratic realities of environmental regulation may be deceptive due to the inherent intragovernmental struggle between "development" and "environmental conservation" attitudes in LDC's.

2. It is probably unrealistic to expect that major environmental expenditures will be undertaken prior to establishing the economic viability of a project.

3. Where the government is committed to environmental protection, it may be to the tactical and negotiating disadvantage of developers to underfund primary environmental fieldwork.

4. The involvement of project implementors (project engineers, environmental scientists, etc.) in addition to planners, lawyers, and financial analysts should go some way toward insuring that contractual financial limits correspond to the reality of agreed environmental work programs.

5. The planning and design of environmental facilities obviously has important profit and tax implications. However, the interplay of various types of tax schemes (such as additional profit taxes) means that an overall impact cannot be determined without a detailed tax assessment.

6. Both sides must recognize and be willing to deal with the existence of genuine uncertainty in structuring environmental agreements. The perceived environmental commitment of developers is vital to the preservation of good public and governmental relations.

7. Rural residents possess a clear sense of "natural justice" based on their traditional values. If prevented from seeking redress (for example, compensation) from a Western-style legal system, the likelihood of costly social disruption may increase.

8. Open-ended environmental obligations may form contingent liabilities and affect the risk assessment of potential project lenders.

9. Some environmental problems may have direct financial advantages through increased resource recovery. Examples may include the commercial recovery of waste rock leachates and the processing of lower grade ores.

10. In an environmental negotiating situation, arbitrary environmental limits or standards may sometimes be preferable to the delay and potential inconclusiveness of trying to establish standards scientifically.

Some Imperatives of Environmental Relations.

*Costs and benefits.* In the hard cost-benefit calculations of resource projects in developing countries, one easily overlooked aspect is the *distribution* of costs and benefits among the participants. The cost-benefit reality of many resource projects is that the investors and the national treasury enjoy whatever benefits flow from the project while the local residents of the area incur most of the costs. Major resident costs often involve environmental degradation and land-use disruption. If some way cannot be found either to compensate residents for such costs or to redistribute some of the benefits, an inequitable and potentially volatile situation is created.

Governments, of course, are not perfect at defining and protecting the public (environmental) interest. Given this inevitable imperfection and the political sensitivity of representative government, it is probably too much to expect that environmental agreements will be sacrosanct. In practice, provisions must be made for the evolution of obligations based on empirical evidence, not simply on a priori assumptions. In this process, area residents must have a real voice and not be heard in the national capital as some distant echo from afar.

Environmental interests are not expressed the same way in developed nations as they are in developing countries. In industrial nations, for example, advocacy groups such as the Sierra Club and Friends of the Earth maintain large memberships and staffs whose primary function is to define an environmental viewpoint and mobilize public opinion in favor of it. In developing nations few, if any, comparable groups exist. Furthermore, with less developed communications networks, public and political opinion is much harder to mobilize, especially where issues involve scientific or technological questions. As a result public opinion on environmental issues in developing countries often emerges *after*, not before, a project is implemented. In turn this ex post facto recognition of environmental costs is often more emotional than rational or judicial. Finally, changes in the physical environment in the Third World are often coupled with traumatic social disruption that is hard for a foreign management to understand. Regrettably, the expression of this largely unarticulated, highly emotional reaction to environmental costs is sometimes violent, unanticipated, and subject to misinterpretation.

Rural people and the environmental ethic of the land. Casual observation suggests that the environmental ethic is strongly rooted in traditions and in rural people's dependence on the land. Although most rural people in developing countries are scientifically unsophisticated, they understand cause and effect intuitively. When the environmental account book gets out of balance as the result of some development project brought in from the outside, such as a mine or a forest project, rural residents are quick to recognize their self-interest in preventing degradation of their land.

However, rural people by and large perceive a conflict between development and environment only when it impinges on their daily activities (such as farming, hunting, cooking, providing shelter, etc.). They have a much narrower environmental focus than exists in wealthy industrial societies, where environmental protection may encompass the preservation of uncommon or unknown species for aesthetic, scientific, or humane reasons.

The LDC Environmental Knowledge Base. Another distinction of some importance in understanding the imperatives of environmental studies in developing versus developed nations is the applicability and extent of the established scientific information base. The existence of a large knowledge base in temperate industrial nations has two implications that deserve mention. First, environmental scientists in industrial nations can, through direct or inferred parallels and with a moderate amount of fieldwork, develop plausible scenarios for environmental impacts. In developing countries conclusions are more highly dependent on fieldwork because the knowledge base is more limited. Therefore both the costs and study time necessary to reach the same level of environmental understanding will be greater.

Second, the lack of an extensive knowledge base means that developing country regulators are less likely to have indigenously developed environmental standards. Typically, standards are either borrowed (sometimes inappropriately) from industrial nations or involve a pragmatic reiteration and adjustment of vaguely defined limits at the submission-of-proposal stage. The result is a transfer of regulatory concepts without also transferring a significant portion of the knowledge base on which the regulatory assumptions were founded.

Environmental Study and Equity Credit. Failure to find some solution to the long lead-time problem of environmental fieldwork has potentially far-reaching consequences. One of these has already been mentioned: the inability of project engineers to incorporate environmentally compatible design or technology choices into feasibility studies. The other problem that may arise is the imposition of costly ex post facto requirements on projects already in operation.

If lengthy field programs are an imperative of developing-country environmental impact assessment and if investors are understandably reluctant to make major expenditures before project viability is established, then the inescapable conclusion is that the government must plan and fund some ecological work in advance. Given the already overstretched budgets of developing-country governments, such a proposal would seem to have little prospect of being realized. However, one way in which ecological field studies might be made more attractive to government budget planners (and perhaps even to outside donor agencies) would be to credit such expenses to the government's eventual equity subscription to the project. Such a contingent equity credit arrangement was successfully introduced at Ok Tedi for funding policy studies related to the capacity of PNG's construction industry and to the selection of a hydroelectric site for the project. International parallels for such arrangements in the mineral industry include the UN Revolving Fund for Mineral Exploration and the exploration subsidy policies of the West German government. In both cases repayment (or credit) of expenses is dependent upon final agreement to proceed with a viable project.

Government Roles in Transition. The Ok Tedi project represents a landmark in the evolution of environmental regulation in Papua New Guinea. Stung by the ecological consequences of the Bougainville mine, the government committed itself through study and negotiation to ensure that the same problems were not repeated at Ok Tedi. That this policy decision was discharged by the implementing agency (the Department of Minerals and Energy) rather than through the statutory framework of the Office of Environment reflects the inherent dilemma that faces Third World countries concerned with both promoting and regulating natural resource projects.

The Ok Tedi implementation experience has been traumatic for PNG. An inadequate administrative capacity in the government, combined with a sometimes indifferent environmental attitude on the part of the mining consortium, has severely tarnished the public perceptions of the project. The pressures of construction schedules and budgetary ceilings have meant that during the early implementation phase, environmental precautions were often subordinated to the imperatives of getting the project into operation. With preproduction construction now completed, Ok Tedi is at an environmental crossroads. Whether the attitude of benign neglect that characterized environmental regulation during the construction period will be replaced by more aggressive environmental enforcement is a question for the future. Certainly, the spirit of the environmental agreements would seem to provide a sufficient basis for government (if not for the local residents) to ensure that the environmental tragedy of Bougainville is not repeated. Regrettably, the national bureaucracy has thus far been unable to abandon its role of project promoter and assume the role of environmental regulator.

# CHAPTER THREE   Multinational Enterprises and

Environmental and Resource Management Issues

in the Indonesian Tropical Forest Sector

Malcolm Gillis

## An Overview of the Role of the Forest Section in Recent Indonesian Development

The Indonesian economy performed well from 1967 through 1983: real GDP grew at an average annual rate of about 7.3 percent.[1] Since the population rose at an estimated 2.3 percent per year, real per capita GDP increased at the rate of 5 percent per year, roughly five times faster than the average for all low-income countries (excluding India and China) over the same period.[2]

After the tragic economic and political turbulence of the mid-1960s and before the first oil boom of 1973–74, the tropical-timber sector played a major role in Indonesia's recovery. Before 1966 timber export earnings rarely exceeded $10 million per year. But with the reopening of the economy to foreign investment after 1967, exports of logs from the virgin rain forest began on a major scale. Virtually all the growth in log exports originated in the dense Dipterocarp stands of Kalimantan and a few Moluccan Islands. By 1973 the gross value of timber export earnings had reached $573 million and timber had become the nation's leading export, representing 28 percent of total export value (see table 3.1). Except for a small drop during the 1975 recession, total timber exports grew rapidly after 1973, reaching nearly $1 billion in 1978. Boom conditions in world tropical-hardwood markets carried gross Indonesian timber export earnings to nearly $2 billion in both 1979 and 1980, even though the total physical volume of exports declined in 1980. Notwithstanding the explosive growth in timber exports, timber's share in total national export earnings dropped steadily after 1973, owing to the effects of the first and second oil booms (1973 and 1979). By 1980 petroleum accounted for 70 percent of export revenues; timber's share had declined to but 8 percent of the total.[3]

The rapid growth in Indonesian tropical timber harvests during the 1970s led to major changes in world markets for this resource (see table 3.2). From virtually nothing in 1967 the Indonesian share of world production rose to nearly 17 percent in 1977, nearly matching that of the biggest producer, Malaysia. By 1981 the Indonesian share in the physical volume of world production had fallen to only 9 percent, but this development masks other important trends in the market for tropical hardwoods.

**Table 3.1**    Export of Tropical Timber: Indonesia, 1965–1982

| Year | Net weight (thousand metric tons) | F.o.b. value (million dollars) |
|------|-----------------------------------|-------------------------------|
| 1965 | 137.5 | 2.1 |
| 1966 | 203.5 | 3.6 |
| 1967 | 400.9 | 6.3 |
| 1968 | 888.2 | 11.5 |
| 1969 | 2,698.7 | 28.2 |
| 1970 | 5,772.5 | 104.3 |
| 1971 | 7,684.3 | 161.4 |
| 1972 | 10,839.6 | 228.7 |
| 1973 | 14,770.2 | 573.6 |
| 1974 | 14,187.9 | 724.7 |
| 1975 | 11,042.0 | 500.0 |
| 1976 | 14,828.4 | 781.8 |
| 1977 | 15,802.4 | 951.2 |
| 1978 | 15,154.9 | 995.0 |
| 1979 | 15,658.1 | 1,796.7 |
| 1980 | 12,656.2 | 1,852.5 |
| 1981 | 6,472.2 | 873.9 |
| 1982* | 2,049.4 | 284.1 |

*January–June

Sources: Biro Pusat Statistik, *Statistik Indonesia 1982* (Jakarta, 1983), 398; Biro Pusat Statistik, *Statistik Indonesia 1979* (Jakarta, 1980), 400; Biro Pusat Statistik, *Statistik Indonesia 1976* (Jakarta, 1977), 664; Biro Pusat Statistik, *Statistik Indonesia 1975* (Jakarta, 1976), 731.

**Table 3.2** World Tropical Hardwood Sawlogs and
Veneer Logs Production (thousand cubic meters)

| Continent | 1977 | | 1978 | |
|---|---|---|---|---|
| | Production | Percent | Production | Percent |
| Oceania[a] | 7,161 | 4.5 | 6,838 | 4.2 |
| Africa[b] | 17,791 | 11.2 | 18,512 | 11.6 |
| Asia[c] | 89,994 | 57.0 | 92,186 | 57.6 |
| Indonesia | (26,630) | (16.8) | (25,550) | (16.0) |
| Malaysia | (27,628) | (17.4) | (31,479) | (19.6) |
| Latin America[d] | 43,236 | 27.3 | 42,491 | 26.6 |
| Total | 158,182 | 100.0 | 160,027 | 100.0 |

Percentages may not total 100 due to rounding.
a. Excludes Australia
b. Excludes South Africa
c. Excludes China, Japan, Republic of Korea, and Mongolia

**Table 3.3** World Sawlogs and Veneer Logs Exports (thousand cubic meters)

| Continent | 1977 | | 1978 | |
|---|---|---|---|---|
| | Export | Percent | Export | Percent |
| Oceania[a] | 1,699 | 3.7 | 1,608 | 3.4 |
| Africa[b] | 6,549 | 14.3 | 6,418 | 13.7 |
| Asia[c] | 37,426 | 81.8 | 38,739 | 82.7 |
| Indonesia | (18,932) | (41.4) | (19,457) | (41.5) |
| Malaysia | (16,118) | (35.2) | (16,717) | (35.7) |
| Latin America[d] | 68 | 0.2 | 70 | 0.2 |
| Total | 45,742 | 100.0 | 46,835 | 100.0 |

a. Excludes Australia
b. Excludes South Africa
c. Excludes China, Japan, Republic of Korea, and Mongolia

By 1977 Indonesian exports of tropical hardwoods had captured 41
percent of the world market, a share that was more or less maintained until
1981, when drastic restrictions were placed on log exports, and the
Indonesian share in the world market fell to 21 percent (see table 3.3).
Nevertheless, from 1977 through 1981 Indonesian exports of timber
exceeded the combined totals of African and Latin American tropical-
timber exports.

| 1979 | | 1980 | | 1981 | |
|---|---|---|---|---|---|
| Production | Percent | Production | Percent | Production | Percent |
| 6,936 | 4.3 | 6,949 | 4.2 | 6,706 | 4.3 |
| 18,991 | 11.9 | 20,678 | 12.5 | 20,836 | 13.5 |
| 88,537 | 55.4 | 89,364 | 54.1 | 79,598 | 51.3 |
| (21,800) | (13.6) | (22,300) | (13.5) | (13,900) | (9.0) |
| (31,479) | (19.7) | (31,479) | (19.0) | (31,479) | (20.3) |
| 45,473 | 28.4 | 48,129 | 29.2 | 47,905 | 30.9 |
| 159,937 | 100.0 | 165,120 | 100.0 | 155,045 | 100.0 |

d. Excludes Chile and Argentina
*Source*: Food and Agriculture Organization, *1981 Yearbook of Forest Products, 1970–1981* (Rome, 1983), 110-11.

| 1979 | | 1980 | | 1981 | |
|---|---|---|---|---|---|
| Export | Percent | Export | Percent | Export | Percent |
| 1,946 | 4.4 | 1,883 | 4.7 | 1,548 | 5.0 |
| 6,314 | 14.2 | 6,144 | 15.4 | 5,189 | 16.7 |
| 36,250 | 81.3 | 31,871 | 79.7 | 24,207 | 78.0 |
| (18,161) | (40.7) | (15,182) | (38.0) | (6,609) | (21.0) |
| (16,500) | (37.0) | (15,151) | (38.0) | (15,859) | (51.0) |
| 87 | 0.1 | 91 | 0.2 | 83 | 0.3 |
| 44,597 | 100.0 | 39,989 | 100.0 | 31,027 | 100.0 |

d. Excludes Chile and Argentina
*Source*: Food and Agriculture Organization, *1981 Yearbook of Forest Products, 1970–1981* (Rome, 1983), 116-17.

The timber sector provided significant tax revenues and employment growth in the early years of the Indonesian recovery after 1967, yet it was probably substantially less than might have been expected given the rapid growth of gross timber export earnings over the period. Taxes collected from the tropical-timber sector never amounted to more than 4 percent of total central government tax revenues over the period, although for the timber-rich province of East Kalimantan, timber royalties and taxes have accounted for as much as 60 percent of revenues.[4]

The early stages of exploitation of the virgin rain forest in Indonesia were characterized by relatively light taxation not only of profits of timber firms (including multinational corporations in timber), but of log exports as well. This pattern was in part due to the liberal income-tax holidays offered to both domestic and foreign investors in the timber sector from 1967 to 1975. Companies entering the sector were exempted from all income taxes for from four to six years. Further, export taxes on logs were relatively low throughout the first period of rapid growth in timber sector activity. From 1967 until 1978, export taxes on logs were 10 percent of export value, roughly half the level imposed in the neighboring Malaysian state of Sabah. Both governments doubled these taxes in 1978.

In Indonesia, the doubling of log-export tax rates was motivated not so much by revenue considerations as it was by official exasperation over the failure of investors, both domestic and foreign, to move into domestic processing of tropical-timber products.[5] Even after a decade of explosive growth in tropical-log exports, processed-timber exports were minuscule (see table 3.4). In 1977 for example, plywood exports were but $2.3 million, about 2 percent of total timber export earnings. After 1978, plywood exports still grew slowly in absolute amounts, reaching $161 million in 1981, which was 18 percent of total log exports.

The forest sector is typically expected to provide substantial numbers of jobs in host countries with significant timber endowments. In at least four African countries, forest-sector employment occupies more than 1 percent of the labor force.[6] But in Indonesia in the late 1970s, forest-sector employ-

**Table 3.4**  Export of Plywood and Wood Products: Indonesia, 1977–1982

| Year | Net weight (thousand kilograms) | F.o.b. value (thousand dollars) |
|------|--------------------------------|--------------------------------|
| 1977 | 5,973.1 | 2,350.9 |
| 1978 | 19,658.7 | 8,685.3 |
| 1979 | 84,883.4 | 31,720.2 |
| 1980 | 164,160.1 | 55,376.5 |
| 1981 | 434,212.3 | 161,410.6 |
| 1982* | 286,964.5 | 114,815.3 |

*January–June

Sources: Biro Pusat Statistik, *Statistik Indonesia 1982* (Jakarta, 1983), 410; Kenji Takeuchi, *Export Prospects for Forest Products in Indonesia, 1983–1990* (Washington, D.C.: World Bank, 1983), table 9A.

ment was a mere 0.1 percent of the labor force.[7] Of total forest-sector employment of 87,000 in 1978, there were only 1,400 professional foresters and about 2,600 trained forestry technicians.[8]

Official perceptions were that large investments, particularly foreign investments, in the timber sector had not created the expected number of jobs for Indonesians. Disenchantment with employment growth in timber led in 1974 to the enactment of special taxes on foreign timber workers and other measures to promote greater employment of nationals.

Still another source of official discontent was the discovery, in 1973, of substantial undervaluation of exports by several national and foreign firms. In some shipments to the Japanese market, firms were said to have understated f.o.b. values by as much as 40 percent, thereby lowering their liabilities for export taxes and, ultimately, income taxes. In response, the government enforced an older "posted price" system for log exports and, for some tree species, raised posted prices by 50 percent or more in 1973.

In sum, because of light tax burdens, undervaluation of export receipts, limited domestic processing, and relatively small job creation in timber, the benefits for Indonesia from logging were not particularly sizable before 1978. Much of the gross export earnings from timber before that time had relatively little positive significance for the country, when measured on a *net basis* (after deducting profit repatriation, values of imported capital equipment and imported materials, and foreign debt service on timber projects). In other words, Indonesia's *retained value* from timber export earnings was then less than one quarter of the gross value of export earnings. By 1979, this figure may have been as high as 50 percent.[9]

Whether the forest-sector contribution to national growth and development was in fact relatively small or relatively large, it fell short of Indonesia's expectations. Chances are that this disappointment over returns during the 1967–78 period helped determine the outcome of discussions on environmental issues between the resource owner—the government—and the multinational firms engaged in extraction. As a result, the government was not predisposed to take a flexible position on environmental issues in the timber sector when these came to the fore in the 1970s and early 1980s. A government may overlook a perceived laxity in firms' reforestation efforts when forest-sector tax collections are perceived to be high. Damage to forest assets from selective cutting practices and over-cutting may elicit few host-country complaints when companies are investing heavily in timber processing. Similarly, the silting of rivers in logging regions may be tolerated when it is a result of harvesting and log transport activities involving large numbers of host-country citizens. But when forest taxes, processing, investments, employment, and other national benefits in the timber sector are all perceived to have been low over an extended period, official tolerance of investor inattention both to reforestation and to other environmental questions is naturally lower.

## Ecological and Technical Features of the Indonesian Forest Sector

The Indonesian constitution of 1945 declares that all virgin forests are the property of the state. Total forest acreage in the early 1980s was 122 million hectares, of which 82 million hectares has been protected or reserved. Therefore, forest land available for production totals 40 million hectares. By 1979 89 percent of this operable forest area was already committed under logging concession licenses.[10] The physical volume of extraction rose at an average annual rate of 22.5 percent between 1968 and 1980, even though production peaked in 1976. Thus, by whatever measure employed, the commercialization of the Indonesian tropical rain forest proceeded at an extraordinarily rapid rate from 1968 through 1980, perhaps too rapidly to meet environmental objectives in a complex ecosystem about which little is known.

The ecological fragility and complexity of the tropical rain forest may be conveyed in numerous ways.[11] Its vulnerability is perhaps best depicted by reference to an important ecological event in 1983: the widespread fires in the dense and humid rain forests of East Kalimantan in Indonesia. Even if not, as termed by the *New York Times*, "perhaps the most severe environmental disaster the earth has suffered in centuries,"[12] the devastation was at least as severe as for any forest area in recent history. Within three months, beginning in March, the fire spread over 13,000 square miles of rain forest, an area about the size of Taiwan. Losses just in terms of the commercial value of trees are conservatively estimated at $3.6 billion. The destruction of prime timber resources was so serious that, for the first time since 1967, Indonesia was forced to import tropical logs as feedstock for plywood mills in 1984. The full ecological consequences are as yet unknown, but preliminary assessments indicate the following: (1) extinction of several species of flora and fauna through direct destruction and loss of habitat; (2) widespread soil degradation through increased erosion and mineralization; (3) hydrological damages, including loss of natural drainage regulation and increased sedimentation of rivers; and (4) climatic change (greater variability in temperature, rainfall, and humidity) caused by destruction of thick rain forest canopies.[13]

This occurrence has major implications for public policies toward extraction in tropical forests. Much of the severity of the fire had its origins in the nature and extent of logging activity in the fifteen years prior to 1983, for reasons heretofore unappreciated.[14] That is to say, a significant social cost of extraction has not been adequately recognized and taken into account in policy decisions concerning methods and scope of timber harvests. The presence of a major, unrecognized cost of logging has meant that the resource owner (the government) has priced the resource too low in the past. The combination of royalties and taxes received by the owner has been well below that required to compensate for the economic and social losses caused by harvesting of tropical timber.

The technical information needed to reduce the scope of such fires and other environmental damages from harvest of tropical timber depends upon advances in both fundamental and applied research on tropical forests. Worldwide, substantial resources have been devoted to basic research but relatively little to applied research. Moreover, fundamental research has focussed primarily upon narrower topics in evolutionary biology of the tropical forest, not upon wider ecosystem processes.[15] Indeed, not until the 1950s was the fragility of the tropical forest ecosystem widely recognized. The forest cover survives not only by drawing on soil minerals, but also by quickly recycling decaying plant material within a delicately balanced closed system. In addition, basic research has been conducted as if human intervention in this complex ecosystem could be ignored.

Much applied research has been highly specialized, short-term in nature, or heavily focussed upon biophysical issues, whereas policy makers require assistance in identifying the effects of human interaction with the tropical forest. Finally, an inherent problem in much research in tropical forestry is that so much of it is site-specific: soils, species, and climate are subject to such wide regional variations that data on the forest ecosystem of, say, Africa may be of only limited relevance to, for example, Indonesian conditions, and only then to specific areas of Indonesia.

In general the quality of technical information on African and most Latin American tropical forests is superior to that available for the dense Dipterocarp forests of Indonesian Kalimantan, where most harvesting has taken place. For one thing, the Indonesian forests are much less accessible to researchers than anywhere in Africa except the Congo—which is one reason it took eight months to get even a preliminary assessment of damages from the forest fires of 1983.

Biophysical information on the dense jungle of Kalimantan is far from complete, if for no other reason than the immense diversity of species.[16] For *commercial* species, technical information is fairly complete regarding growth rates, growing cycles, incidence, density per hectare, and commercial characteristics (durability, water-resistance, hardness, etc.). But fewer than a dozen of the 3,500 species of tropical trees comprise over 90 percent of the harvest, and little is known about the others. Even less is known about the underlying soil characteristics, the hydrology of the jungle, and the interaction between fauna and flora in this complex ecosystem. In addition, researchers have only begun to accumulate technical information on the uses and economic value of tropical forests' non-wood products. Nor is it known to what extent selective cutting (as opposed to clear-cutting) will result in the extinction of highly localized species. According to Kuswata, firms with timber concessions ordinarily return to logged-over areas after five years.[17] Data cited by him suggest that each concessionaire entry into a stand destroys or damages up to half the stems *not* taken, depending on the method of harvest. Given that many of the most attractive commercial species require forty to seventy years to flower, a harvesting cycle of even thirty years (the typical duration of a concession) may mean that many of these species will disappear from their original habitat, if not from the jungle itself.

Finally, the quality of technical information on the Indonesian tropical forest is limited because neither the government nor (with one exception noted later) any multinational timber enterprise has undertaken controlled experiments with replanting in jungle areas. There is thus a dearth of data on the efficacy of replanting programs for most mixed Dipterocarp forests.

### Foreign and Domestic Investment in Tropical Forestry

From almost nothing in 1967, total foreign direct investment in the Indonesian forest-based sector grew to $376 million by 1979 (see table 3.5). Most investments prior to 1971 involved 100 percent foreign equity ownership in timber operations. However, changes in government policies in the early 1970s precluded this form of foreign investment, so that operations initiated by foreign enterprises increasingly took the form of joint ventures with domestic firms. But by 1975 foreign investors were no longer allowed to form new joint ventures in simple logging activities. Still, by January of 1978 there were seventy-seven foreign enterprises active in

**Table 3.5**   Foreign Investment in Indonesian Timber Sector as of
January 1, 1979: Size, National Origin, and Area

| Country | Investment (million dollars) | Total area of concessions (thousand hectares) | Joint venture | 100% Foreign equity | Total |
|---|---|---|---|---|---|
| | | | | Form of entry | |
| Philippines | 72.6 | 1,380 | 10 | 1 | 11 |
| Hong Kong | 53.0 | 1,387 | 13 | 2 | 15 |
| Malaysia | 49.1 | 2,419 | 17 | 2 | 19 |
| United States | 48.7 | 1,081 | 2 | 2 | 4 |
| Japan | 46.2 | 1,263 | 11 | 1 | 12 |
| South Korea | 33.3 | 890 | 5 | 2 | 7 |
| Singapore | 10.3 | 420 | 5 | 0 | 5 |
| France | 7.2 | 260 | 0 | 1 | 1 |
| Italy | 3.5 | 110 | 1 | 0 | 1 |
| Others | 52.0 | 236 | 2 | 0 | 2 |
| Total | 375.9 | 9,336 | 66 | 11 | 77 |

*Source*: Directorat Jenderal Kehutanan, *Kehutanan Indonesia 1978* (Bogor, October 1979),
10–11.

the timber sector. Of these, sixty-six were joint ventures and only eleven involved 100 percent foreign equity.

Table 3.5, which ranks investments by the country of origin, shows that investors from three neighboring *developing* countries accounted for nearly half the total of all foreign investment. Altogether investors from other developing countries were responsible for two thirds of total investment before 1980; multinational firms from industrial countries accounted for the other third. Of the nearly 500 firms operating in the timber sector in 1980, only 29 were based in industrial countries. Of these, three were U.S.-based, twenty-two were Japanese, two were French, and one was British. Although investments by Japanese firms expanded between 1978 and 1981, developing-country foreign investors nevertheless controlled more than half the total amount of foreign investment in timber by 1981.

Reported domestic investment in the Indonesian timber sector is almost three times greater than reported foreign investment. Official figures indicate that investment by domestic firms totaled almost $1 billion by early 1971[18] (see table 3.6).

Both government policies and domestic attitudes toward foreign invest-

**Table 3.6** Domestic and Foreign Investment in the
Indonesian Forest-Based Sector, January 1, 1979

|  | Investment (U.S. $ millions) | Percent of total |
|---|---|---|
| Investment by domestic firms with forestry agreements (407 firms) | $ 999.0 | 72.5 |
| Foreign investment (77 firms) | 377.7 | 27.5 |
| Total | $1,376.7 | 100.0 |

*Source*: Indonesian Foreign Investment Board, *The Almanac of Investment in Indonesia* (Jakarta, 1983).

ment in the forest sector have changed since 1974. From 1968 until then, foreign investment in all aspects of this sector was eagerly sought. After 1974, however, the Indonesian government restricted foreign investment in the forest sector, partly because local partners complained about unfair treatment by foreign enterprises and partly because the government perceived many multinational corporations (MNC's) as unresponsive to environmental issues (particularly reforestation) and to the need for processing investments (plywood, molding, etc.). A series of policy measures discussed below were adopted from 1974 through 1983 in an effort to induce enterprises to take corrective action in all these areas.

Perhaps the most significant source of the Indonesian government's dissatisfaction with foreign investors in timber stemmed from delays in undertaking investments in processing facilities. Although concession contracts signed between 1968 and 1973 contained ambiguous clauses regarding company obligations to invest in such processing facilities as sawmills, plywood, particle-board, and pulp and paper plants, government spokesmen repeatedly stressed during the 1970s the necessity for companies to meet good-faith commitments to investments in processing. For various reasons, these blandishments went largely unheeded. Beginning in 1978, the government took several steps to induce companies to invest in processing—doubling log-export taxes and reducing export taxes on processed items (sawn timber and veneer) to 5 percent and to nothing on plywood and particle-board. Delays in enterprise responses to these measures prompted Indonesia in April of 1980 to follow the Philippines and Malaysia in imposing restrictions on log exports. In addition, a one-million-hectare concession held by a Philippine-based company was revoked in 1979, primarily on grounds that the company had implemented less than one-fourth of the investments originally scheduled in its original concession agreement (signed in 1969) and had undertaken no reforestation.

Company inattention to reforestation was the second major source of continuing friction between government and foreign investors. By 1979, only one foreign firm, the U.S.-based Weyerhaeuser Corporation, had begun significant reforestation programs, and these affected only about 15,000 hectares. By contrast, central and regional government reforestation programs had been extended to nearly 1 million hectares by 1979, and reached 1.4 million hectares by early 1981, according to government data.[19] In response to perceived laxity of enterprises in implementing reforestation, in April 1980 the government imposed refundable deposits of $4 on each cubic meter of logs exported, with the deposits to be returned to the companies only after they presented evidence of an adequately maintained replanting program.

Friction between foreign investors and domestic joint venture partners began to surface in the mid-1970s. As a result, a few foreign investors reduced their shares in equity ownership below 50 percent. Weyerhaeuser agreed, with some reluctance, to full divestment in 1981. Within a few months, the only other large U.S.-based multinational, Georgia Pacific, announced its intention to wholly divest all of its forest-based operations in Indonesia. Weyerhaeuser's announcement came after years of differences with local partners proved irreconcilable, while Georgia Pacific concluded that a continued presence in Indonesia was no longer consistent with company objectives, particularly given the pressures for large investments in Indonesian timber processing. Earlier (in 1978) Bowaters had sold its only Indonesian operation. By 1984, Lever Brothers was the only large Western-based MNC still operating in the Indonesian timber sector. Some twenty Japanese-based multinational firms remained, however, led by subsidiaries of Mitsui, Mitsubishi, Sumitomo, and C. Itoh. Virtually all other remaining foreign timber firms were from other Asian developing countries, including South Korea, Hong Kong, and Malaysia.

## The Structure of Government Regulation of Foreign Investment in the Forest Section

Since 1967 entry terms and conditions for foreign investment in manufacturing have been coordinated and administered by the National Investment Coordinating Board, known by its Indonesian acronym, BKPM. However, BKPM has no jurisdiction over foreign investment in natural resources, including the forest-based sector.

Jurisdiction over foreign investment proposals as well as projects in forestry were handled from 1967 to early 1983 by the Directorate-General of Forestry of the Ministry of Agriculture. (This influential entity was given ministerial status in March 1983, and is now the Ministry of Forestry, hereinafter, the Forestry Department). Since 1975 foreign firms have not been able to enter the forest sector as owners or joint venture partners in logging operations. Rather, foreign participation is now limited to equity shares in timber processing projects.

Since most multinational corporations entered the timber sector between 1967 and 1974, the status of regulations at that time is germane to the present discussion. Until 1984 the Forestry Department, together with the Ministry of Finance, determined the duration and scope of income-tax incentives awarded to foreign firms. Decisions concerning location and size of concession areas are the responsibilities of the Forestry Department. Before 1978 no further environmental clearances were required since any vetting of concessions to prevent infringement upon reserve forests or endangered species habitats or to proscribe logging in erosion-prone areas was left to the Forestry Department. In 1978, however, a new State Ministry for Development Supervision and Environment (later, the State Ministry for Population and Environment) was created (hereinafter, the Ministry for Environment). This office, headed by an environmentally conscious minister since its creation, coordinates environmental management across sectors. Forestry investment proposals must now be evaluated for environmental impact by this ministry. While the task strains the small staff, the ministry has successfully modified some proposals that would otherwise have encroached upon reserved forest areas.

Responsibility for determining and monitoring environmental and resource management standards in the operation of forest projects was, until 1978, split between the Forestry Department and the Ministry of Industry. After 1978, the Ministry for Environment began to play a role as well. The Forestry Department determines an "annual allowable cut" for each concession holder, prescribes harvest methods, oversees and enforces timber grading and scaling, and imposes and collects timber royalties and license fees.[20] Harvesting methods are restricted to selective cutting, and clear-cutting has so far been proscribed. Under selective cutting, only stems of merchantable size—on average, about two trees per hectare in the best stands—may be taken.

The Ministry of Industry promotes and regulates forest-based industrialization. Primarily through the single-minded effort of this agency, 60 plywood mills had been established by 1982, another 45 were constructed in 1983, and plans made for another 27 to be built in 1984–85.[21] Of these 132 mills, only 22 are foreign-owned (none by U.S.-based multinational firms). As late as April 1984 at least half the mills were reportedly near bankruptcy, owing to the Kalimantan fire of 1983 and to government harvest restrictions.[22] The ministry also oversees timber-processing activities in pulp and paper. As the short-fibered trees of the rain forest are not well suited for pulping, this agency has had little contact with foreign investors in tropical timber.

As a coordinating and advisory body, the Ministry for Environment has had almost no contact with foreign timber firms. But it does monitor reforestation programs, and even though it lacks enforcement powers it has successfully persuaded the Forestry Department and the Chief Executive to tighten reforestation requirements and penalize errant firms. Indeed, the primary initiative for a major reforestation measure in 1980, described below, was undertaken by the Minister for Environment.

Foreign investors in tropical timber are subject to various governmental regulations imposed by other agencies too. The most significant of these, from the investor's standpoint, have been the Ministries of Trade, Finance, Manpower, and the Directorate-General of Immigration.

The Ministry of Trade quarterly determines the posted prices (check prices) for numerous exports, including timber. In turn, the check prices form the basis for the valuation of timber in conjunction with the 20 percent export tax on logs. Check prices are determined by referring to information on log prices in Japanese and Hong Kong markets.

The Ministry of Finance formulates and administers all taxes and fiscal charges affecting the timber sector, except timber royalties and license fees and special taxes on foreign timber workers. As mentioned earlier, until 1984 it granted income-tax holidays to foreign investors; the ministry also approved or rejected proposals for duty-free import of materials and equipment.

The Ministry of Manpower grants work permits to people issued visas by the Directorate-General of Immigration. The ministry was responsible for adopting and enforcing an annual tax of $1,200 on all foreign timber workers enacted in 1974. Foreign investors in timber have claimed persistently since 1969 that such officially sanctioned taxes constituted only a small portion of total payments made to government agencies at various "pressure points" where investors need clearances. This was probably true for the early 1970s when official taxes on timber were small, but more recent claims that large unofficial payments must be made to public officials remain to be documented.

## Conflicts in Regulation

Conflicts between multinational corporations and the Indonesian government over environmental issues have occurred only relatively recently. Earlier conflicts were largely confined to issues in processing, taxation, and the use of expatriate labor. But these earlier disputes and, particularly, delays in their resolution have charged the atmosphere under which environmental disputes have been discussed and have affected the outcomes of such discussions. We first examine those conflicts that preceded emergence of serious environmental issues.

Of nonenvironmental conflicts, two types plagued foreign investors in Indonesian tropical timber between 1968 and 1984. The first, "frontal conflicts," originated in direct disputes between investors and a particular regulating agency. The second, "peripheral conflicts," arose from clashes of objectives between different agencies of the government itself, though they ultimately affected investors.

The locus of frontal conflict has been primarily outside the main agency that regulates forestry. Disputes between MNC's and the Forestry Department have never been frequent or protracted, largely because the agency has until recently been interested primarily in expanding the number and size of timber extraction projects so as to maximize timber production and exports. Certainly, when expansion in foreign investment in timber was most rapid (1967–74), virtually every public pronouncement relating to departmental performance equated size of harvest with official regulatory effectiveness. In this period, and to some extent later, the wood-producing capacity of the tropical forest was clearly viewed as the most important, if not the only, service provided by the forest. Few conflicts arose between multinational corporations and the Forestry Department over such questions as annual allowable harvest, harvest methods, and grading and scaling, since the firms and the department had more or less the same objectives. (One exception was the occasional allegation of investor fraud in grading and scaling of logs.)

Conflicts over timber royalties were brief but sharp. MNC's protested vociferously over a 1971 "additional royalty" enacted by the department (amounting to about 2 percent of the value of log exports) to finance the dredging of rivers used for log rafting and transport and to cover ecological damage from silting caused by timber harvest. (Initially, one large U.S./Philippines-based multinational firm refused to pay the royalty.)

Frontal conflicts with other government agencies have been more frequent and acrimonious. Enactment of sharply higher timber check prices (posted prices) by the Ministry of Trade beginning in late 1972 set off a decade-long dispute with investors. The ministry revised check prices upward on evidence that most companies had for several years substantially undervalued log exports. Investors did not vigorously contest the initial increases in check prices, but claimed repeatedly (and with some justification) that over the next eight years downward revisions in check prices to reflect cyclical downturns in world markets were often late and insufficient, resulting in excessive payment of log export taxes.

Disputes with the Ministry of Finance were rare until 1973, although there were recurring complaints from MNC's of delays and irregularities in customs clearance of duty-free machinery imports. Indications of tax evasion by some firms first surfaced in 1973, and these issues continued to cause disputes between the ministry and the companies through 1984. For example, at least one timber multinational corporation from a developing country paid no income taxes in the twelve years of its Indonesian operations, yet it did not have its extraction license revoked by the Forestry Department. Other abuses of tax holidays were common among investors in this sector. In the 1970s several firms attempted to evade income taxes by overvaluing duty-free machinery imports, thereby gaining artificially large depreciation deductions. The scope for such abuses and the disputes arising from them will diminish in the future since Indonesia greatly simplified its income tax laws and abolished all special tax incentives in 1984.[23]

Disagreements involving multinational corporations and the Ministry of Manpower were rife from the beginning of the timber boom in 1968 until about 1982, by which time few foreign workers and managers were still employed by the remaining MNC's. Press reports (1972–74) of the intensive use of Philippine and Malaysian logging crews in Kalimantan, Sulawesi, and the Moluccan islands led to official complaints and later crackdowns on the use of foreign workers.

Peripheral conflicts—those originating largely from discordant pressures from within the government, causing a stream of mixed signals to investors—were at least as serious as frontal conflicts between MNC's and the government. Frontal conflicts involved environmental issues only in a marginal sense (royalties earmarked for dredging), while peripheral conflicts ultimately had a significant environmental content. As often as not, the

Forestry Department found itself on one side of an issue and other government departments on the other. Although disagreements over objectives between agencies were rarely open (and even more rarely acrimonious), they became serious problems for investors because they took so long to settle and because investors failed to heed the at first polite and then strident admonitions of agencies other than the Forestry Department. But once settled, the outcomes of peripheral conflicts were announced with little warning, leading firms to charge the Indonesian government with unilaterally altering the rules of the game.

Most peripheral conflicts fell into three categories. The first stemmed largely from differences between the Forestry Department and the Ministry of Industry over the speed at which forest-based industrialization should proceed. The initial concession contracts with MNC's did not legally bind them to move quickly into the domestic processing of tropical timber, nor did it penalize them for failure to do so. But officials in the Ministry of Industry and in the Ministries of Finance and Planning took the view that all MNC's had a moral if not a legal commitment to begin plywood and/or chipboard manufacture. When few firms had made such investments by 1978, the Indonesian government decided, in the absence of penalties, to provide clear financial incentives for processing investments by doubling the export tax on unprocessed logs. This was undertaken not by or with the Forestry Department, but on the advice of the Ministries of Industry and Finance.

Still, timber companies (both domestic and foreign) proved reluctant to invest in processing facilities, particularly given the high log prices that prevailed in world timber markets from 1978 through 1980. Inasmuch as no concessions were revoked for this reason, and no penalties applied by the Forestry Department, the investors were taken aback when further measures to promote domestic processing were announced. In April of 1980 the Ministers of Industry, Trade, and Agriculture jointly decreed a complete phaseout of log exports by 1985, beginning with a limit in 1982 of one cubic meter of log exports for every four cubic meters of processed timber.

A second source of peripheral conflict affecting foreign investors has been the different perspectives of various agencies toward large-scale timber extraction. While the Forestry Department has until recently consistently measured national benefits from timber endowments in terms of the growth of gross foreign exchange earnings from the forestry sector, other ministries saw the issue in a different light.

As noted, the Ministry of Industry tended to measure national benefits from timber in terms of the number of new plywood pulp and paper and chipboard plants, while the Ministry of Finance tended to calculate benefits in terms of taxes originating in the sector, and the Ministry of Manpower focussed on the number of new jobs created. Unfortunately, these measures of success are not wholly consistent with one another. As indicated in the first section of this chapter, maximization of gross timber foreign exchange earnings does not provide any useful measure of national benefits from the sector. Maximum budgetary revenues are consistent with continued high levels of log exports, but not, in the short to medium term, with a full phaseout of log exports. Maximum employment is not in the short run possible when there is a phasing out of log exports, particularly since upwards of 30,000 loggers have become unemployed since export quotas on logs were first enforced in 1981. And many processing activities, particularly pulp and paper operations, are among the least labor-intensive of all activities.[24]

There is no shortage of environmental and resource management questions related to large-scale harvests in the Indonesian tropical forests or, for that matter, in lowland tropical forests elsewhere in the world. While viewed as serious problems among plant scientists and foresters, many of these have not yet become issues of contention between MNC's and governments, including that in Indonesia.

Selective cutting methods[25] practiced by all concessionaires remain uncontroversial, notwithstanding earlier and more recent demonstrations of the extent of forest damage from selective cutting, the growing body of biophysical evidence that the effects may be devastating in terms of reduction in species diversity,[26] and preliminary evidence suggesting that present harvest methods may predispose the forest to ruinous fires. Except in the Ministry of Environment, the effects of commercial harvests in increasing the attractiveness of the forest for squatters and slash-and-burn agriculture have not been formally voiced. Few government agencies in Indonesia have focussed at all on the implications of deforestation for irreversible losses in potentially valuable non-wood products, reduced gene pools, or loss of animal habitats, although the Ministry for Environment has in recent years sought to arouse public awareness of these problems. Some expatriate observers have commented on the environmental implications of forest-based industrialization for imbalanced regional development, including costs of "boom-town" phenomena,[27] but this has not yet become a widely recognized problem at the official level, nor has it given rise to much conflict between investors and government.

If controversy on these environmental issues has been rare or mild, disputes over essential resource management questions have been almost absent. The multinational corporations have not contested the thirty-year limit on concessions imposed by the Forestry Department. Although lengthening the contract tenure would be in the long-term interests both of the companies and of sensible resource management (owing to the 70- to 100-year growing cycles of commercial species in the tropical forest), the nearer-term interests of the firms and the department dictate a much shorter time horizon for harvesting. Finally, beyond the usual governmental exhortations for companies to "develop markets for secondary species," the focus of all harvesting activity remains the dozen or so species currently regarded as commercial. Exploration for and use of non-wood products of the forest, including utilization of fruits, flowers, bark, roots, and leaves for medicinal or cosmetic purposes, remains largely a nonissue from the point of view of firms and the government alike.

Quite possibly, the neglect of these environmental and resource management issues is not neglect at all, especially given the dearth of technical information available and disseminated. Rather, it may be that these issues are subsumed under the larger controversial issues of deforestation and reforestation. It may be that questions of vanishing gene pools, reduction in species diversity, losses of animal habitat, macroclimatic changes, silting of river systems, and other possible consequences of the large-scale harvest of tropical hardwoods are too distant or amorphous to incite public or governmental demands for action. But the claims of "denuding of forests" that are often raised in the popular Indonesian press do capture attention, even if denuding is not (as the press usually implies) a result of clearcutting methods proscribed in Indonesia but of the more gradual (but nonetheless dramatic) changes in the forest ecosystem arising from present selective cutting practices.

In any case, some inappropriate corrective measures have been taken for some of the wrong reasons. After the Chief Executive (but not the Forestry Department) repeatedly warned concession holders of the consequences of their failure to initiate reforestation programs, a by-now-familiar Indonesian pattern was set in motion. First, as in 1978 when the government doubled the export tax on logs, a financial incentive for reforestation was established. In 1980 a special deposit (tax) amounting to $4 per cubic meter on every log exported was established. This tax is refundable once the firm demonstrates that a satisfactory reforestation program has been established. For an average Indonesian stand of tropical timber, the tax annually amounts to about $180 per hectare harvested. Although the revenues from this measure may be significant, it provides a very weak incentive for reforestation, since the present value of the refundable tax (deposit) is much less than the cost of reforestation.[28] (Similar measures employed in the Philippines and Malaysia have proved equally ineffective.)

Firms have no real incentive, then, to reforest, and most would not know how to do so in the context of a tropical forest even if required. Thus, the reforestation controversy may worsen, and along with it relations between firms and the government. Past patterns of government decision-making on forest issues suggest that if this market-related incentive does not yield results (as with the export tax in 1978–80), the Indonesian government will resort to a nonmarket measure. Elsewhere, these have taken the form of revocation of concessions and establishment of minimum per-hectare requirements for reforestation outlays. In the depressed world market for tropical hardwoods during 1981–83, the latter measure would have meant, in Indonesia, closing down most logging operations—which is perhaps why it has not yet been required.

Although not intended as such, two policy tools have had significantly greater positive environmental impact in the tropical-timber sector than official exhortations and refundable taxes for reforestation combined. The first was the doubling of the export tax on logs to 20 percent. Coming at a time of historically high world prices for tropical hardwoods, the tax reduced the rate of harvest below what would have occurred at lower tax rates. Stands formerly attractive at the lower tax rate became uneconomical propositions, particularly those in more remote upriver locations. (These tend to be upland forests in any case, where harvests lead to the most damage from erosion.) The second tool was the enactment of export restrictions on logs beginning in 1981. Since log exports were limited to one cubic meter per four cubic meters of processed exports, and since there was insufficient processing capacity to handle even half the logs that would ordinarily be harvested in a year, the rate of harvest was curbed significantly from 1981 to 1983. From the point of view of the balance of payments and returns to loggers, this was damaging. But it did allow more time—while there still are tropical forests—to come to grips with complex environmental questions involved in harvesting of tropical timber.

### Involvement of MNC's in Environmental and
### Resource Management Efforts

As noted, two distinct types of multinational corporations have been active in the Indonesian forest sector since 1967: large MNC's based in industrial countries and small MNC's based in neighboring developing Asian countries. Predictably, these two groups have somewhat different objectives. The larger MNC's can be expected to pursue a complex mix of profit and strategic objectives wherein profit objectives are defined not so much in terms of individual projects per se but in terms of those projects' effects on global MNC profits.[29] Strategic objectives include maintaining world market shares for the MNC in wood-product sales and reducing the uncertainty facing the enterprise (by, say, assuring steady supplies of logs for plywood mills located elsewhere—a particularly important consideration for Japanese MNC's in the past).

Smaller multinationals, particularly those from nearby Asian countries, may be expected to pursue more prosaic objectives. Operating on a regional rather than global scale, such firms tend to focus much more on the profit implications of particular investment projects: each investment "tub" is expected to stand on its own bottom.

Owing to these differences in outlook and objectives, large MNC's can be expected to have a longer investment horizon than would smaller corporations based in nearby countries and, accordingly, more concern with longer-term issues in relations with host countries—principally environmental and resource management questions in the case of tropical timber.

In general, experience in Indonesian timber extraction before 1983 bears out these generalizations. The larger MNC's from the United States and Britain have shown somewhat greater concern about environmental and related questions, though not to the degree the differences between them and the smaller MNC's would suggest. But since the larger MNC's have also been viewed as having greater financial and technological *capacity* for dealing with environmental issues, their perceived shortcomings in responding to environmental and resource management problems have been judged more harshly. Furthermore, the biggest, most visible MNC's (Soriano, Georgia Pacific, Weyerhaeuser, Lever Brothers) secured much larger concession areas (one million hectares in one case) than did smaller firms, so complaints over their conduct were magnified proportionately. In addition, these larger corporations were much more visible than the numerous smaller logging operations of enterprises based in Malaysia and Hong

Kong. As a result, widespread press reports of abuse of forest resources and of fiscal and other obligations tended to be associated with the larger firms, even when—as in the case of employment of nonIndonesians in logging—smaller MNC's were at fault.

Host-country disenchantment with various aspects of foreign investment led, in 1979, to the revocation of the largest MNC concession. Although inattention to environmental questions was often mentioned as a reason for revocation, other factors mattered more. Official concern over lack of reforestation efforts by concessionnaires led to the special refundable reforestation deposit in 1980, and environmental arguments came to be used increasingly in condemnation of foreign investment in the forest sectors. Within three years two of the three remaining large MNC's based in industrial countries (Weyerhaeuser and Georgia Pacific) had initiated or completed divestment in Indonesia. In neither case were environmental issues primarily at issue, but widely held perceptions of environmental abuse by logging firms in general clearly undercut the companies' positions. In both cases it was delay in implementing investments in domestic processing of timber that ultimately led to their departure from Indonesia, although for neither company was this the precipitating factor in divestment. Had any of the larger MNC's moved substantially into such investments before 1978, it is doubtful that any real or perceived shortcomings on their part would have resulted in an impasse leading to divestment.

Although smaller MNC's from nearby nations may have initiated environmental and resource management programs, none is documented. Similarly, only in one case (Weyerhaeuser) did a foreign firm mount significant research and development projects in the Indonesian tropical forest.

Weyerhaeuser began its reforestation program in East Kalimantan in the early 1970s. With over thirty years of experience in tropical forest extraction in Sabah, the company was ideally suited for the task. The effort involved experimental work using introduced (nonnative) tree species in a plantation establishment.[30] The experimental area reportedly involved 15,000 hectares. Tropical foresters from international agencies who visited the facility in 1979–80 praised the design and monitoring of the experiment. Early on, however, the project encountered problems arising from what one report described as "the rigidity of legal and concession agreement restrictions,"[31] including problems of insecure land tenure.

Elsewhere local joint-venture partners including governments-as-owners of timber stands have been unwilling to reinvest profits in this type of experiment since the financial rewards are, at best, in the distant future.[32]

This consideration may have been a problem in the Weyerhaeuser case as well. Indeed, according to its president, "the company could not persuade the government to go along with . . . longer term investments in new plantings. . . . [A]ccordingly we were forced into a short-term extractive program."[33]

### Environmental Disputes in a Broader Perspective

The record of disputes between government and the multinational corporations involves few clear-cut instances of conflict traceable to any specific incident. Rather, the history of investor-governmental relations since 1968 has been one of inconsistent and miscommunicated signals from government on the one hand and their misinterpretation or neglect by investors on the other. Governmental complaints about MNC's have been duly noted here, but investors also cited a litany of complaints, some related to environmental issues.

Chief among investors' complaints was that of instability in the environment for investment. As the implementation of many policies, including forestry policies, can be changed in Indonesia by decree, regulations vital to investors can be altered overnight. Companies have thus long argued that the rules of the game have been unstable. Indeed, from the companies' point of view, several key regulations—among them, the timber royalty policy (1971), Indonesianization of the labor force (1974), timber export taxes (1978), log export quotas (1980), and reforestation policies (1980)—were revised with little advance warning. From the government's perspective, all but the first of these policy adjustments did not represent overnight changes, but were merely delayed governmental responses to perceived intransigence by investors in the face of repeated governmental exhortation over a long time.

Another major investor complaint has been that local joint-venture partnerships pose difficulties. Companies alleged, for example, that all their attempts to move into domestic processing and/or reforestation programs were blocked by local partners mainly interested in short-term gains from logging, rather than in long-term resource management.

Finally, the workings of other aspects of the Indonesian legal system, particularly with regard to land-tenure questions, has been a continuing irritant. Companies with valid concession agreements specifying their fiscal obligation to the central government reacted sharply to the many demands for taxes imposed by regional and county governments, many of which had perfectly valid claims that were simply not covered in the agreements signed by firms. The inability to obtain secure tenure of land rights to conduct reforestation experiments was a problem not only for Weyerhaeuser but also for several other firms.

## The Future Role of MNC's in Environmental and Resource Management Issues

Multinational corporations' capacity to cope with environmental issues in Indonesian forestry is secondary to the question of the future presence of MNC's in forestry. All but one of the larger Western-based firms—those with the greatest capacity and interests in environmental and resource management issues—have already left. Smaller MNC's from nearby countries have to date displayed little concern for such problems.

Further, any role for the larger MNC's in the forest sector generally will not be in the extractive stage, where most of the serious environmental and resource management problems have been present, but in processing of domestic logs for export as plywood or moulding. New foreign investments in logging have been actively discouraged since 1975. By 1984 it was clear that any new foreign investments in processing would have to rely on local logging firms for feedstock.[34] European and, perhaps, U.S.-based firms will, however, probably be involved in several future projects involving pulp and paper plants, where potential environmental problems abound. But constraints on these projects, particularly limits on the supplies of long-fibered wood, have already caused long delays for many planned pulp and paper projects, and the future of this industry in Indonesia remains uncertain.

Even where foreign firms might have a role in extraction, the continuing lack of scientific data on soils, species, regeneration rates, forest hydrology, and the like serve to limit prospects for success of future programs in environment and resource management in the tropical forest of Indonesia. In conjunction with constraints arising from lack of secure tenure for land used in experimental projects, these limitations bespeak a limited role for multinationals in the future.

Still, MNC's might help resolve environmental and resource management problems in the Indonesian tropical forest. There are areas of need that MNC's are best equipped to service, though whether they have any incentives to do so is unclear. Multinational corporations such as Lever Brothers, Weyerhaeuser, and Georgia Pacific have perhaps the most extensive experience in mechanically processing logs into final products. Anything that is done to increase recovery of usable materials during this process will reduce the need to harvest the virgin forest. And anything that reduces demands on this fragile ecosystem is likely to be good for the environment. But recovery is as low as 33 percent in some developing-country sawmills and veneer mills versus over 55 percent in some Japanese, U.S., and Gabonese mills.[35] The marked shift to on-site processing in Indonesia and elsewhere means that as long as such recovery rates persist, more stems will have to be cut to obtain a given volume of final product. Providing training as well as expert consultants from large MNC's could enhance recovery in Indonesia, but financing for this activity remains a question.

Similarly, quality-control problems persist in Indonesian plywood manufacture. Every sheet of Indonesian plywood rejected in U.S. or Japanese markets means additional demands for harvest in the forest. Technical assistance in establishing and operating a quality-control institute for Indonesian plywood would be best supplied by MNC's with long experience in plywood fabrication. Such an institute could test existing and potential commercial species intensively to determine their suitability for use in veneer panels; they could also test adhesives, other binding agents, and waterproofing substances commonly used in Indonesian plywood plants. The institute would disseminate results to all producers, and its stamp of approval could be withheld from all shipments that failed to meet quality-control standards for strength, waterproofing, and lamination. Again, although MNC's are best suited to render such assistance, at present they have little incentive to do so.

It is perhaps more plausible to expect multinational corporations to create and fund host-country research institutes where both fundamental and applied forestry research would be conducted on biophysical, economic, and cultural aspects of forest-based activity. Particularly critical is research that might indicate ways of making undisturbed forests more valuable. Many useful and valuable nonwood forest products may be extracted without cutting stems and incurring the consequent damages. Such products include those derived from bark, leaves, flowers, and fruits, and those used to produce gums, resins, oils, pharmaceutical products, spices, and cosmetics. Many of these products are unique to the tropical forest.

The problem is that the larger MNC's with the most extensive experience in the tropical forests are by and large no longer active in those forests, except in the Malaysian state of Sabah. Joint efforts between these firms and those industries standing to benefit most from such research (cosmetics, pharmaceuticals, specialty foods, naval stores) might, however, be fostered by foreign aid.

Large MNC's from developed countries can sometimes be induced to support such activities even in the absence of clear short-term financial benefits. An example was a proposal by Weyerhaeuser in 1982, made when the firm began to divest its holdings in Indonesia. The Weyerhaeuser experimental research plots in East Kalimantan were among the largest and best designed anywhere in the vicinity of a tropical forest. The company offered a sizable sum (about $1 million) to be used to continue the experiments after it left the area. The funds were to be split between one or more forest departments in U.S. universities and Indonesia's Agricultural Institute at Bogor. The U.S. universities and the Bogor Institute would jointly monitor the experiments over the next few decades, and would take responsibility for both keeping up the plots and disseminating the results. Valuable insights on reforestation programs of interest to Indonesia and the world at large would thereby be made widely available. In many ways, this was a model proposal. But it was ultimately rejected—not by the government, but by the local joint-venture partners, who saw little merit in the proposal.

### Conclusion

Participants in the continuing degradation and deforestation in the tropical forest include multinational firms large and small, host-country holders of concession rights, host governments, and consumers of tropical hardwood products. History is unlikely to award any prizes for stewardship of this natural resource to any of these participants. Perhaps none should be expected: the costs of degradation and deforestation are essentially long-term in nature, while the benefits from present harvests are certain and accrue rapidly. Paying greater attention to environmental and resource management questions will primarily benefit future generations, not those alive today. As with so many natural resources it turns out that because property common to all (government-owned virgin forests) is the property of no one, there is little incentive to maintain its economic value. Because the vesting of rights to virgin forests in private hands, particularly foreign private hands, is probably politically unthinkable in Indonesia and most other developing countries, the world may soon face a shortage of virgin rain forests even in the absence of any shortage of wood.

**CHAPTER FOUR**   Foreign Toxins: Multinational

Corporations and Pesticides in Mexican Agriculture

Louis W. Goodman

## Introduction

Pesticide use in developing countries is a controversial subject.* One aspect of the controversy is the apparently harsh choice between the benefits of increasing agricultural yields and the regrettable but likely environmental and health costs of pesticide use. Another aspect is allocating responsibility for widespread misuse and abuse of pesticides between host government ignorance, inadequate training, regulatory neglect, and the practices of agricultural producers and host-country and multinational pesticide firms.

The pesticide industry in Mexico makes a useful case study. Mexican agriculture is in crisis, the country is increasingly dependent on food imports. Pesticides have been used intensively in Mexican agriculture since 1948, but their use remains concentrated in the irrigated export-agricultural areas of the North. At the same time, there is considerable evidence of serious pesticide pollution in the country, affecting human health and the

*Solon L. Barraclough, Henry J. Frundt, Kitty Richeldeurfer, and Robert Wasserstrom advanced the work of this chapter with advice and encouragement. Any faults are the sole responsibility of the author. Unless otherwise noted, data on the importation and domestic production of pesticides, and the structure of the Mexican pesticide industry, were supplied by Belfor Portilla of the Instituto de Proyectos Agroindustriales, S.A., of Mexico City drawing upon information provided by Fertilizantes de Mexico (FERTIMEX) and the Asociacíon Mexicana de la Industria de Plaguicidas y Fertilizantes.

environment. The victims are frequently field workers and migrants separated by a huge social gap from large growers who make pesticide use decisions. Despite an extensive regulatory apparatus, there is broad consensus that state control over pesticides remains ineffective.

The structure of the Mexican pesticide industry also suggests that a case study is fruitful. Mexico has a mature and relatively advanced domestic pesticide industry. Fertilizantes de Mexico (FERTIMEX), a state-owned company, is the biggest single producer of pesticides. At the same time, multinational corporations (MNC's) play a key role at each stage of production and distribution. More than fifty foreign companies are active in Mexican pesticide production and importation. The more complex the manufacturing process, the more important the role of MNC's. FERTIMEX produces most of the relatively technologically simple organo-chlorides and much of the more complex organo-phosphates. Foreign firms produce all the most technologically complex pesticides (carbamates and synthetic pyrethroids) used in Mexican agriculture.

These characteristics—a critical need for higher agricultural yields, serious pesticide pollution, inadequate regulation, strong state leverage through a parastatal enterprise, and a technologically sophisticated foreign-owned industry segment—are, or soon will be, typical of many Third World countries. An analysis of pesticides in Mexico can be instructive for other developing countries.

The immediate issue addressed in this chapter is how MNC's might make a more effective contribution to avoiding pesticide abuse and more effectively managing the production and use of pesticides. The questions, however, cannot be answered without an understanding of the importance of pesticides for Mexican agriculture, the structure of the Mexican pesticide industry including the role of MNC's, and the nature of the pesticide regulatory framework. This matrix guides the structure of the paper. The first section provides background information on the use of pesticides in Mexican agriculture, the terms of the pesticide debate, and evidence of pesticide pollution. The next section examines the Mexican pesticide industry and demonstrates the critical role of MNC's at each stage of production and use. The third section describes state control of the pesticide industry and analyzes reasons for weakness. Returning to the original question, the final section considers more positive roles MNC's might play in improving pesticide management.

## Background

*Pesticide Use in Agriculture.* During the 1940s and 1950s pesticides were mainly used for cotton cultivation. At that time cotton was grown on nearly one million hectares and provided the country with 25 percent of its export earnings. In recent years land in cotton has fallen to between 200,000 and 300,000 of Mexico's 16 million harvested hectares. With the Mexican oil boom, cotton's $300 million in earnings provided, in 1985, only 1.5 percent of the nation's foreign exchange, and cotton has fallen to second place, behind coffee, among agricultural exports. In 1983 cotton cultivation still used more than 20 percent of Mexico's pesticides, with the balance used in the cultivation of other crops, including coarse grains (16 percent), winter vegetables (12 percent), fruits (10 percent), sugar (6 percent), and oilseeds (6 percent).[1]

While pesticides are applied in all of Mexico's highly varied agricultural regions, use is concentrated in the often irrigated export agriculture in the North. Growers with large holdings are typically fully mindful of their customers' requirements when making decisions about type and frequency of pesticide applications. The typical Mexican agricultural pesticide user is not a small-holder eking out a living on a tiny plot, but a commercial farmer growing cotton, winter vegetables, or animal feed, all of which are committed before planting and grown to customers' specifications. If, as is often the case, the customer is a food exporter, varietal and quality specifications are set in terms of ultimate consumer preferences, and pesticide use is limited by Food and Drug Administration (FDA) standards needed to gain U.S. import certification. If the grower fails to meet these standards, the rejected crop spoils or is consumed in Mexico.

Few Mexican "peones" use pesticides for their small corn and beans plantings. Yet they and their landless counterparts become pesticide porters, mixers, loaders, and sprayers when they find work on the big export-oriented farms. They become pesticide *sprayees* when the poisonous mists dropped by crop dusters drift from empty fields to adjoining ones, or onto their homes, families, and drinking water sources—often located dangerously close to the fields. And they become pesticide consumers when they drink contaminated drinking water or eat food containing pesticide residues. Thus pesticides raise serious questions regarding the social distribution of the benefits and costs of their use.

*Terms of the Toxin Debate.* Reliable and systematically gathered information on pesticide poisonings does not exist for Mexico, but there is enough circumstantial and anecdotal evidence to suggest that it is a serious problem. Critics argue that pesticides are overused in Mexican agriculture and in public health programs.[2] They suggest that this results in unnecessary poisoning and environmental contamination. They maintain that pesticide use is ultimately self-defeating since its use generates pest populations that are pesticide-resistant and that pesticide imports waste foreign exchange critical for Mexico's development ($30 million in 1983). They claim that production could be significantly increased through the use of integrated pest management (IPM) techniques that rely more on naturally occurring pest controls.[3]

Advocates argue that pesticides are needed to increase agricultural productivity and to control disease vectors. Industry sources claim that pesticide use prevented more than $1 billion worth of crop loss in 1983, that it hastens agricultural modernization, and that it has a net positive effect both on gross domestic product and on the Mexican balance of payments.[4]

Part of the background of this debate is that Mexico's agriculture is in crisis. A strong food exporter through the 1960s, in recent years Mexico has become increasingly dependent on imported food to feed its population, running a $2-billion food trade deficit with the United States from 1981 to 1983. Mexico has twice as many farmers as the United States crowded onto one-eighteenth as much arable land, with rural unemployment running over 20 percent and malnutrition as high as 90 percent.[5] With pesticides used on less than 50 percent of Mexico's farmland, agricultural modernizers often become pesticide advocates.

On the other hand, nearly half the pesticides produced in Mexico are organo-chlorides that are severely restricted or prohibited by members of the Organization for Economic Cooperation and Development (OECD). Furthermore, the Bhopal pesticide disaster has caused new anxiety about the safety of pesticide production in developing nations. With pesticide production and use in Mexico more dangerous than in industrial countries, critics fear that long-term systematic pesticide use will result in great harm and in long-term degradation of the environment. New research suggests that Mexican pesticide use is already a clear hazard to farmworkers, farm product consumers, and the environment.

Arguments on both sides are far from fully substantiated. However, there can be little doubt that pesticide use is growing in Mexico, that substances banned elsewhere are used there, that substantial pesticide pollution is already occurring, and that Mexico sorely needs to find ways to make its agriculture more productive.

Pesticide Pollution: Evidence. While the Bhopal methyl isocyanate poisonings have raised a red flag for producers and regulators of hazardous chemicals, smaller yet similar flags have been raised by reports of commonplace poisonings and sloppy application of hazardous chemicals in Mexican export agriculture. For example:

> On this warm spring day, Jorge Muñoz stands on a farm lane with several younger boys, smoking as he mixes buckets of canal water with poison dust from a plastic bin. The label on the product says "Sencor, Metribuzin." The product, an herbicide, is made by Bayer of Mexico.
>
> On the label are 13 warnings in Spanish.
>
> The first says, "Read instructions carefully."
>
> Jorge cannot read.
>
> "People under 18 should not apply this product," the label says. "Mexican law says it is illegal for growers to employ anyone under 16 to do hazardous work."
>
> Jorge is 16. His companions are 13, 14, and 15.
>
> Other instructions warn workers to keep the mixture away from skin, clothing, and food, to avoid spillages or mixing the poison near drinking water sources and to wear protective clothing. Within 10 minutes, the young workers have violated every warning and numerous labor laws as well. . . .
>
> On any winter day, you can watch as crop dusters roar low over the valley, casually dropping loads of poison mist that drift over workers in the fields and their families in ditch-bank labor camps. A *Times* photographer was sprayed as he took pictures of sick children in one squalid labor camp.
>
> You can see barehanded and barebacked men mix chemical cocktails and load them onto grower-owned crop dusters, wearing no masks and no gloves to protect their skin and lungs. . . .
>
> One group of workers said someone in their camp dies every two or three days. Another group said they figure 150 workers have been given antidotes after being overcome by pesticides.[6]

While reports such as this largely highlight grower negligence, it does not take too much imagination to see how other actors in Mexico's pesticide industry might, rightly or wrongly, become implicated. Huge and foreign, multinational corporations could become easy targets.

Satisfactory documentation of the complex ways in which pesticide-related substances can affect the environment, the economy, and human health requires massive amounts of expertise and resources in any country. Sheer physical size and ecological and social heterogeneity make this particularly difficult for Mexico. Not surprisingly, no satisfactory comprehensive study has been carried out to date. However, some reports of pesticide-related pollution do exist—enough to suggest the need for immediate and long-term concern.

Most of the systematic studies have been carried out in the area of human health. The leader in this research is Dr. Lilia A. Albert, of the Department of Chemistry of the National Polytechnic Institute in Mexico City and Director of the Environmental Pollution Program of the National Institute for Research on Biological Resources. For the past ten years Dr. Albert and her research team have conducted studies designed to detect levels of pesticides in raw and processed Mexican foods.[7]

In a program begun in 1973 Dr. Albert's team analyzed pesticide levels in potatoes, carrots, cabbage, lettuce, spinach, avocados, strawberries, tomatoes, rice, cheese, eggs, butter, chickens, and pasteurized milk. Very few of the vegetable samples were free of organo-chlorides (oc) residues and they often contained organo-phosphates (op) residues as well. Furthermore, these residue levels frequently exceeded internationally recommended limits. High levels of residue were also found in foods of animal origin. Dr. Albert's general conclusion was that "the situation regarding the use of pesticides in Mexico and the presence of these residues in foods and in the environment is potentially very dangerous."[8]

Although Dr. Albert's studies initially focussed on foods in Mexico City, in 1976 she began to examine the question of whether exposure varied by region. An initial study was carried out in the cotton-growing region of Comarca Lagunera. There, oc residues were examined in pasteurized milk and, in a parallel study, in human milk samples. The pasteurized samples were compared with similar samples analyzed from Mexico City. In both places, traces of more than a half dozen different oc pesticide residues were found, with samples of DDT-derived compounds considerably higher than the practical limit advised by the California Administrative Code (cac).[9] A study of nursing mothers yielded similar results. Nine different residues were found in this 1976 study and DDT levels were reported in a range approximating the highest found in parallel studies in other countries.[10]

While oc residue was the focus of this research on food of animal origin and of early studies of potatoes and other root crops, studies of vegetables also revealed the presence of OP. In a 1979 study Dr. Albert reported that 50 percent of samples of strawberries, tomatoes, and avocados purchased in Mexico City had concentrations of parathion and methyl parathion in excess of those recommended by the CAC.[11]

Another study carried out by Dr. Albert reported OC pesticide residues in human adipose tissue in three Mexican cities—Mexico City; Torreon, the most important city in the Comarca Lagunera cotton-growing region; and Puebla, a city surrounded by traditional agriculture.[12] The principal result was that, although DDT concentrations higher than CAC recommendations were found in all three, those found in the Torreon sample were unusually high compared with research carried out worldwide. This suggests that the excessive use of DDT in the past in this cotton-growing region has resulted in wide distribution of its residue in the environment, foods, and feed of the area.

Other pesticide pollution reports lack the systematic basis of Dr. Albert's research but still deserve attention. For example, a former employee of a major pesticide-producing firm reported that company studies of cotton farmers working in insecticide-protected fields have shown abnormal levels of carcinogens in serum technology tests on urine. Comparisons of DDT residue in tissue of humans in Ciudad Juarez and El Paso reported that the Juarez tissue had twice the level of DDT of the El Paso tissue.

Unsubstantiated reports suggest that less than 30 percent of the employees of Mexico's ninety-six pesticide-formulating plants are provided with adequate protection in their place of work. Knowledge among pesticide workers of the types of risks to which they are exposed and the means required to reduce the risks has been reported as generally low. Similarly, it has been noted that only about one-third of pesticide users have received proper information about its application and that 60 percent of them use no protection during application, with many considering such protection unnecessary. An early 1983 *Excelsior* article stated that Mexican cotton workers using Ciba-Geigy-produced Galecrom did not use gloves, masks, or protective clothing due to costs to growers, with resulting residue levels sixty times higher than those permitted by Ciba-Geigy and 3,000 times higher than World Health Organization standards. *Excelsior* also reported workers' refusals to complain of sickness for fear of losing their jobs.[13]

The impact of pesticide residue on human health in Mexico is of particular concern because of the general health condition of its population. Mexican studies have reported that up to 90 percent of rural populations, especially children, suffer from malnutrition.[14] Dr. Albert's studies suggest that pesticide use in farming areas likely leads to widespread contamination and introduction of residues into the food chain. The juxtaposition of physically vulnerable individuals and pesticide residues makes this a special cause for concern.

Pesticide use has impacts other than those on human health through the food chain. The use of OC pesticides for agricultural production in Southern Mexico and Guatemala has resulted in the resurgence of malaria, due to the development of inbred tolerance resulting from intensified agricultural application of pesticides.[15] This parallels many reports of inbred tolerance to pesticides applied elsewhere for both public health and agricultural reasons.[16]

Another relevant problem is the "broad spectrum" effect, where damage to insect, animal, and plant life beyond that intended by initial pesticide application results in harm to desirable aspects of the environment.

No claim is made, least of all by this researcher, for the comprehensiveness of this research report. To get a full picture of the problem, more studies in more regions of poisonings and of residues in human tissues, food products, and elements of the environment would have to be carried out. However, in one sense, this is not necessary. What Dr. Albert and other researchers have demonstrated is that there is reason for concern about pesticide pollution in Mexico, due to its impact on human health and on the environment. As will be discussed, Mexican pesticide legislation is generally good. What is lacking is the ability or will to enforce it. Although substantial work needs to be done to better demonstrate the precise dimension of the pesticide pollution problem in Mexico, more good work is especially needed on mechanisms for enforcing control of pesticide use. Before examining controls, however, we will describe the structure of the pesticide industry.

### The Pesticide Industry

The world pesticide industry is importantly integrated by multinational corporations. Several features of the world industry require examination before turning to the Mexican pesticide industry.

The World Pesticide Industry. An estimated $12 billion worth of pesticides were produced worldwide in 1980. Although the industry grew rapidly during the 1970s, with a 40 percent increase in shipment value, output has slowed in the 1980s, in part due to market saturation in developed countries and in part due to the reduced purchasing power of developing nations. Still, developing countries are considered an important growth market for pesticides.

Approximately one-third of the pesticides produced worldwide are used in the United States; another third, in the EEC and Japan; and of the balance, developing countries are the largest consumers, purchasing 25 percent of world supplies, with Latin American purchasers accounting for half of this. The developing-country market has traditionally been split between U.S. and European firms, with the former dominant in the Western Hemisphere and European firms dominant in Africa and Asia. Japanese shipments, however, have become increasingly important in recent years, especially in India and other Asian nations. Japanese manufacturers, as a result, have predicted a growth in overseas pesticide sales of nearly 15 percent a year, while the other OECD countries predicted a growth rate of only 1.3 percent.

The pattern of pesticide use in developing countries is somewhat different from that in industrial nations. Pesticides are generally divided into three groups: herbicides, which kill weeds; insecticides, which eliminate harmful insects; and fungicides, which prevent fungal plant disease. These are applied variously to all types of crops, but each has special relevance for some types. *Insecticides* are used for export crops such as coffee, cotton, and bananas, which are major developing-country products; *herbicides*, for grains, oil seeds, and grasses, such as soya beans, corn, and wheat, that are grown worldwide, but most importantly in OECD countries; *fungicides*, which account for less than 10 percent of worldwide pesticide sales, for fruit and vegetable production. As developing nations replace manual weed control with chemicals, and as they strive for self-sufficiency in food grains, herbicide use will increase. Fungicide and insecticide use will continue to be higher in developing than in industrial countries due to the importance of perennial crops for Third World agriculture.

On a country-by-country basis, the worldwide pesticide industry is quite highly concentrated. Of the more than thirty major producers worldwide, the top twenty control nearly three-quarters of world production, and the top eight control 60 percent. In the United States, the top four firms control 54 percent of sales; in France, the figure is 60 percent; and in the United Kingdom, 60 percent. Nearly half of all pesticides are produced by chemical companies; oil companies produce 20 percent, and pharmaceutical companies produce approximately 15 percent. The industry may be viewed as even more highly concentrated if analysis is done on a crop-by-crop basis. For example, the market for herbicides or insecticides used on a particular crop is generally largely dominated by one or shared by only two firms. For example, FMC and American Cyanamid together sell 56 percent of the ingredients used in corn insecticides in the United States; Ciba-Geigy and Shell sell 76 percent of the herbicides that kill broad-leaf weeds; Monsanto and Stauffer sell 92 percent of the herbicides that control grasses.[17]

Such concentration is alleged to make pesticide division sales more profitable than those of other divisions in the firms that produce pesticides, although the picture is far from clear. Some chemical industry sources estimate that profit on initial pesticide investments is two to four times as high as that for other divisions and that profits for such divisions can be as much as four times as high as those of other divisions with sales revenues of similar sizes. However, this is disputed by some pesticide analysts who claim that pharmaceutical earnings exceed those of pesticides in the same firm.

Industry concentration is partly related to the lengthy and costly process of product development. Major firms spend approximately 8 percent of their sales for research and development and smaller firms attempting to break into the market may spend as much as 20 percent. These costs include original synthesis and screening, toxicological studies on mammals and the environment, field plot testing, metabolism and residue analysis, formulation and process development, registration, and distribution expenses. Costs have been rising in recent years. An official of one of the industry's top ten firms estimated that his company has increased screenings eightfold since the 1960s, with consequent cost increases of 300 percent. He stated that the time needed to develop a new product has increased from five to ten years and that annual registrations for his firm have dropped from ten to two. The OECD has estimated that each new product requires $20 million in development costs.

Products receive partial protection through patents. But firms also try to protect expensive product development costs by creating complex distribution networks and measures to promote demand. Both have implications for effective pesticide-control programs.

The Mexican Pesticide Industry. Among developing nations, the Mexican pesticide industry is one of the oldest and most fully developed, with current sales near $160 million per year.[18] The industry structure has four stages of production: (1) the provision of basic materials; (2) synthesis of active ingredients; (3) formulation of the commercial product; and (4) distribution of the commercial product.

*The provision of basic materials.* There are three sources of pesticides: direct importation, importation of the basic materials or intermediate goods for their combination within the country, and synthesis from domestically produced basic materials.

Multinational corporations play a tremendously important role in this stage of the Mexican pesticide industry. Through headquarters coordination, they exercise control over a large portion of the worldwide chemical industry and thereby guarantee the provision of basic inputs for the production of active ingredients. This can perhaps best be demonstrated by comparing the number of pesticides imported with those produced domestically. Of the 132 pesticides used in Mexico, 86 were imported in 1982 and 46 produced domestically, FERTIMEX reports. However, imports of the most important pesticide category, insecticides, shrunk from 65 percent of Mexico's consumption in 1969 to barely more than 25 percent in 1979.

The importance of multinational corporations can also be shown by the amount imported of a specific pesticide product. Between 1969 and 1979, the principal importing firms for each group of pesticide products were MNC's. These are listed below for OCs, OPs, and carbamates: The OC importers were Bayer Mexicana (GFR), Ciba-Geigy Mexicana (Swiss), Distribuidora Shell de Mexico (USA), Quimica Hoest (GFR), Union Carbide Mexicana (USA), Vimsa (USA), and Fertilizantes Mexicanos. For OPs, the importers were Bayer Mexicana, Ciba-Geigy Mexicana, Union Carbide Mexicana, Diamond Chemical Mexicana (USA), Cyanamid Mexicana (USA), Dow Quimica Mexicana (USA) and Stauffer Mexicana (USA). Last, along with Union Carbide Mexicana and Bayer Mexicana, Du Pont (USA) was a principal importer of carbamate.

The role of domestically produced basic materials varies by type of product and a steadily growing stream of new products has been produced domestically since the late 1940s. Some OCs are produced wholly from domestically provided basic materials. These include DHC, DDT, and toxaphene. Other OCs are produced in part from domestic products and in part from imported ones. For example, 60 percent of endrin is produced from domestic product and a significant proportion of it, including the intermediate product isodrin, is imported. Domestic product is used significantly less in OP pesticides than for OCs. No phosphorate pesticide is made 100 percent from Mexican basic materials. Raw materials for carbamates and for the most technologically advanced pesticides are imported virtually entirely by multinational corporations.

*Synthesis of active ingredients.* The second phase of production is the fabrication of active ingredients within the country. From 1970 to 1980 installed capacity of active ingredients grew at 8.8 percent per year, reaching 44,000 tons in 1980. Eighty percent of this capacity is for insecticide production, with the balance roughly divided between fungicides and herbicides. Actual production grew at a 5.6 percent annual rate, reaching 20,000 tons in 1980.

This phase of the pesticide industry consists of twenty-four firms that produce forty-six active ingredients. For most, pesticides constitute one of a number of lines of production. Closely tied to these are the ninety-six formulator companies that produce commercial products. Fourteen of these twenty-four firms produce insecticides; ten, fungicides; nine, herbicides; and two, soil fumigants.

In 1983 the overall installed capacity for insecticide production reached 24.5 thousand tons. FERTIMEX accounted for more than half of the installed capacity, with multinational corporations making up most of the balance. The industrial profile for fungicides, which had an installed capacity in 1983 of 10,220 tons, is dominated by multinational corporations. A similar pattern exists for herbicides.

In summary, while FERTIMEX is the most important individual firm in Mexico's pesticide industry, it controls only 40 percent of the industry, and its power is strongest for the least technologically sophisticated products, the organo-chlorides. Multinational corporations control the importation and production of more than 60 percent of the active ingredients for Mexico's pesticide industry and dominate the technically advanced part of the industry.

*Formulation of the commercial product.* The third stage of pesticide production is the formulation of the commercial product from active ingredients. The Mexican Association of the Pesticide and Fertilizer Industry estimates that the country has an installed formulation capacity of 320,000 tons, of which 100,000 are for liquid formulation, 180,000 for powder, and 40,000 for granule.

There are four different types of pesticide formulators in Mexico—each with a different sourcing pattern for active ingredients:

1. *Formulators linked to multinational corporations.* These largely use active ingredients, either produced domestically by subsidiaries of multinational corporations or imported through them. To a lesser degree, they

use active ingredients produced by Mexican companies, especially FERTIMEX.

2. *Formulators tied to the National Rural Credit Bank (*BANRURAL*).* Their formulations are largely based on FERTIMEX products obtained through BANRURAL's distribution company, Servicios Ejidales, S.A.

3. *Independent Mexican Companies.* These are largely controlled by private agricultural associations that have integrated this phase of pesticide preparation into their general operations. They utilize both foreign and domestically produced inputs.

4. *Importer Industry Formulators.* These formulate pesticides under special contracts for re-export to the United States.

Mexico's ninety-six pesticide-formulating plants are located throughout the country but are most heavily concentrated in areas where cotton and other export crops are grown, such as Baja California, Chiapas, Chihuahua, Coahuila, Durango, Michoacan, Sonora, and Tamaulipas.

Pesticide formulation began in Mexico prior to national production of the product, and installed capacity is estimated to be substantially underutilized. The Mexican government operates fifteen formulating plants with a capacity of 100,000 tons of power but it is reported that these operate at less than 15 percent capacity. Affiliates of MNC's also carry out production far short of their installed capacity, though not to the extent of the state-owned firms.

Multinational affiliates, both through domestic production and through importation of raw materials, work with a much wider variety of active ingredients and produce a substantially more diverse set of products than do the state formulators. By and large, these are sold to a relatively small number of specialized formulators who produce a relatively small number of products with these inputs. On the other hand, state production of active ingredients such as methyl parathion and ethyl parathion are distributed to nearly three-quarters of the industry's formulators. Methyl parathion is produced in seven different formulations under 142 different trademarks; ethyl parathion in thirteen formulations under 86 different brands. FERTIMEX sells 37 percent of its product to BANRURAL and Health Ministry formulators; the rest is sold to private-sector firms.

The great variety of formulations (178) and the significant number of brands (917) of pesticide reported for 1980 show the complexity of the market for insecticides. This permits substantial price differences among brands, especially for MNC's with strong control over the production and importation of active ingredients for sophisticated and specialty products. *Distribution of the commercial product.* In the distribution of pesticides, the provision of technical assistance to the ultimate user is a crucial influence on purchase decisions. Affiliates of multinational corporations employ more than 600 agronomists specialized in parasitology, entomology, and phytopathology as well as many less highly trained technicians who lend technical assistance to users. MNC's also provide technical assistance to pesticide distributors and to technicians of government organizations during inspection trips to the countryside, where diseases and pests are detected and products are recommended to combat them.

One technique used in the provision of technical assistance is market segmentation. Affiliates of multinational corporations take into account, for each region of the country, the types of pests and crops and the level of technological sophistication in providing technical assistance.

This is complemented with promotion through farming magazines and brochures strategically located at distribution centers and along highways in farming areas. Firms also carry out free applications in experimental plots to demonstrate utility of a particular product in the hope that it will be adopted in future agricultural production.

State-supported technical assistance relating to pesticide use exceeds that of the private sector. This assistance is provided through thousands of technicians employed by the Ministry of Agriculture and Water Resources, largely through their offices for irrigation districts, dryland farming, and plant sanitation. In addition, technical assistance is provided by the many decentralized functional and crop-specific institutions, such as the National Institute of Agricultural Research, the Mexican National Tobacco Company, the Mexican Coffee Institute, and the Mexican Fruit Council.

A second and more important state influence on distribution is the credit management system of the National Rural Credit Bank. Bank credit managers not only determine the schedule for payment and repayment of agricultural loans but also the products on which those monies will be spent, including agricultural machinery, water, seeds, fertilizers, and pesticides. As a result, the credit management services of BANRURAL are critical for pesticide use decisions by farmers. They are an important source of pesticide purchases not only for the formulators and the state-owned Servicios Ejidales, but also for all of the private-sector formulators, including those associated with MNC's.

From the analysis of the four stages of the production of pesticides, it is clear that multinational corporations play a decisive or important role in each stage of production. For highly technical products they control every phase of production from the provision of basic materials to their distribution. For less highly specialized products, those that currently have the widest distribution in the country, they play a more secondary role complementing the activities of FERTIMEX. In the area of formulation, this pattern continues, but the state-owned company is the formulator division of Servicios Ejidales. With regard to distribution, multinational corporations employ a large number of individuals who provide technical assistance to farmers and officials who make decisions about pesticide use. The state provides a substantially larger number of technical advisors through a wide variety of organizations. In addition to farmers, the prime targets they attempt to influence are the credit managers who supervise the financing of Mexican agriculture, especially those in the national rural credit bank, BANRURAL.

### State Control of the Pesticide Industry

One aspect of state control of the industry, direct participation, has already been discussed. FERTIMEX is the largest single producer of raw materials for the Mexican fertilizer industry, concentrating on the less technically demanding products. The state has an impact on the industry in two additional ways: first, various agencies of the state simultaneously promote pesticide use and authorize control of its production. Second, another set of state agencies attempts to control pesticide use for environmental protection.

The agency assigned responsibility for controlling pesticides is the Ministry of Agriculture and Water Resources (SARH) through its office of Plant Sanitation (SV). SV has the following responsibilities:

1.  To determine the authorization process for the use of a new pesticide.
2.  To grant a product provisional registration.
3.  To approve annually those pesticides authorized for use in the country.
4.  Through regional committees, to establish the type and pesticide requirements for different crops.
5.  To publicize plant sanitation practices and information.
6.  To establish and maintain laboratories for quality control of pesticides and for the analysis of residues in agricultural products that are sold for human consumption and forage.

To oversee these functions, sv has constituted a committee called the "National Input Evaluation Committee," whose auxiliary group on pesticides, in 1985, was made up of representatives from the National Institute of Agricultural Research, the SARH Office for Rainfed Farming, the National Rural Credit Bank (BANRURAL), the national seed producer, FERTIMEX, the Mexican Union of Producers and Formulators of Pesticides, and the Mexican Association of the Pesticide and Fertilizer Industry (whose members include multinational affiliates). Absent from this committee are representatives of the Ministries of Health and of Ecology and Urban Development.

In addition sv joins with the U.S. Food and Drug Administration on bilateral agreements for the detection of pesticide residue in food products. At the international level it participates in the meetings of the Food and Agriculture Organization and the World Health Organization.

Despite all this apparatus there is broad consensus that there is little effective state control of pesticides in Mexico. As a result it is difficult to measure effective pesticide use or contamination because of the lack of available statistics and the difficulty of gathering new statistics. The problem is not loose standards. Mexico has strong legislation controlling which pesticides can be produced and imported and for the implementation of a nationwide monitoring system. The problem is a widely reported but unsystematically documented inattention to safety measures at all stages of pesticide production, storage, mixing, application, and residue monitoring. Parallel to this is a lack of political consensus and resources for implementing the legislation. One result is self-regulation in the Mexican vegetable-growing industry. In 1981 the President of the National Union of Produce Growers, J. Cuauhtemoc Bernal, stated that his organization, acting through state-level confederations of associated producers, "polices itself, has stopped certain farmers from exporting products violating U.S. standards, tries to educate its members in U.S. regulation concerning pesticide use, and itself inspects shipments leaving Mexico."[19] This is a clear indication that in at least one important area, the state does not itself effectively enforce pesticide regulation.

This ineffectiveness is compounded by the fragmentation of state attempts to control the pesticide industry. The industry is partially state-controlled through the competition afforded by FERTIMEX production, through the extension services of Servicios Ejidales, and through distribution controls exercised by BANRURAL. Parallel to this (and sometimes in conflict), SARH is authorized to approve pesticide products and to control their importation and production. The Ministry of Commerce and Industry is in charge of monitoring proper labeling of pesticide products. SARH's office, SV, together with specialized institutes, disseminates information on proper pesticide use, both for enhancing agricultural productivity and from a health standpoint. The Ministry of Work and Social Welfare regulates work conditions and contamination in pesticide production and formulation at work sites. Finally, the new Ministry of Urban Development and Ecology, under a newly implemented law largely modeled after U.S. legislation, has widespread authority but little effective control in environmental and health monitoring. Each of these functions was assigned at different times as a result of different political processes. Efforts to eliminate duplication and to consolidate disparate operations within one authority are, not surprisingly, the subject of fierce political infighting.

In addition to this, separate problems exist with respect to relations with the United States: Mexican growers claim that U.S. administration of import controls is unreliable and cite the 1984 ban on imports of EDB-sprayed Mexican citrus as an example. Their claims of unreliability were fueled by hearings of the Senate Subcommittee on Agriculture, Nutrition, and Forestry in 1978 that "made it evident . . . that U.S. inspection of imported (fruits and vegetables) is not rigorous . . . samples of incoming products are very small . . . and the analytic process itself is not very good for detecting certain chemicals."[20] A 1979 GAO report showed that the FDA had released food shipments for public consumption before completing tests that showed them to be in violation of U.S. health standards.[21] Furthermore, Mexican producers of fruits and vegetables for the American market report variations in FDA standards tied to domestic demand. When U.S. producers cannot satisfy domestic demand, some have alleged that there is far less pressure to impose FDA standards than when U.S. demand can be more fully satisfied by domestic production. United States officials deny such variations in standards.

Another problem is the cross-border flow of pesticides. Many products that are suspended, cancelled, or heavily restricted in the United States are alleged to be routinely exported to Mexico. These products include Dieldrin, Aldrin, Heptochlor, Chlordane, Lindane, Paraquat, Chlorobenzolate, Endrin, Captan, DDT, BHC, and Toxaphene. Parallel to this, it is reported that there is substantial illegal cross-border trade in products manufactured in Mexico but prohibited for use in the United States, such as DDT, BHC, and Toxaphene.[22]

**The Future Role of Multinational Corporations
in the Mexican Pesticide Industry**

The problem of pesticide pollution in Mexico will not vanish soon. To make progress, growers need to find ways to improve worker safety; storage and transport of pesticides must be closely monitored; producers —especially the largest firm, FERTIMEX—must enforce safety standards; the government must find ways to streamline its fragmented set of regulating agencies and to enforce its generally excellent legislation; and care must be taken that pesticides are not overused, either in agriculture or in disease eradication.

This is a tall order. It is so tall that many experts feel that the real issue is not how to reduce pesticide pollution in Mexico but how to prevent it from getting worse. Mexico's economic crisis, its chronic food production shortfalls, and its under-productive and overcrowded countryside suggest that disaster scenarios are indeed reasonable.

In this complex situation, multinational corporations are but one actor. Furthermore, most findings on negative pesticide environmental impact relate to organo-chloride residues—chemicals largely produced by Mexican national firms. Nevertheless, multinational corporations are in a particularly advantageous position to take action. Their "foreignness" and salience in developing countries make positive action highly desirable if they hope to retain large shares of developing-nation pesticide production. In fact, some firms have already begun to take positive action.

To be effective, MNC action would have to be taken in concert with the other actors in Mexico's pesticide industry and should address the problem in its broadest possible dimension. Viewed broadly, there are three interrelated policy problems to be confronted. These are:

1. *The environmental problem.* The extent to which pesticide manufacture and use in Mexico creates health problems and places stress on Mexico's physical and social environment.
2. *The industrial structure problem.* The extent to which current patterns of Mexican pesticide production impede efficient economic development through poor management of existing facilities, through lack of full integration into parallel development processes (for example, the broader chemical industry), and through drains on scarce foreign exchange.
3. *The technology-transfer problem.* The extent to which the existing industry changes too slowly, does not move quickly to develop the latest

worldwide technologies, and remains internationally uncompetitive.

In dealing with the environmental problem, multinational corporations, working with other actors, can lead. Officials of Mexican private-sector industrial organizations such as COMPARMEX and the Union of Fabricators and Formulators of Pesticides and Fertilizers report that foreign firms are largely passive members. They solve their problems by themselves and, while they maintain membership in industrywide organizations, they try to keep a low profile. Although this may be sound day-to-day business practice, it does not put MNC's in a position to deal with major social and industrial problems, and it can leave the industry defenseless against unilateral and industry-disruptive acts such as the nationalization of the fertilizer formulators carried out by the government of Luis Echeverria in 1972.

What would a higher profile mean with respect to the environmental problem? It would mean pushing, in concert with Mexican pesticide fabricators and formulators and other private-sector groups, for joint public-sector/private-sector cooperation in pesticide monitoring and in review of existing pesticide legislation. A positive step forward has been made in this regard with the membership of the two private industrial organizations of the pesticide group of the National Agricultural Input Authorizing Committee. However, private-sector initiatives forged in a broad public spirit could separately advance improvement of the environmental problem.

A second area of leadership could be the financing of independent research on the environmental impact of pesticides. Funds could be provided by the pesticide industry for the kind of independent research pioneered by Dr. Albert, funds currently in short supply in Mexico. These could be paralleled by studies carried out by firms themselves (many of which already exist but are not made public). Providing support for such research would advance the knowledge base needed to understand dispassionately the dimension of the pesticide-environmental problem in Mexico so that adequate steps could be taken for its improvement.

Parallel steps could be taken to improve the industrial structure problem. Although Mexico's largest producer of pesticides is the state company, FERTIMEX, the vast majority of pesticide production or importation is carried out by the private sector, largely through affiliates of multinational corporations. MNC's can play a positive role within the structure of Mexico's pesticide industry by being both cooperative and dynamic. Reports in the literature that multinational corporations have an advantage over domestic firms, not only in capital availability but also in quality of research, development, and engineering, in management skills, and in experience in diverse environments, has a firm base in the experience of the pesticide industry. Mexico's existing national industry and its plans for growth of that industry give foreign firms an unusual opportunity. They can accelerate both their own and Mexican national participation in the industry by developing cooperative research and development projects with Mexican private and public-sector firms, bringing world-quality research to bear on local problems. This would respond to the frequent complaint that products available in Mexico are not specifically tailored to Mexican needs but are adapted from those developed elsewhere, largely in industrial nations, and would also strengthen an important research community.

The technology transfer problem is, in a sense, the dynamic aspect of the industrial structure problem. The experience of MNC's in diverse business environments around the world gives their management unique perspective and skills. Multinational corporate managers understand that they are engaged in dynamic industries that are not necessarily wedded to a particular technology. In fact, corporate advantage is often strongest in the areas of sales and distribution, and adjustments in technology are often seen as a response to changing user needs.

The business of the pesticide industry is improving the physical environment to reduce disease and to increase the potential for food and fiber production. Review of the state-of-the-art of world technology reveals that the application of chemical-based substances to the physical environment is only one way in which important technological advance is being carried out. A second parallel area of substantial technological development is integrated pest management. Research on the coordinated use of pest-resistant plant varieties, together with specially designed tillage techniques and the introduction of beneficial insects, has been shown to produce substantial monetary and environmental savings with little or no reduction in output compared with pesticide-intensive production, especially in situations of labor-intensive farming. Integrated pest management, rather than being a threat to the pesticide industry, is a parallel technology that is available for all interested parties to develop, including firms traditionally involved in pesticide production. In fact these firms' long experience with agricultural conditions and needs, and their capacity for innovation and imaginative research would likely give them a comparative advantage in the exploitation of this technology. Since population and employment problems in developing nations are particularly acute and some integrated pest management techniques lend themselves well to labor-intensive agriculture, this technology could be particularly appropriate to the growth market for the pesticide industry—developing nations.

For the present, then, the nature of industrial structure and technology transfer in the Mexican pesticide industry suggests that multinational corporations can take a higher-profile role promoting research and development designed to improve both enforcement of Mexico's existing pesticide use regulation and the technological capacity of Mexico's industry. For the future, in part based on such cooperative programs, multinational corporations can anticipate local private and public-sector firms successively appropriating technologically simple areas of the industry and MNC's introducing new technologies to Mexican agriculture, especially innovative ones such as integrated pest management.

These suggestions are intended to involve multinational corporations more fully with many actors involved in Mexico's pesticide industry. Such actions will generate healthier and fuller public and private-sector relations in the Mexican industry, which are sorely needed. It will also generate new and solid opportunities in an economy of special interest to the United States. This is an important challenge for multinational corporations in an industry of great importance not only for the world's economic well-being, but also for building a healthy environment for healthy human beings.

# III International Trade and Investment Issues:
Pollution Havens, Hazardous Exports,
and the Workplace Environment

International trade and investment link the environmental practices of industrial and developing countries. At one time there was considerable concern that rigorous standards in industrial countries would drive polluting industries to countries with weak regulations or none at all. A second concern has been the appropriate role for home governments in industrial countries in regulating the export of such hazardous products as pesticides and in controlling the workplace environmental policies of MNC's in their overseas operations.

Both concerns contain an element of paternalism suggesting that developing countries cannot or will not establish environmental protection measures that will meet their own economic and social needs. But the question cannot be so easily dismissed. Differences in environmental measures might distort trade and investment patterns and might cause considerable economic adjustment costs in industrial countries. And if for no other reason than foreign policy interests, industrial countries do have a legitimate concern over their hazardous exports and MNC workplace environment issues.

These interlinked questions are considered by Jacob Scherr, Barry Castleman, and me in the following three chapters. I conclude that differences among countries in environmental protection regimes are unlikely to distort international trade and investment significantly, so both industrial and developing countries should feel free to pursue environmental protection policies suited to their own particular circumstances. Scherr analyzes the evolution of domestic and international regulation of the export of hazardous products, often through multinational corporations, and concludes that the principle of "informed consent" is being slowly, sometimes grudgingly, accepted as the basis of regulation. Finally, Castleman makes a vigorous plea for eliminating a double standard in MNC workplace practices and for bringing international companies' Third World performance up to their industrial-country levels. One implication of all three studies is that MNC's wishing to cultivate a favorable climate for international business must be concerned with their image in their home country as well as in their Third World operations.

# CHAPTER FIVE  Environmental Standards,

## Industrial Relocation, and Pollution Havens

## Charles S. Pearson

A major concern in discussions of environment, development, and multinational corporations (MNC's) has been that differences among countries in environmental standards and costs may cause relocation of economic activity, especially "dirty" industries, from strictly controlled countries to those with few or no standards.* Extensive relocation might create substantial adjustment costs for countries losing production, and environmental abuse and social costs in countries attracting polluting industries. This concern is sometimes known as the "pollution haven" issue.

MNC's, which are deeply involved in foreign trade and investment, could be the agents for such industrial relocation and have a direct business interest in the issue. Industrial relocation also has public policy implications and has been used by both industrial and developing-country governments as a reason for delaying strict environmental protection measures.

This chapter examines the theoretical, empirical, and policy aspects of industrial relocation. To do so requires a discussion of appropriate environmental standards and an explanation of how traditional international trade and investment theories can be modified to accommodate environmental resources as a factor of production. The first section considers the question of appropriate environmental standards in the Third World. The

*Portions of this chapter were originally published in Charles S. Pearson, *Down to Business: Multinational Corporations, the Environment, and Development* (Washington, D.C.: World Resources Institute, 1985).

second section develops the argument that environmental resources are an additional factor of production that, together with the traditional productive factors of capital, labor, and natural resources, helps determine the pattern of international trade and investment. The next section reviews the empirical evidence of effects on international trade and investment, and the final section considers policy responses in industrial and developing countries. A principal conclusion is that strict environmental regulations in developing countries, if explicit, certain, and stable, are unlikely to result in widespread loss of investment and industrial production.

### Environmental Protection Standards

A common concern in industrial and developing countries has been that if rigorous environmental protection standards are established, production costs will increase and the country will be at a competitive disadvantage vis-à-vis nations with lower standards. Two opposite conclusions have been drawn from this concern: first, that internationally uniform environmental standards should be established, to eliminate any competitive advantage based on differences among countries in environmental control costs. Second, that developing countries, because they are at relatively low levels of industrialization and hence have not exhausted the "assimilative capacity" of their environment (the natural capacity to absorb wastes and render them harmless), and because they are poor and hence have a low demand for environmental services, should choose low or even no environmental protection standards.

Both propositions contain a kernel of truth, but closer analysis reveals that both are a poor guide for policy. There are two errors—one a misconception of the relation between standards and costs, and the other a misunderstanding of the supply and demand for environmental services in developing countries.

Environmental protection standards take many forms:[1] ambient standards specifying permissible levels of pollution in ambient environmental media (for example, nitrogen oxide levels in urban areas); emission and effluent standards specifying permissible discharge levels for economic activities, often with required dilution and specified per unit time or production level (for example, particulates per cubic meter of stack gases); environmentally related product standards (for example, pesticide residue levels for food products); and exposure standards (for example, maximum daily exposure to radiation in the workplace). A moment's reflection reveals that the economic costs of achieving a particular ambient air or water quality standard depends, among other things, on the level of economic (industrial) activity, the composition of that activity (dirty or clean processes), the spatial dispersion of the activity, and the topographical and climate conditions (atmospheric inversions, levels and several variations of rainfall and river flows, etc.)—all of which vary among countries. Thus, internationally uniform ambient environmental standards would not harmonize environmental control costs and competitive positions internationally, even if that were a desirable objective.

Moreover, the benefits associated with a particular ambient environmental standard (the environmental damages avoided) depend upon the extent and vulnerability of receptors (for example, crops sensitive to air pollution, commercial fisheries vulnerable to pollution) and the values attached to environmental services, which are related to income levels. These factors also vary among countries. Internationally uniform ambient standards therefore would fail to account for the differences among countries in benefits, and would be uneconomic.

Similar conclusions emerge if internationally uniform effluent and emission standards are considered. Costs would vary at different sites depending in part on the availability of alternative pollution abatement and waste disposal opportunities. Benefits would also vary depending in part on other sources of pollution and environmental stress. Hence, internationally uniform effluent and emission standards would neither equalize control costs internationally nor be economically efficient.

This points to two important conclusions. First, an attempt to establish internationally uniform standards for the purpose of harmonizing the international competitive position would be neither successful nor desirable on economic efficiency grounds. Second, the correct general principle in both industrial and developing countries is to establish ambient standards on the basis of a local calculus of costs and benefits, and to support these with effluent and emission standards on individual sources in a least-cost fashion.[2]

Identifying the general principle is easy. Translating it into policy is not. A major problem, discussed below, is the difficulty in determining monetary values for the benefits of environmental protection measures. What price should be attached to preventing illness, preserving a species or saving a wilderness area for later generations to enjoy?

There are also two valid exceptions to the general principle of international diversity of standards based on local calculations of costs and benefits. Some environmental degradation transcends national boundaries, the so-called transfrontier pollution. Examples are pollution of regional seas, the global carbon dioxide problem, and acid precipitation that affects several countries. Closely related is damage to resources of global significance, such as gene pools and genetic diversity of wildlife and wilderness areas of worldwide value. Clearly, in these instances, cost-benefit analysis done at the national level is too narrow, and adequate protection requires consideration of global damages.

There is also a strong economic argument for international harmonization of some environmentally related product standards for internationally traded goods. Uniform product standards reduce the cost of adapting products to different markets, allowing longer production runs at a lower unit cost. Uniform product standards (and testing procedures), as for example in radiation emission levels for consumer electronics, are easier to establish when scientific opinions on a health hazard are uncontroversial and when the costs of adapting products to separate markets are high. A pragmatic reason for adopting uniform product standards is to avoid having product standards used as covert trade barriers.[3] Multinational corporations, which operate in many markets, generally support uniform product standards.

There is one troublesome point. Internationally uniform standards, especially for the workplace environment, are sometimes advocated not on the grounds of equalizing international competitive positions, but because of the universal value of human life. This raises important and difficult ethical problems, especially in developing countries. It can be argued that the scarcity of economic resources in poor countries and other pressing health needs mean that less money should be spent on protecting workers than in rich countries. But this fails to persuade many. A more convincing assertion is that reasonable protection measures are generally not costly, that employers have good business reasons for maintaining a healthy, productive, and loyal work force, and therefore the dilemma is more apparent than real. But this, too, is not fully persuasive, as the costs of worker protection in a few industries may be quite high.

The workplace environment issue is especially salient for MNC's, not because their performance is worse than national firms, but because they are guests in the host countries, because they comply with high standards in their industrial country operations, and because they generally command superior technical and financial resources. These features suggest a leadership role for MNC's. Castleman, for example, is strongly opposed to a double standard in the workplace environment.[4]

A word should be said about the practical difficulties of using cost-benefit analysis to help establish environmental standards. One problem is that good analysis requires a team effort involving engineers familiar with pollution-abatement technology; physical scientists who measure and model the sources of pollution and their dispersion in ambient environmental media; ecological scientists who measure and monitor the effects of ambient concentrations on ecological communities, biological resources, and humans; and economists who investigate the economic sources of environmental stress. This is difficult enough in industrial countries, where baseline environmental data and technical expertise are relatively abundant, and where market prices may reflect economic scarcity. The task is obviously more difficult in developing countries.

Another major problem is determining monetary values for environmental damages. When the damages are to productive resources such as soils, fisheries, crops, or to international tourism—the types of damage of great concern in the Third World—valuation is quite straightforward, at least in principle. The value is the opportunity cost, or output forgone, as these resources are damaged. Even here, however, there are problems in discounting future costs and in treating uncertainty. Damages to human health or to amenities are equally real costs but despite great ingenuity by economists, the monetary valuation techniques are quite imperfect.[5]

These are formidable difficulties and should not be underestimated. But decisions concerning environmental protection must be made. Even the decision to forgo protection measures is an implicit standard. It is better to have decisions guided by an explicit principle, even when analysis falls short of what is desired. And the process of cost-benefit analysis encourages a systematic and rational consideration of alternatives, which is at the heart of sensible decision making.

### The Environment and Trade and Investment Theory

The opposite proposition can now be examined: that developing countries should choose lower standards than industrial countries. The theory of comparative advantage (traditional international trade theory) says that in order to allocate resources efficiently and hence maximize global output and income, countries should specialize in the production and export of products that use in their production a relatively large amount of the resources the country has in relative abundance. Countries should produce and export products for which they have a comparative advantage, and they should import products in which they have a comparative disadvantage.

At first glance, extending the theory to include environmental resources or environmental quality appears straightforward. Environmental media (air, water, soil) provide a supply of assimilative capacity for waste disposal. Where demand for these services is modest relative to supply—due to, say, low income levels, the absence of industry, or low competing demands for environmental services—the economic price (the implicit or "shadow" price) of the waste disposal service should also be low. A low price implies relative abundance. Other things being equal, a country with abundant supply would then have a comparative advantage in goods whose production generates high levels of residuals discharge, as well as a comparative disadvantage in "clean" industries. Conversely, countries or regions where assimilative capacity is exhausted and incremental residuals discharge has a high cost would have a comparative disadvantage in dirty industries and a comparative advantage in clean industries. Thus, the theory goes, specialization through comparative advantage and international trade (or investment) efficiently allocates resources, increases production, and improves world welfare.

One problem with this simple formulation is that countries may not know or act on their true comparative advantage. Unlike labor and capital, most environmental services do not pass through markets and hence, there are no explicit market prices to indicate abundance or scarcity.[6] Implicit prices are established by government regulation, but the process is imperfect at best. Hence, governments may deliberately or inadvertently undervalue environmental services so as to gain a competitive advantage in world markets. The danger of undervaluing environmental services is compounded when damages are cumulative, indirect, and long-term, as they frequently are. Comparative advantage based on environmental resources is not "obvious."

A more serious problem arises if the additional assertion is made that developing countries *in general* have a comparative advantage in "dirty" industries. The supply of unused assimilative capacity is not inevitably higher in the Third World. Sketchy evidence on physical environmental attributes such as level and seasonal distribution of rainfall, river discharge per unit of land surface, and variability of river flows (all measures of flushing and dispersal capacity), as well as on soil types and structures, suggests that developing countries have a lower inherent physical capacity to absorb wastes and render them harmless, and a lower capacity to tolerate environmental stress.[7] Generally poorer health and nutrition in developing countries also increases the damage from a given level of ambient pollution.

Moreover, industrial production, although smaller in aggregate than in industrial countries, is highly concentrated in small urbanized countries (for example, the Republic of Korea) and in highly industrialized areas within larger countries (for example, the state of São Paulo in Brazil). The spatial concentration of economic activity within countries determines exhaustion of local assimilation capacity. Industrial relocation is likely to increase existing concentration in the Third World, and this again argues against automatically assuming a comparative advantage in dirty industries.

Nor do low incomes necessarily imply that the demand for environmental quality is weak. Recall that many types of environmental damages affect productive resources and that the very scarcity of such resources in developing countries suggests the demand for some types of environmental protection should be strong. Also natural resources, which are prone to environmental stress, account for a larger proportion of the economy in developing countries. It is only for environmental amenities, for example, the absence of unpleasant odors or noise, that one can assert a stronger demand for higher environmental quality in industrial countries.

The conclusion, then, is that the traditional theory of international trade—comparative advantage—can be extended to incorporate the supply and demand for environmental services as an additional factor of production, and that an efficient pattern of world production will reflect that factor. But the resulting pattern of production and trade is by no means obvious, and a general presumption that developing countries can neglect the environment and pursue a "pollution haven" strategy is ill-founded.

A second conclusion is that as countries systematically establish and enforce environmental standards, some alteration in the pattern of international trade and investment is likely and desirable. Until recently, a significant social cost of production—environmental externalities—was not included in private production costs, and hence resources were misallocated. The inclusion of these costs will alter production, trade, and investment patterns, but the move will be toward a more efficient pattern.

Two points concerning industrial relocation and multinational corporations can be made. First, there is no theoretical reason why MNC's should account for a disproportionate share of industrial relocation. One question is the amount of reallocation, if any, and this is a question of differences among countries in environmental control costs. A wholly separate question is whether additional production in countries with low environmental costs will be captured by domestic producers or by foreign investors (MNC's). On this latter question, there is nothing in the theories of international investment that suggests that MNC's have an advantage vis-à-vis their domestically based competitors.

A more interesting question is whether MNC's have an advantage over their local competitors in meeting new environmental regulations in developing countries. Most foreign investment theories that attempt to explain how MNC's can surmount the barriers of distances, language, custom, control, and knowledge of local conditions and compete effectively with local firms are variations on the themes of monopolistic advantage due to superior knowledge and technology, oligopolistic behavior, and the characteristics of the product cycle theory. The concept of monopolistic advantage based on firm-specific intangible assets offers a clue. To the extent that environmental control measures require sophisticated technology or technical and management expertise, MNC's may be better able to comply, and to comply at a lower cost, than local firms, thereby gaining a competitive advantage. For example, MNC's may have superior technology and more experience than national firms in preventing and containing oil pollution in offshore oil production.

The combination of in-house technology, expertise, and prior experience —all intangible assets that form the basis of the monopolistic advantage theory—suggests that the introduction of environmental regulations in developing countries will promote foreign direct investment, not block it. This point, however, remains speculative and would only apply to industries requiring sophisticated pollution control or to natural resource industries that require considerable skill in efficient management.

### Empirical Studies

Numerous empirical studies have been done to determine if differences in environmental control programs have significantly affected trade and investment. Most have focussed on the possible relocation of industry to developing countries on the premise that such nations have generally lower standards.[8] Several limitations on these analyses should be mentioned. First, no unambiguous definition of environmental control costs exists, and attempts to relate trade and investment changes to these costs are tenuous. For example, environmental considerations accelerated the shift from sulfite to sulfate pulp, but the shift was underway in any event and the cost attributable to environmental control alone cannot be ascertained. Second, data on control costs are fragmentary and incomplete, especially outside the Organization for Economic Cooperation and Development (OECD). But since it is the *difference* in control costs among countries that prompts trade and investment change, foreign control costs should also be known to estimate the effects. Third, neither MNC's nor host governments wish to declare publicly that foreign investment seeks to escape stringent environmental controls, and empirical analysis must look to inferential evidence. Finally, virtually all studies have concentrated on industrial pollution control. Whether environmental regulations have affected the international pattern of natural resource production and trade (oil and gas, mining, renewable resources) is largely unexplored.

The studies differ, using different methodologies and data. Some studies use analysis of investment data by location and industry, using regression analysis or tabular array; others attempt inferential analysis from environmental control cost data. Still other studies rely on surveys of firms to analyze locational determinants, surveys of business literature, case studies of firms and countries, or anecdotal evidence.

With respect to trade, in early research Richardson and Mutti examined the price and output effect of environmental control costs on the United States, taking account of effects through international trade.[9] Eighty-one industries were examined. The results showed generally modest effects, with price increases under a polluter-pays regime ranging from 0.19 to 5.12 percent, and a weighted average of 1.2 to 1.7 percent, depending on elasticity assumption. The weighted average output effect was a negative 1.75 percent under a polluter-pays regime, implying that on average U.S. output would decline less than 2 percent as a result of U.S. environmental control costs. The small output effect suggests that the trade effect is also small.

In a study for the UN Conference on Trade and Development, I used U.S. environmental control costs data for eighteen industrial sectors to estimate the increase in exports that developing countries might expect as a result of differences in environmental control costs.[10] The results showed the range of likely increases in developing country exports to have been $129 million to $257 million annually from 1973 to 1977, and from $116 million to $232 million annually from 1978 to 1982. These figures represent 2.1 to 4.6 percent of then-existing levels of Third World exports of manufactures. Overall, these increases would have been modest in relation to the 8 percent annual growth of manufactures exports from developing countries during this period.

Duerksen and Leonard examined trade and investment data to determine if environmental factors have influenced production and investment decisions.[11] They found that:

1. U.S. foreign investment in pollution-intensive industries grew no more rapidly than for all manufacturing.
2. The share of U.S. foreign direct investment in pollution-intensive industries that went to developing countries compared with other industrial countries did not increase significantly.
3. Host countries that received the most overseas investment in pollution-prone chemicals, paper, metals, and petroleum refining sectors were other industrial countries, not developing ones.
4. U.S. import of products manufactured by pollution-intensive industries grew at about the same rate as total imports.

They concluded that there is no credible evidence that environmental regulations have caused a widespread relocation of U.S. industries to so-called pollution havens, or that they will. Duerksen and Leonard did find environmental and workplace regulations may have motivated relocation in two types of industries—those producing highly toxic products (asbestos, benzidine dyes, and a few pesticides) and those processing copper, zinc, and lead.

Stafford and his colleagues have analyzed relocation within the United States, using corporate survey data and content-analysis techniques.[12] Their principal conclusions are that environmental factors are more important today than in 1970 but are still not major location determinants, that the speed and efficiency of the permit-granting process is important, and that environmental factors may influence siting within a region. This research tends to confirm the findings of Gladwin and Wells that uncertainty and delays in obtaining necessary permits may be a greater deterrent to construction of new plants than environmental control costs per se. Duerksen's research also strongly confirms this conclusion.

Knödgen examined environment and industrial siting for West German foreign investment, with a view toward identifying relocation in developing countries.[13] Her findings, broadly consistent with studies of the United States, indicated that there is no evidence that West German firms have reallocated production to pollution havens in the Third World in any major way. One reason may be that the cost advantage is narrowing as firms must build now to meet expected high future standards in developing countries. An interesting finding was that 90 percent of firms surveyed claimed to use the same environmental protection techniques in developing countries as in West Germany. Old, highly polluting equipment and technology are apparently unprofitable compared with modern clean equipment and technology, which conserves materials, energy, and water.

Castleman focussed on industries with serious workplace environmental hazards (for example, asbestos, arsenic, mercury, and benzidine dyes).[14] Control of workplace hazards can be difficult and costly, and it provides the same incentive for relocation as other environmental control costs. In his initial study, Castleman found evidence of imminent significant relocation, although his subsequent research, reported in this volume, found no wholesale exodus of the U.S. industry in response to regulations by the Occupation Safety and Health Administration.

Finally, Leonard has recently published very useful detailed case studies of four rapidly industrializing countries—Ireland, Spain, Mexico, and Romania.[15] He found that, for a period, Irish authorities did seek polluting industries with a view toward accelerating economic growth and exploiting assimilative capacity, but for unrelated reasons the investments did not materialize, and the strategy was quickly reassessed and abandoned. Spain did not deliberately attempt to attract foreign investment in polluting industry on the basis of weak environmental controls, in part because resentment against foreign polluters is strong in the bureaucracy and among local and regional political groups. Leonard found that there has been some migration of hazardous industries (for example, asbestos textiles and building supplies) to Mexico, and nonferrous metal smelting and refining operations (highly polluting) have expanded. But he concluded that Mexico did not explicitly encourage the migration, and that factors unrelated to workplace health and safety and to pollution control costs (such as labor wage rates, proximity to the U.S. market, and incentives for domestic processing of materials) are largely responsible for the expansion of these industries in Mexico. Finally, Leonard found that in the 1970s Romania became a major exporter of a variety of chemicals and chemical products the production of which was banned or strictly regulated in the West. Romanian officials claim that technological improvements have allowed them to produce these products safely, but this has not been adequately documented. Recent increases in East-West political tension and product purity standards in the United States have reduced Romanian penetration of the U.S. chemical market.

Despite difficulties with the data and analytical techniques, some reasonably strong findings emerge. First, environmental control costs are a small fraction of production costs in virtually every industry, and the effect on trade is correspondingly small. Although there may be some discernible competitive advantage in a very few industries (such as copper smelting and refining), developing countries should not expect any major improvement in export earnings from this source. Conversely, a putative trade advantage would not justify environmental neglect.

Second, there is no evidence of widespread reallocation of production by MNC's on the basis of environmental cost considerations. Thus industrial countries need not fear extensive loss of industry as they pursue environmental quality objectives, and the developing countries need not fear the loss of prospective foreign direct investment in industry if they implement tighter standards.

Third, efficiency in the granting of permits and stable, predictable environmental regulations are important. Both influence how potential investors perceive the overall business climate, which is an important locational determinant.

Fourth, there is weak evidence, especially from Knödgen, that MNC's may have an inherent advantage over local firms in meeting environmental control regulations. This advantage arises from the coincidence of clean and efficient (profitable) technology, and it suggests that MNC's have a constructive role to play in transferring environmental control technology and in meeting new market demand in developing countries for pollution monitoring and control equipment.

In short, these findings tend to confirm that environmental factors have not been and are unlikely to become major determinants of either international trade or investment patterns.

### Policy Considerations

Taken individually, the relations between environment and development and those between multinational corporations and development are complicated and often controversial. Considering environment, development, and MNC's together, the problem is compounded. For this reason a careful analysis and search for evidence has added importance as a guide for policy.

A principal conclusion for developing countries is that reasonable measures to protect their environment, especially if the measures conserve productive resources and maintain human health, are essential for sustainable development. If these measures are explicit, stable, and certain, it is unlikely that they will forgo significant industrial production or investment by multinational corporations. If some marginal investment is lost, the social cost to the host country of that investment would probably be excessive. To the extent possible, environmental standards in any country should be established within a local cost-benefit framework, to reflect local environmental and economic factors. In implementing environmental regulations, a policy of national treatment of foreign investors (that is, nondiscrimination between foreign and domestic investors) makes good sense.

It is also important to avoid subsidizing environmental control costs for either foreign or domestic investors. The polluter-pays principle, agreed to within the OECD in 1972, calls on member governments to refrain from such subsidies. This makes good economic sense. Not only are market prices aligned with the social costs of production, a requirement for economic efficiency, but international trade distortions that would occur if one country subsidized and another did not are minimized. Developing countries should consider a similar policy. Also, environmental objectives can easily be subverted if basic inputs—water, energy, pesticides—are subsidized and used in excess. A policy of removing such subsidies would improve the environmental performance of both MNC's and local firms.

The importance of explicit, stable, and certain environmental regulations for attracting foreign investment has been discussed. For those developing countries that have already established ambient environmental quality objectives and supplemented them with industry-specific effluent and emission standards, there is little play for discussion on pollution abatement during investment negotiations. MNC investors would be expected to comply with existing environmental standards and the concern would shift to enforcement. This situation, however, is likely to be the exception, either because ambient and emission and effluent discharge standards have not been adopted, or because the MNC investment involves environmental protection issues wider than just pollution—for example, erosion control in tropical forestry projects or measures for safe storage and transport of highly toxic materials, which by their nature are project-specific.

In these other, more frequent situations there is scope for environmental negotiations, and certain policies and procedures by host governments can be highly useful. Perhaps most important, the MNC should be required to submit a complete environmental impact assessment (EIA) for each proposed major investment. The statement should be more than a pro forma description of anticipated effects and should include baseline environmental data, environmental protection and pollution abatement technology (and the cost thereof), standards and control measures taken at other plant locations, procedures for environmental and pollution emergencies, and targets for environmental protection. The purpose is twofold: first, to transmit useful information to environmental regulators and, second, to form the basis for explicit environmental provisions in the investment agreement. The process itself of preparing an EIA forces the firm to consider better environmental practices.

If these procedures are to be successful, several conditions should be included. First, the environmental authority of the host government should be brought in early in the investment negotiations and be given authority to veto investments that are financially attractive but environmentally disastrous. Too often environmental agencies in developing countries are consulted after investment agreements have been reached, or their advice is overridden by powerful development, finance, and foreign ministries. The need to involve environmental agencies also applies to purely domestic investment. Second, negotiators for developing countries must themselves have high-quality technical and environmental expertise if they are to bargain on equal terms with foreign investors. There is an active international commercial market in such services, and development assistance agencies also provide these services for countries that require outside assistance. Third, however painful, the corporate environmental impact assessment and the environmental provisions of the investment agreement should be made public. Public disclosure not only provides a check on cozy investor-government deals, it can defuse subsequent controversy and provide some protection for the MNC's against charges that might emerge later.

A complete corporate EIA and its review by host-country environmental authorities is the first step. Many MNC investment agreements would benefit from explicit environmental provisions spelling out the host country requirements and the MNC's responsibilities. Such provisions could then be used as a basis for monitoring performance and, if needed, compensation for unanticipated damages. Negotiating environmental provisions and assigning responsibility may be especially important in joint-venture arrangements with local partners. Some modified procedures could also be used for licensing and subcontracting agreements with local firms that involve environmentally sensitive products and production techniques.

Industrial countries, generally the home countries of MNC's, confront two policy issues. First, is there any case for restricting imports from low environmental cost countries? Second, what responsibilities, if any, do home country governments have to regulate the overseas environmental performance of their MNC's?

The case for restricting imports on environmental cost grounds—by tariffs, quotas, or border equalization taxes—is weak. Some change in the pattern of international trade represents a movement toward more efficient global production and should be welcomed. It is only when an exporting government deliberately sets low environmental protection standards to gain an artificial competitive advantage that the exports receive an implicit subsidy. Even then an offsetting tariff ("countervailing duty") is undesirable on practical grounds. A precise determination of the amount of the subsidy cannot be made, and an attempt to do so would be controversial and invite covert protectionist actions. Finally, the international trade effects of environmental control programs are generally small, and the need for a policy response is correspondingly minimal.

Setting aside the contentious issue of controlling hazardous exports, examined by Scherr in this volume, what should home government policy be toward controlling foreign environmental performance of their MNC's? An automatic extension of U.S. environmental norms to all U.S. MNC operations in developing countries is not desirable. Internationally uniform environmental standards are uneconomic, and extension of the U.S. regulatory jurisdiction would create problems of extraterritoriality. But at the same time, a home-country government such as the United States does have a larger foreign policy interest in avoiding environmental disputes between its MNC's and other countries and in maintaining a generally favorable climate for private foreign investment.

The question becomes easier when the home-country government itself promotes private foreign investment, as is done through the insurance and financing activities of the U.S. Overseas Private Investment Corporation (OPIC) and parallel agencies in other industrial countries. OPIC's mandate is to promote development (its mixed public/private sector board is chaired by the administrator of the U.S. Agency for International Development) and this confers some responsibilities for sound environmental practices. OPIC does screen projects for environmental effects and recommend improvements, and it has refused to insure certain projects deemed environmentally unacceptable. Although OPIC has generally taken a constructive approach to environmental considerations, some further steps—such as placing an environmentalist on the board of directors, adding to its environmental staff, and transmitting environmental reviews to developing-country officials with environmental responsibility—would all be useful.

The final policy consideration is international environmental regulation of MNC's also analyzed by Gladwin in this volume. The rationale for international regulation is that MNC's are too large, complex, and internationally mobile to effectively regulate at the national level. Strict national regulation by one host country might divert foreign investment to a neighbor; strict controls by one home country might divert exports or investment opportunities to other industrial country competitors.

No effective and comprehensive intergovernmental environmental codes or guidelines for MNC's now exist. The OECD did establish a voluntary code in 1976 that is concerned with many other aspects of MNC investment performance, but a recent effort to expand the code to include environmental provisions appears stalled. The United Nations Commission on Transnational Corporations has been working on a comprehensive code that would include environmental provisions, but early agreement is unlikely.

The case for international regulation through codes or guidelines can be overstated, as the evidence suggests that strict standards at the national level, if certain and stable, do not deter significant foreign investment. Thus regulation at the national level is generally a feasible action. But at the same time, some international regulation would be helpful in bringing hazardous export policies within a common framework and in compelling MNC management to pay greater attention to environmental performance. Moreover, a carefully drafted code that requires a corporate EIA could encourage the transfer of valuable information on environmental control technology and costs, thereby supplementing efforts at the national level in host countries.

# CHAPTER SIX   Hazardous Exports:

## U.S. and International Policy Developments

## S. Jacob Scherr

The protection of public health and the environment against hazardous substances and products has long been a matter of societal concern.* Virtually every nation has taken actions to assure the purity and safety of food and drugs. In light of the exponential growth in the use of chemical substances after World War II and the deepening scientific understanding of dangers they pose, the United States and other industrial countries have established controls on the production, sale, use, and disposal of pesticides, toxic chemicals, and chemical waste products. Consumer goods, which may present chemical and other safety hazards, also have been regulated.

Generally, national statutes that control these substances exempt exported goods from domestic testing, labeling, and other regulatory requirements, and government regulatory agencies often lack any authority over exports.[1] Thus, substances that are banned or severely restricted where they are produced may be freely sold abroad. This laissez-faire policy reflects national desires to expand foreign trade and the traditional view that each nation has the sovereign obligation to protect its own citizens and environment, along with the right to take action to halt imports of hazardous goods. The prevailing standard in international trade remains caveat emptor — "let the buyer beware."

*The author wishes to acknowledge the assistance of Laird Lucas, Yale Law School, in the preparation of this paper.

### Dimensions of the Problem

The catalyst for international attention to the export of hazardous substances was the 1977 TRIS incident. Acting on evidence that TRIS, a flame retardant, could cause cancer by absorption through the skin, the Consumer Product Safety Commission (CPSC) banned the domestic sale and distribution of all fabrics treated with the chemical.[2] Several months later, CPSC decided to prohibit the export of such fabrics.[3] By the time the export ban went into effect, however, millions of dollars worth of TRIS-treated sleepwear had been shipped overseas.[4]

The TRIS case was not an isolated one.[5] A number of cases of exporting banned or severely restricted substances have been reported,[6] a few of which resulted in serious harm. Yet it remains impossible to determine the full extent of such exports worldwide due to a lack of adequate, up-to-date data. Industrial nations, which account for a high percentage of the world's production and export of hazardous substances, generally exclude from domestic regulatory requirements products destined for export, and do not routinely monitor exports of banned commodities. The United States is the only country so far to attempt to ascertain the volume of exported banned or severely restricted substances.[7] Available information nonetheless indicates that a significant amount of products banned or restricted in the country of origin are moving in international commerce.

The so-called dumping of banned products in developing countries reflects the broader problem of hazardous exports. The widespread use of pharmaceuticals, pesticides, and other dangerous products has spread across national borders much more quickly than the capability to assure their safe use. In some cases, such products may become much more dangerous in the Third World, where literacy and educational levels are lower and where protective equipment and other precautions are absent. As a result, widespread abuse of chemicals has been reported in many countries.

Pesticides. According to the U.S. General Accounting Office, approximately 29 percent of the 522 million pounds of pesticides exported from the United States in 1976 were not registered for use in this country. About 20 percent of these unregistered pesticides had been cancelled or suspended by the U.S. Environmental Protection Agency (EPA) because their use posed unreasonable risks to health or the environment.[8] No comparable statistics are available for the European Economic Community, which exported five times as much pesticide in 1978 as the United States did.[9] Overall pesticide exports to the Third World have grown rapidly in recent years—at an average annual rate of 15 percent through most of the 1970s—and are expected to continue growing in excess of 5 percent a year through the 1980s.[10]

Pesticide poisonings are becoming a major public health problem in a number of developing countries. In 1973 the World Health Organization (WHO) estimated the annual pesticide poisoning cases in the Third World at a quarter million, of which about 6,700 are fatal.[11] David Bull of Oxfam more recently projected that pesticide poisonings have increased to 375,000, with 10,000 deaths a year in the developing world.[12]

A number of pesticide poisonings involving exported banned or restricted products have been reported. The most infamous such incident involves leptophos, a pesticide never registered for use in the United States but produced here for export to some fifty countries. In 1971, the use of leptophos in Egypt resulted in death and illness among rural people and the death of over 1,000 water buffalo.[13] Perhaps the largest mass pesticide poisoning in history occurred that same year in Iraq, where some 100,000 Iraqi peasants became ill and some 6,000 may have died from eating imported seed grains treated with methylmercury, a fungicide that had been banned in the United States and other countries.[14]

Less dramatic but far more pervasive examples of pesticide poisonings abound.[15] In Ecuador, for example, mortality statistics indicate that pesticide misuse may be a significant contributor to death and disease, and shrimp and fish from the coastal waters have been found to have high levels of DDT. Ecuador continues to import DBCP for banana cultivation, although the use of this pesticide has been suspended in the United States with the exception of on pineapples in Hawaii under carefully controlled and monitored conditions. EPA requires those workers handling DBCP to wear respirators and full-body impermeable clothing. Such protective gear is either unavailable, extremely expensive, or impracticable in tropical countries.[16]

Pharmaceuticals. In the early 1960s concern first surfaced about the quality of pharmaceuticals in international trade, particularly those exported to developing countries. In 1963 the World Health Assembly passed a resolution requesting an examination of methods of assuring that exported medications comply with regulatory requirements in the country of origin.[17] In 1980 President Daniel Arap Moi of Kenya charged that foreign pharmaceutical companies were continuing to dump unproven, ineffective, and outdated drugs in the developing world.[18] The marketing practices in developing countries of American and British pharmaceutical firms also have been severely criticized for grossly exaggerating their claims[19] and for failing to provide the information and warnings that are required for domestic sales. In one case, the misleading and excessive promotion of chloramphenicol contributed to the deaths of 20,000 victims of a 1972–73 typhoid epidemic in Mexico, when the medication proved ineffective against resistant typhoid bacteria.[20]

Illustrative of the reverse side of this export dilemma is the controversy over Depo-Provera, an injectable contraceptive. In 1978 the U.S. Food and Drug Administration (FDA) denied approval for the domestic use of Depo-Provera as a contraceptive due to evidence that linked the drug to risks of fetal malformations, mammary tumors, and bleeding irregularities.[21] Under U.S. law, drugs not approved for domestic use cannot be exported. Yet several developing-country leaders have specifically asked that the United States permit the export of Depo-Provera to their nations, arguing that it is needed to curb rapidly growing populations. Also, their assessment of the drug's risks differed from the FDA's since women in their nations faced a much greater danger of death in childbirth and pregnancy-related illnesses.[22] Although the manufacturer renewed its efforts to obtain FDA approval, women and consumer groups fought against the increasing use of Depo-Provera in the Third World on the grounds that it is frequently administered needlessly and without women's knowledge or consent.[23]

Consumer Goods and Food. Prior to 1978 the Consumer Product Safety Commission did not compile data on exports of banned or noncomplying consumer products. Yet, in addition to the TRIS exports, CPSC learned that other banned products have been sold abroad, including defective electrical toys and baby pacifiers that had caused choking deaths in infants.[24] Several hundred thousand of the dangerous pacifiers were shipped overseas between June 30, 1977, when the ban was announced, and February 26, 1978, when the ban became effective.[25] The problem of dumping unsafe products abroad continues. The *Washington Post*, for example, reported in May 1984 that American companies "are considering" selling kerosene heaters that do not meet new U.S. safety standards in developing countries that do not have heater standards.[26] The situation appears to be similar in other industrial nations, such as the United Kingdom and Sweden, where domestic product bans do not extend to exports.[27]

Equally little information exists on international commerce in banned food products. FDA does not generally inspect foods to be shipped abroad and maintains no records on exports of banned foodstuffs. By chance, its inspectors have noted a few cases of exports of adulterated or contaminated foods, including 6,796 boxes of rice intended for Chile that were contaminated with insects and 3,250 pounds of moldy flour headed for the United Arab Emirates.[28] Contaminated fish that do not meet U.S. standards or that contain excessive levels of PCB's, mercury, or illegal additives are also routinely shipped overseas.[29]

The baby formula controversy illustrates yet another aspect of the hazardous-export problem—situations in which a product safe in normal use in industrial countries can be highly inappropriate and dangerous when marketed under very different social and economic conditions in many developing countries. The primary marketer of infant formula, Nestlé, has conducted an extensive advertising and distribution campaign in the Third World including the provision of promotional samples and material to medical clinics. The evidence indicated, however, that babies being fed on infant formula were frequently malnourished and prone to disease, often dying, because the formula was being prepared under unsanitary conditions or with dirty water, or was being mixed with far too much water by families unable to afford sufficient amounts of the dry formula. Nestlé refused to alter its promotional campaign even after being confronted with this evidence, and a long boycott was mounted against the company. It finally agreed in December 1983 to alter substantially its marketing practices in the Third World.[30] A similar controversy is now developing over the marketing of condensed milk.[31]

Hazardous Waste. The most recent hazardous-export problem involves hazardous wastes. In 1980 EPA implemented new, strict regulations on the generation, transport, treatment, storage, and disposal of hazardous wastes.[32] EPA estimated in 1979 that some 90 percent of the hazardous wastes generated annually were not being handled in accordance with new federal standards.[33] Facing increased waste disposal costs and growing local opposition to new waste storage and disposal facilities, companies began a search worldwide for countries willing to accept American hazardous wastes.[34] In November 1979 a Colorado company offered the President of Sierra Leone $25 million to allow the disposal of hazardous mining wastes in his country.[35] Other nations approached with similar proposals included Chile, Liberia, Nigeria, and Senegal.[36] There have also been reports of plans to ship to Haiti wastes from the paint industry in New

Jersey and sewage sludge from Washington, D.C.[37] In late 1980 an Alabama firm announced plans to dispose of U.S. hazardous wastes in the Bahamas.[38] In each of these cases media attention to plans to ship hazardous wastes to developing countries resulted in public concern. As far as can be told, none of these proposals went forward as a result. Other companies, however, reportedly shipped PCB's to Mexico and the Dominican Republic for disposal in February 1980.[39]

Little is known about exports of toxic wastes from other industrial nations, although there was one very well documented incident in Europe. In March 1983 an uproar followed the revelation of the "disappearance" from Italy of forty-one drums of dioxin wastes resulting from the 1976 Seveso disaster. The Hoffman La Roche company refused to divulge where the wastes had been sent, which led to a frantic search for the drums throughout Europe and sharp exchanges between several European governments. The missing drums were finally found improperly stored in an abandoned abattoir in a tiny village in northern France.[40]

### U.S. Hazardous Exports Policy Developments

The development of a single overall U.S. policy on hazardous exports has been an elusive goal of the last two administrations. The Reagan administration has taken a number of highly visible stands against restrictions on the international free market in hazardous goods, but it has failed to weaken the existing U.S. statutes and regulations affecting exports of a number of products. Due in part to a lack of significant industry support for its proposals, the administration has now relented somewhat and publicly expressed its support for existing policies and acted to obtain international acceptance of them.

Virtually every one of the more than a dozen product-control statutes passed by the Congress over the last forty years has addressed the issue of exports. Their export provisions vary widely, however, from a total exemption from domestic requirements to a complete prohibition on exports of materials banned from domestic sale.

At one end of the spectrum, prior to 1978, banned or unregistered pesticides and banned or noncomplying consumer products could be freely exported. The sale abroad of regulated toxic chemicals requires notices to importing governments and can be totally curtailed if there would be a resulting serious risk to health and environment in the United States. Unapproved medical devices and investigational drugs can be sold abroad only with the prior consent of the importing country. At the other extreme, drugs not approved for domestic use cannot be exported at all.[41] This inconsistency in the treatment of exports of various products and substances is not surprising given that these statutes were enacted over a long period.

The sales overseas of banned TRIS-treated baby pajamas stimulated the first major government investigations of U.S. exports of hazardous products in 1978. A subcommittee of the House Government Operations Committee conducted an extensive survey of federal regulatory agencies and held three days of hearings. The full committee articulated a view of U.S. responsibility for exports that continues to be widely held: "The United States has a significant responsibility for the safety of the goods it sells abroad. It cannot condone the export of regulated products which it knows to be harmful either to foreign consumers or the local or world environment. . . . This responsibility must be exercised in a way that respects the sovereignty of other nations and accounts for differing conditions which may affect judgments of health and safety."[42]

The committee found the existing export provisions in the statutes administered by CPSC, EPA, and FDA to be highly inconsistent and inadequate. It recommended that these laws be amended to provide for (1) agency monitoring of exports, (2) adequate notification to foreign governments, (3) agency discretion in dealing with exports of banned products, (4) adequate protection of U.S. citizens from reimportation of banned products, and (5) adequate labeling of exported banned goods.

The House committee report came too late to influence legislation already moving through the Congress to tighten requirements for exports of banned pesticides and consumer products. The November 1978 amendments of the three statutes[43] administered by the Consumer Product Safety Commission added an export notice requirement for products not meeting U.S. standards and gave CPSC the authority to prohibit export of a banned or otherwise noncomplying product if there is an unreasonable risk of injury to American consumers.

The 1978 amendments to the Federal Insecticide, Fungicide, and Rodenticide Act (FIFRA) placed limited requirements on pesticide products to be exported. The amended FIFRA now requires that prior to the export of a pesticide not registered for domestic use, the foreign purchaser must sign a statement acknowledging the understanding that the product cannot be sold in the United States. A copy of the statement must be submitted to EPA and then forwarded to the government of the importing nation.[44]

In addition, the amended FIFRA establishes minimum labeling requirements for all exported pesticides. Labels now must include an ingredient statement and warning and caution statements, and, if highly toxic, bear a skull and crossbones and statements of practiced treatment in the case of poisoning. All unregistered pesticides to be exported must also carry the statement "Not Registered for Use in the United States." The most critical information, particularly any precautionary statements, has to appear in both English and the language of the importing country.

During this same period, the Carter administration began its own review of U.S. hazardous substances export policy (HSEP) with the creation of an interagency working group. The passage of the consumer product and pesticide export amendments removed much of the impetus for the work and it remained inactive until early 1980. EPA and CPSC began to implement their new export procedures with little complaint from industry. The situation changed in late 1979 with the revelations mentioned earlier of attempts to dump U.S. hazardous wastes in developing countries. In addition Representative Michael Barnes introduced in February 1980 a bill to place export licensing controls on banned products, arguing that the existing export notice provisions did not go far enough.

The Subcommittee on International Economic Policy and Trade of the House Foreign Affairs Committee held hearings on the Barnes bill in June 1980. The administration testified in opposition, stating that the HSEP working group would soon be proposing a comprehensive U.S. policy. In August the working group took the unusual step of publishing in the *Federal Register* for public comment the fifth draft of its report.[45] A final day of committee hearings, on September 9, 1980, examined the draft report of the HSEP working group. Representative Barnes held open the possibility of reintroducing his bill even if the HSEP were adopted by the administration. He expressed concern that the HSEP was the result of many compromises and that an Executive Order might not be an adequate solution.

During the last four months of the Carter administration, there was a furious fight over the working group's proposed HSEP. Despite extensive White House lobbying by industry representatives, on January 15, 1981, President Carter signed Executive Order 12264 entitled "On Federal Policy Regarding the Export of Banned or Significantly Restricted Substances."

Building upon the existing statutory framework, the Executive Order had four major components. First, it sought to improve the export notice procedures already required. Second, it called for the annual publication of a summary of U.S. government actions banning or severely restricting substances for domestic use. Third, it directed the State Department and other federal agencies to participate in the development of international hazard-alert systems. Fourth, it established procedures whereby formal export licensing controls would be placed upon a very limited number of "extremely hazardous substances" that represented a serious threat to human health or the environment and the export of which would threaten U.S. foreign policy interests. Export licenses for such substances would be granted only in "exceptional cases" where the importing country, when fully informed, had no objection.

The Executive Order was attacked immediately by the Pharmaceutical Manufacturers Association as "an eleventh hour act of arrogance" that cost Americans jobs.[46] (This statement is somewhat perplexing since the drug industry, which was already prohibited by statute from shipping unapproved drugs abroad, would be virtually unaffected by the Executive Order.) The transition team for the new administration had already identified this order as an early target of its anti-regulatory crusade. Just thirty-four days after its promulgation, the order was rescinded by President Reagan.[47] In an accompanying memorandum, Reagan said that the implementation of the Carter Executive Order, particularly the imposition of export controls, would result "in a cumbersome regulatory program, costly to both the public and private sectors." He requested the Secretaries of Commerce and State to assess the existing procedures for notifying and consulting with importing countries regarding harmful substances, and he asked that they recommend "specific revisions in regulations or statutory authorities that will make our implementation of hazardous substances export policy more consistent and cost-effective." The review by the two departments was to be completed within 180 days.[48]

Four years later, the administration had yet to make any public proposals for changes in existing export provisions. Commerce Secretary Malcolm Baldrige and Secretary of State Alexander Haig submitted their recommendations and a report to William Brock, U.S. Trade Representative, on May 10, 1982.[49] Although never made public, copies of the report were leaked to the press. The Baldrige-Haig report proposed two major changes in U.S. hazardous-export policy:

1.  The elimination of existing requirements that the U.S. government alert foreign governments as to the shipments of toxic chemicals and pesticides that are banned or restricted here.

2. The repeal of a forty-four-year-old prohibition on the export of drugs that the FDA has not approved for domestic sale.[50]

The accompanying fourteen-page report is extremely short on facts and appears to have been written to please the preferences of the free market ideologues in the administration. It asserts without any documentation that export notifications represent "a burdensome regulatory procedure that fails to achieve its intended purpose."[51] In support of this claim, the report cites only the view of "U.S. industry," which reports that in many cases export notice requirements have proved "ineffective and costly."[52] It appears now that the Baldrige-Haig proposals are dead. In the fall of 1983 at the Organization of Economic Cooperation and Development, the United States began to express once again its support for export notifications for toxic chemicals. And in July of that year a State Department official testified that the export notice procedure for pesticides "appears to be working well."[53]

The seven-year-long search for an overall U.S. policy on exports has been all but abandoned. As of spring 1985 the administration had not yet released any proposal. In the Congress, Representative Barnes reintroduced his bill as H.R. 638, which would amend the Export Administration Act of 1979 to require export licensing for the sale abroad of products that are subject to U.S. prohibitions or restrictions. However, prospects for the passage of such legislation do not seem to be bright.

A May 1984 decision of the CPSC, dominated by Reagan administration commissioners, on exports of banned products marked perhaps the last attempt by rigid free marketeers to undo existing U.S. export policies. The commissioners voted three to one not to lift the long-standing prohibition on the export of items that had been marketed here and then recalled or banned.[54] They rejected a proposal by Commissioner Terrence Scanlon that in the pursuit of "uniformity" would allow the export of all banned hazardous products. He asked: "Are we here at the Commission to be international nannies or does our duty to protect consumers stop at our territorial borders?"[55]

The one legislative area in which there has been real progress is hazardous wastes. Prodded by public concern in the United States and repeated reports of attempts to ship such wastes overseas, the Congress enacted in fall 1984 new, much tougher requirements for exports.[56] Under the previous regulations, persons who wished to export wastes had to notify EPA four weeks prior to the initial shipment of a given hazardous waste each year. EPA in turn had to transmit the notice to the importing country. The notification did not include details of the amounts to be exported, ports of entry in the importing country, or the methods of treatment and disposal there. The new law contains a provision to enable the importing country "to make an informed decision as to whether it will accept the waste and, if so, how it will deal with that waste."[57] EPA is to issue regulations requiring exporters to notify the agency of proposed exports of hazardous wastes. Once a notice is received, the State Department, on behalf of the EPA, would inform the receiving country and seek written consent. Only then may the shipment proceed. The new law does permit flexibility when the United States and the receiving-country government have entered into an international agreement that establishes different procedures for notifications of such exports.[58]

The leak at the pesticide-manufacturing facility in Bhopal, India, in 1984 did stimulate increased congressional awareness of the problems of pesticides in developing countries. Its lessons are not directly applicable to exports, however, since the situation involved a hazardous manufacturing facility overseas and not the sale abroad of a chemical that is banned or restricted here.

### International Developments

Over the last decade new voices have been heard for the first time in discussion of international commerce in potentially dangerous goods. In the past the focus was on the impact of differing national standards and regulations upon the free flow of trade. There have been efforts to establish international standards for some products, to harmonize varying national regulatory schemes, and to avoid or settle disputes over whether national and environmental standards pose nontariff barriers to imports. In the mid-1970s developing countries began to express concern about industrial countries' exports of products, particularly drugs and pesticides, that were banned or unapproved for domestic use. Concerned environmental consumer organizations worldwide joined in the call for international standards and controls on exports of hazardous products and substances, particularly to the Third World.

The first widely noted expressions of concern occurred at a United Nations Environment Programme (UNEP) Governing Council meeting in May 1977. Dr. J. C. Kiano, then Minister for Water Development in Kenya, charged that developing countries were being used as "dumping grounds" and their peoples as "guinea pigs" for drugs. He called for the establishment of "international rules and procedures . . . to protect mankind, particularly people in developing countries."[59]

The fifty-eight-nation UNEP Governing Council adopted a statement on sales abroad of banned or restricted production. Acknowledging that "there have been unethical practices concerning the distribution of chemicals, drugs, cosmetics and food unfit for human consumption" and that "there is a need for harmonious cooperation . . . between exporting and importing countries," the Governing Council urged that "governments . . . take steps to ensure that potentially harmful chemicals, in whatever form or commodity, which are unacceptable for domestic purposes in the exporting country, are not permitted to be exported without the knowledge and consent of appropriate authorities in the importing country."[60]

The same concerns have now been reflected in a number of decisions of the UNEP Governing Council and resolutions of the United Nations General Assembly. They contain slight variations on the general statement of shared responsibility of exporting and importing countries and the need for information exchange, and, in some cases, stronger measures to discourage export of banned products.[61]

In response to this statement a number of international agencies have begun to develop new information standards and procedures. At the same time, the adoption of international codes of conduct for marketing practices of potentially hazardous goods continues.

The responses of the Organization for Economic Cooperation and Development (OECD) are particularly significant since its twenty-four members, all Western industrial nations, are the major producers and exporters of chemical substances and consumer goods. On April 4, 1984, the OECD Council adopted a recommendation on "Intermediate Exchange Related to Export of Banned or Severely Restricted Chemicals."[62] The recommendation calls upon exporting nations to provide information to permit the importing country to make "timely and informed decisions" about such chemical exports. It incorporates a set of Guiding Principles that were the result of three years of study and negotiation. They called for a minimal notification scheme that consists of two notices: one when a government takes a control action (that is, bans, severely restricts the use or handling of a product, or refuses a required authorization for its use), and a second notice when the initial export of the product following such action is expected or about to occur.

The United States remains the only nation to have an operating export notice procedure and was the somewhat erratic leader in the effort leading to the recommendation's unanimous acceptance by the OECD. The issue of hazardous exports is increasingly a matter of concern in other industrial countries. The OECD recommendation, while not binding, will increase the pressure for the adoption of some standards and requirements for exports.

The OECD action set a precedent for consideration by a UNEP ad hoc expert group examining the issue of the "exchange of information on trade and management of potentially harmful chemicals, in particular pesticides." At a meeting in March 1984 fifty government representatives from twenty-nine countries abandoned a broad set of guidelines drafted by the UNEP Secretariat and agreed to a provisional scheme of export notifications that is almost identical to that of OECD.[63] UNEP's International Registry of Potentially Toxic Chemicals (IRPTC) was given the role of assisting in the operation and monitoring of the information exchange. The UNEP Governing Council in May 1984 agreed that the scheme should be implemented over the next two years and then reassessed.[64]

The UN General Assembly has taken a different, but complementary, course. In 1982 the assembly adopted Resolution 37/137, entitled "Protection Against Products Harmful to Health and the Environment," over the sole negative vote of the United States.[65] The resolution restated the call for an end to the export of "products that have been banned from domestic consumption and/or sale" in the exporting country, unless requested or officially permitted by the importing country.

To aid in achieving this objective, the Secretary-General was directed to prepare a consolidated list of products "whose consumption and/or sale have been banned, withdrawn, or severely restricted or, in the case of pharmaceuticals, not approved by Governments." Such data had never been pulled together in one document. Not even the United States has readily available a list of products and substances that have been banned or restricted by federal agencies. The consolidated list should be of value to governments and organizations worldwide in identifying products in international commerce that in the judgment of one or more nations pose a threat to health or the environment.

The Secretary-General released a first version of the consolidated list on December 30, 1983. Information was obtained throughout the UN system. In addition, in response to a note from the Secretary-General requesting information on national regulations and product data, some thirty-four nations provided details for the list.[66] Although the State Department refused to comply with the request for information, materials about U.S.

banned and severely restricted products were gathered from UN sources and U.S. public records. On November 25, 1983, the General Assembly passed Resolution 38/139, which reemphasized the importance of the list and directed the Secretary-General to continue to gather information from member states and to update the list. A revised first issue of the consolidated list was issued in July 1984.

The controversy over this list has continued. The United States and other industrial countries argue that it is a wasteful duplication of the efforts of some of the UN specialized agencies and that its summary presentation of data on the legal status of chemicals could lead to hasty, ill-informed decisions by nations to prohibit a listed product. In December 1984 the United States was again alone in its opposition to General Assembly Resolution 39/229, which called for the further development and annual publication of the consolidated list.

A third major area of activity involves the development of codes of conduct that are not directed primarily at governments, but rather at the marketing practices for various dangerous goods. The first such code to be the subject of considerable controversy involved infant formula and was the focal point of the major international boycott of Nestlé. In May 1981 the United States was the only country to vote against the International Code of Marketing of Breastmilk Substitutes adopted by the World Health Organization. The Nestlé Corporation later agreed to abide by the code.

The U.S. representative to the UN at that time, Jeane Kirkpatrick, later explained that this vote was taken in part to discourage the development by the UN of similar codes for other products. Yet developing countries will continue to demand such codes when they recognize that their very limited resources make it difficult to develop their own standards and controls over often very large multinational corporations.

In October 1982 a resolution was adopted by the UN Food and Agriculture Organization (FAO) to devise an international Code of Conduct on the Distribution and Use of Pesticides. The final resolution calling for the code specified that it should cover a wide range of topics, including user information (labeling, storage, and disposal), information exchange, training and education of users, and advertising and marketing practices. A final draft of the code was submitted in March 1985 to the FAO Committee on Agriculture for its review, prior to consideration by the FAO conference.

The preamble to the code indicates that it represents a voluntary "self-commitment by the industry concerned and by all those engaged in trade" to standards regarding the marketing and use of pesticides.[67] However, article 2 states that the code is also "designed to encourage the introduction and enforcement of the necessary regulatory measures" needed to put those standards into effect. Article 6 emphasizes that "it is for the government of each individual country to assume responsibility for pesticide usage . . . [but that] manufacturers, importers and traders have important roles in bringing about safe, efficient and acceptable practices in the use of pesticides." The proposed code urges that a pesticide that has not been fully evaluated and registered in an individual country should not be registered in a developing country unless that country determines its benefits outweigh its risks, and it recommends that the WHO Recommended Classification of Pesticides by Hazard be adopted by all countries.

The Thirty-Seventh World Health Assembly adopted on May 17, 1984, a resolution on the "Rational Use of Drugs."[68] It was opposed by U.S. and industry representatives as a step toward a code of conduct on drug sales.[69] The resolution called upon the Director General to arrange in 1985 a meeting of governmental and nongovernment experts to discuss "the role of marketing in . . . respect [to the rational use of drugs] in developing countries" and to report to the Thirty-Ninth World Health Assembly.

The impetus for all this international action has come in part from increased activities and cooperation by citizens' groups in industrial and developing countries. Over the last few years, the International Organization of Consumers Unions has become active on the problem of dumping, with a particular focus upon consumer goods. Other coalitions—such as the Infant Formula Action Coalition, Health Action International, and Pesticide Action Network International—have been created to press for national and international responses to the problems associated respectively with infant formula, drugs, and pesticides. With improved communications and increased access to international organizations, these coalitions are beginning to have a substantial impact.

Industry groups, such as the International Group of National Associations of Agrochemical Manufacturers, are also beginning to develop their own guidelines and codes concerning international sales. In the United States citizen groups and the pesticide industry have cooperated in the preparation of guidelines for "product stewardship" in developing countries, including advertising and labeling of pesticides. In October 1983 the Board of the National Agricultural Chemicals Association adopted guidelines for Advertising Practices in the Promotion of Pesticide Products in the Developing Areas of the World, devised by an Agricultural Chemicals Dialogue Group consisting of industry representatives and church, environmental, and other citizens' groups. A second set of guidelines on labeling practices developed by the group was adopted in March 1985. This experience may provide a model for cooperation by such groups in addressing other elements of the hazardous export problem.

### Areas of Consensus and Contention

This review of recent U.S. and international discussions of hazardous exports reveals a growing consensus among industrial and developing countries in some areas, but a number of issues that remain to be resolved. A hazardous export problem exists about which something should be done, it is agreed, but how to allocate responsibility and what remedial actions should be taken are questions still in dispute.

Perhaps the most successful aspect of all the attention given to this issue in recent years is the increasingly broad acceptance of the notion of "informed consent." This concept is reflected in U.S. statutes and intergovernmental decisions regarding hazardous exports. U.S. industry has repeatedly voiced its agreement with this approach. At 1983 hearings a representative of the National Agricultural Chemicals Association testified that his industry is "a proponent of information exchange," has undertaken numerous conferences and other activities to promote better understanding of the uses of pesticides, and sought to leave "the door [opened] wide to future information exchange on any questions any government would have relative to any aspect of concern about an unregistered pesticide."[70] Finally, as noted earlier, the Reagan administration now accepts the notion of "informed consent" as a basis for national and international hazardous export policy.

Yet there remain strongly held views on both sides of the question of informed consent. A few U.S. government officials still perceive attempts to place any restrictions on trade in hazardous goods as a conspiracy among developing countries, citizens' organizations, and UN bureaucrats to redistribute the world's wealth and to hamper capitalism.[71] On the other hand many Americans see hazardous exports as fundamentally a moral issue and cannot understand why the United States would permit under any circumstances the sale abroad of banned products. There is often an accompanying concern about the impact of such exports upon the reputation of the United States, as illustrated by the remarks of Representative Sam M. Gibbons (D-Fla.) in 1980: "The exportation of any product considered unsafe for Americans should be condemned. . . . It would be unconscionable on our part to stand back and allow this traffic in hazardous products to continue. . . . I urge the Administration to forge an export policy that protects the health and safety of consumers wherever they may be and preserve the integrity of the label "Made in U.S.A."[72]

The usual reply to such calls for absolute prohibitions on exports of banned products is that the United States cannot impose its standards on other countries that may reach a different judgment about the benefits and costs posed by the importation and use of a particular product. To do so, the argument goes, would be to infringe upon other nations' sovereignty.[73] Such vigorous defenses of the sovereign rights of other nations almost always come from representatives of industry, who generally have not been loath to ask the U.S. government to intercede in the internal affairs of other countries when their own interests are affected.

In contrast, developing-country officials have supported complete bans on hazardous exports. In July 1980 the Nigerian Ministry of Housing and the Environment communicated to Representative Jonathan Bingham (D-N.Y.) its support for "the moves being discussed by the U.S. Government . . . to ban the exports of products [from the United States that have been found to be hazardous to the public health and are prohibited from use in the United States], particularly with reference to Nigeria."[74] Similarly, the initial version of the hazardous export resolution introduced by developing countries and later adopted by the UN General Assembly in 1982 called for a total prohibition on exports of banned products.

Debate continues over the best means to assure that importing countries are able to make well-informed decisions about hazardous products. Much of the discussion focusses on the value of export notice procedures as now required by U.S. statutes and reflected in the OECD Recommendations and UNEP decision. *Mother Jones* magazine, in an award-winning series on hazardous exports, labeled notifications as the "liberal compromise."[75] Not surprisingly, citizens' groups, as well as industry representatives, have complained that such procedures are unwieldy and ineffective.

Both *Mother Jones* and the Baldridge-Haig report argue that many developing countries are poorly equipped to act upon export notices. Health and environmental agencies in these nations often do not have adequate scientific and administrative resources and sometimes lack legal authority over imported hazardous goods. Industry, as well as citizens' groups, claim that determined or less scrupulous exporters can easily evade such a process.

Citizens' organizations complain that export notices alone are insufficient to assure that importing governments have actually received the notices and had time to decide about a proposed export. The route a notice must travel is quite involved, with plenty of opportunities to go astray. A notice may typically go from an exporter to the U.S. regulatory agency, then to the State Department, then to the U.S. Embassy in the importing country, and finally to the appropriate governmental official. In 1979 the General Accounting Office reported that one U.S. embassy official admitted that he never forwarded notices of U.S. regulatory actions regarding particular chemicals because "it might adversely affect U.S. exporting."[76] A more recent review of effectiveness of EPA's pesticide notice procedures in three East African countries found that such notices are a "low priority" in U.S. embassies.[77] Thus, they have called for licensing or permitting of exports, dependent upon the receipt of an approval or other response from the importing country.

Industry representatives argue that export notifications are too burdensome and costly, and that other means of information exchange are already available and more effective. They express the concern that such notices, or summary lists of banned products such as the one prepared by the UN, are not "useful" and may cause foreign regulatory agencies to make rash decisions.[78]

There has been no definitive study of the U.S. experience with export notices, but there are a number of cases where export notices have worked. In late 1979 CPSC received a notice of intent to export to Canada children's nursery lamps coated with lead-based paints that could not be sold in the United States. CPSC then notified the Canadian government, which in turn requested more information and eventually told the exporter not to ship the goods to Canada.[79] An export notice from EPA enabled the South Korean government to reject a shipment of PCB-contaminated animal fats. State Department consultations with Sierra Leone, Haiti, and the Bahamas helped to head off plans to ship American hazardous wastes to those countries.[80]

In the wake of the Bhopal tragedy, both citizens' groups and industry representatives more than ever perceive exports of banned products as part of a larger problem of chemical misuse in developing nations. Industry representatives agree that more has to be done to provide better information and training to consumers, workers, and farmers handling hazardous goods. The disagreement concerns whether and what further steps are required to respond to the problem. Citizens' organizations and some health and environmental officials question the capabilities of developing societies in the foreseeable future to cope with a deluge of drugs, pesticides, and other potentially hazardous products. They argue for stricter limits on developing-country markets (such as use of the WHO Essential Drug List), the development of international standards for marketing practices, and reliance on alternatives more appropriate to developing world conditions. These are all highly controversial issues and will be at the center of international debate in the years ahead.

## Recommendations

The hazardous export problem might be considered, in a sense, a tragedy of the commons. It involves potentially dangerous goods or processes that may be moved across the globe and cause or threaten damage thousands of miles away from the point of origin. Such transfers may involve a large number of parties, including producers, exporters, shippers, importers, distributors, users, consumers, and governmental officials in two or more nations. Thus, the risks and responsibilities are shared all along the chain and, as a result, may likely fall upon the weakest link.

Multinational industries are perceived as the major engine propelling the transfer of hazardous products worldwide. Their economic and technical resources are enormous, dwarfing those of many of the developing nations of the world. Given this central role, the demand will continue for multinational industries (and their home countries) to assume more responsibility and accountability for their actions and practices. In the past, many corporate representatives have tried to evade these tasks or to shift them to other parties. These tactics have failed to stifle the debate and only led to adverse reactions and increased concern on the part of the public. Dialogue and cooperation among interested nongovernmental and governmental organizations is possible and can result in policies that further the interests of all.

In the United States, the public has not wavered in its strong support of government's role as a protector of health and environment through the imposition of limits on the marketplace, and U.S. industry has learned to accept some regulation as necessary. Multinational corporations now operate in a virtually free international marketplace and should realize that the development and imposition of certain limits there is inevitable. Some industry representatives have asserted that international rules are unnecessary since they maintain the high standards they follow in the United States wherever they operate.[81] If this is indeed the case, U.S. industry should support efforts to raise international standards to this nation's level for no other reason than to avoid possible competitive disadvantages. Corporations should also demonstrate their own self-restraint and willingness to incur costs to protect citizens abroad from undue hazards.

Governments also have a major role to play in accepting a shared responsibility to cooperate in addressing hazardous export issues. Industrial countries must see themselves as both producers and consumers, as exporters and importers benefiting from international health and environmental standards. Developing countries must strengthen their own abilities to protect themselves and to choose wisely the most appropriate products and substances to meet their own, often different needs.

While progress has been made over the last decade, the global challenge of controlling potentially hazardous products remains. There is no single simple solution. Yet increased commitment, communication, and cooperation among governments, industry, and citizens' organizations can make a difference.

# CHAPTER SEVEN Workplace Health Standards and

## Multinational Corporations in Developing Countries

Barry I. Castleman

Occupational diseases and injuries are large and growing by-products of Third World industrialization. At the same time, the development of laws and regulations to protect workers from health hazards in industrial countries has widened the disparity in workplace safeguards around the world. U.S.-based multinational corporations (MNC's) meet the standards of the Occupational Safety and Health Administration (OSHA) at home but are not required to do so elsewhere. Many companies nevertheless follow corporate policies of meeting U.S. standards worldwide, and others claim that some of their corporate standards are stricter than OSHA's or cover substances that OSHA doesn't regulate.

Despite such assertions, numerous examples suggest that worker protection in the multinationals' Third World plants has been markedly poor compared with that in U.S. operations. The increasing scale of occupational and environmental disease from MNCs' Third World subsidiaries has caused a backlash both in the developing countries and at home. Because they are uniquely open to the charge of following a double standard for worker protection, MNC's can expect increased labor unrest, as well as consequent pressure from foreign governments and affected communities. At home the multinationals face media exposés and lawmakers' concern about the implications of double standards for employment, U.S. foreign policy, and international relations.

Given this backlash and the increasing transfer to developing countries of expertise on workplace safety by union federations and other international bodies, the multinationals may decide to take the lead in working with governments and unions in the Third World to raise national standards of worker protection and compensation for work-related disability.

### The Nature and Extent of Occupational Diseases and Injuries in Developing Countries

The scope of occupational disease is not well known even in industrial countries. Most of these illnesses develop slowly and insidiously over a number of years. Moreover, their symptoms are seldom specific to any one occupational health hazard, and the diseases that they can lead to—tuberculosis in silicotics, pneumonia and lung cancer in asbestotics—may render occupationally caused deaths hard to distinguish from other common causes of death.

Occupational cancer typically arises thirty years after the onset of the causative exposure, sometimes years after cessation of the work that caused it. Usually nothing about the cell type or target organ distinguishes occupationally related cases from other cancers. The long latency of these diseases and the relatively small number of industrial chemicals adequately tested on laboratory animals for chronic effects has led to the sad discovery of one human carcinogen after another, with decades of future cancer cases "already in the pipeline" by the time each risk is discovered. To varying degrees the same applies to substances that cause chronic neurological effects, damage to the kidney or liver, and impairment of the blood and circulatory system.

In developing countries the extent of the problem is still more obscure. The prevalence of malnutrition and chronic diseases clouds the picture, and relatively few professionals in government and medicine are trained to identify occupational causes of disease. Ignorance and illiteracy increase the incidence of workplace mishaps. In the Brazilian state of São Paulo alone, 2,000 deaths a year are ascribed to pesticide poisoning.[1] In Trinidad one doctor has witnessed fatal paraquat poisoning at the rate of almost one case per week.[2]

Where endemic diseases have already taken a toll, people are more susceptible to organ injury from occupational exposures. In someone whose liver has been damaged by schistosomiasis, for example, moderate exposure to common chlorinated solvents could have devastating effects. In Southeast Asia, where many people don't have enough of the enzyme glucose 6-phosphate dehydrogenase, exposure to toxic chemicals is more likely to cause or exacerbate liver injury and hemolytic anemia.[3] Studies with laboratory animals indicate that chronic protein undernutrition and bladder parasites enhance susceptibility to cancer development.[4] The hot climates of developing countries also present special problems, including greater skin absorption of chemicals and extreme discomfort from personal protective equipment.

Occupational injury and death rates are extremely high in developing countries. According to a 1980 International Labour Office (ILO) survey, workplace injuries in the Third World claim the life of one worker in 3,000 each year—more than five times the rate in industrial countries.[5] In Latin America one worker in four suffers temporary or permanent disabling injuries annually, which is about ten times the rate in the United Kingdom.[6] The ILO has also estimated that economic losses from occupational diseases and workplace injuries run as high as 5 percent of the gross national product in some countries.[7] Clearly this is a large and growing health problem in developing countries.

### Governmental Resources for Monitoring Workplace Health and Safety in Developing Countries

Policymakers in developing countries view occupational health as only one of many serious public health problems. Governmental commitments to occupational health are minimal, and trained people and laboratory support are sorely lacking.

Some developing countries (such as Brazil, Peru, and Colombia) legislate limits for workplace exposure to toxic substances. But few enforcement agencies have the sampling and analysis equipment needed to do proper inspections. Indeed, when Brazilian authorities decided to bring large asbestos companies under surveillance in 1980, they had to ask the companies to train government employees in the use of the companies' monitoring equipment.

Recognizing the need for people trained in industrial hygiene and medicine, Brazil has adopted as law ILO Recommendation 112 (1959), which requires the establishment of medical services in large plants. To fulfill this requirement 16,000 physicians and 16,000 engineers have received training in occupational health since 1976. Managers have proved receptive to the contributions of these professionals, since they help control costs by selecting "healthy" workers, cutting down absenteeism and labor turnover, and reducing worker-compensation costs. The fact that virtually all employment for occupational health professionals is in industry no doubt has a restraining effect on developments in this field. Moreover, unethical practices — such as the use of erroneous medical diagnoses as pretexts for firing union activists — are also a problem. Even though large industries in Brazil must provide occupational health services, only 30-35 percent of the industrial labor force is covered. Workers in smaller plants and agricultural workers, who are at high risk from occupational health and safety dangers (80 percent of the total labor force), must be reached in other ways.

Given the lack of regulation to prevent occupational diseases, how effective are the workers' compensation systems for job-related disability? The scarcity of independent occupational health physicians in developing countries all but assures that only the most acute or well-recognized occupational illnesses will be considered for compensation purposes. Even so, some employers prefer to lobby to get the law changed rather than implementing better protective measures. In Bolivia, a desperately poor country where multinational corporations mine tin, silicosis is appearing in ever greater numbers of workers between the ages of twenty-five and thirty. The compensation law now provides that affected workers do not have to keep working until they are totally disabled from silicosis and tuberculosis in order to be eligible for compensation. But employers in Bolivia are pressing to weaken these "early silicosis" provisions.

One constructive approach to industrial health and safety problems is to create and empower safety committees composed of labor and management representatives. Where labor representatives have legal or contract protection against retribution and a real say in workplace-protection issues, much can be accomplished through constructive negotiations. On the other hand, a law establishing merely token committees composed strictly of management appointments only further poisons labor-management relations. South Africa's Machinery and Occupational Safety Act of 1983, for example, calls for management-appointed labor representatives.

Considering the paucity of governmental resources and training in developing countries, the assertion that multinationals should only have to meet government requirements is impossible to justify. Indeed, MNC's acknowledge their obligation to not destroy their employees' health, irrespective of governmental failures in lawmaking and enforcement, official corruption, and the ignorance about industrial causes of illness that prevails in much of the world today.

## Double Standards in Worker Protection

U.S.-based multinational corporations and their trade associations have been consistently vociferous in claiming that both OSHA and environmental regulations threaten to drive industry out of the country. In hearings about establishing specific rules and in the courts, OSHA has been challenged on every front by these corporations, whose technical grasp of the implications of proposed regulations is quite sophisticated.

Since OSHA and EPA imposed only a few highly controversial regulations, and did so gradually, no mass exodus in the affected industries occurred.[8] In most cases the standards were met and industrial growth continued. But the existence of U.S. workplace standards presented a challenge worldwide to the multinationals. Would the companies insist that OSHA's rules were needlessly strict? If so, did this justify a "double standard"—a lower standard of worker protection outside the United States? When pressed, most U.S.-based companies say that their policy is *at a minimum* to observe OSHA's provisions the world over. Some firms, such as Du Pont, claim also to have company limits for newer substances not regulated by OSHA.[9]

Unfortunately, policy and practice frequently differ. A strong commitment is needed to assure that a large multinational corporation's far-flung operations do in practice meet U.S. worker-protection standards. Expertise must be committed to the field on a large scale, and it must be backed by the authority to order and implement improvements in plant design and operation that entail significant initial and operating costs. Corporate headquarters must conduct thorough, unannounced safety audits, and hold plant managers personally responsible for performing well in these audits and making improvements where deficiencies are found. When profits are low, economy measures that compromise safety and health must be forcefully discouraged. Plants must be staffed with people with sufficient expertise and training to operate them safely. Further, without continuing worldwide training of management and labor, the improvements will not be self-sustaining. These are the responsibilities of executive management in the multinational corporation.

Double standards in worker and community health protection are sadly commonplace in the world today (see table 7.1).[10] Extreme examples of the lack of health safeguards for Third World workers by MNC's have been reported in the asbestos, vinyl chloride, pesticide, chromate, steel, and chlor-alkali industries, among others. Abuses are rising throughout Asia, Africa, and Latin America as industrialization occurs, and dramatic double standards are easy to identify without police powers of plant entry or sophisticated air-sampling equipment. Often it is enough to visit the plant site's environs, look at the workers' clothes and hair as they come off a shift, and ask about the working conditions. Do products carry warning labels? What type of personal protective equipment is available and in use? What are workers told and what do they suspect about the chronic hazards of their jobs? Are disabled employees dismissed? How does the plant dispose of wastes? Is hazardous work subcontracted to day laborers? Have there been any signs of government standards and inspections? How irritating are the various vapor concentrations to the nose and eyes? Is local exhaust ventilation used? If so, how well is it operated and maintained? Do workers receive periodic medical examinations? If so, are they ever told of adverse health effects attributable to their work? The picture obtained by asking these and similar questions can sometimes be supplemented by a visit to a nearby government office, medical clinic, university, or newspaper.

In Johns-Manville Corporation's India affiliate, all the applicable OSHA requirements for handling asbestos were disregarded for years, and this was well known to the parent corporation.[11] Elsewhere, Johns-Manville's double standards extended to product warnings and manufacture. Asbestos thermal insulation manufactured by the company first bore warning labels in the United States in 1964, the year epidemiologists showed that 40 percent of insulation workers died from occupational diseases. The same products made in Brazil by the company did not carry warnings until 1976, by which time the sale of such insulation products as "Thermobestos" had been banned in the United States by the Environmental Protection Agency. Not until Brazilian labor officials took an interest in the asbestos industry in 1980 did Johns-Manville finally stop manufacturing asbestos insulation in Brazil. The needless exposure of millions of U.S. workers to asbestos dust from thermal insulation in past years now accounts for thousands of deaths each year from occupational cancer and asbestosis. Safer substitutes have always been available.[12]

Double standards in occupational health arise in various areas, including exposure to recognized hazards, warnings to those exposed, notification to employees of medical conditions discovered by industrial physicians, compensation of the injured worker as an employee or as a consumer of products used in industry and agriculture, and exposure to technologies that have been widely replaced by less dangerous alternatives.

Some economists seek to explain or justify such disparities with cost-benefit analyses based on imprecise estimates of job risks, compounded by

**Table 7.1**  Double Standard Cases

| Industry | Location | Type of hazard reported | Multinational affiliation | Type of affiliation |
|---|---|---|---|---|
| Asbestos milling | South Africa | Children with severe asbestosis | Cape Asbestos (UK) | Subsidiary mining operation |
| Alpha maphthylamine manufacture | Outside the UK | Bladder cancer | Imperial Chemical Industries (UK) | Not known |
| Benzidine dye manufacture | Outside the UK | Bladder cancer | — | — |
| Asbestos textile manufacture | Agua Prieta and Juarez, Mexico | Not informing workers, not providing clothes change, neighborhood pollution | Amatex (US) | Subsidiary |
| Trichlorophenol manufacture | Seveso, Italy | Workplace and air pollution with dioxins, failure to inform workers, inadequate safety controls in plant design | Givaudan (of Hoffmann-LaRoche) (Switzerland) | Subsidiary |
| Asbestos insulation manufacture | Brazil | Failure to affix product warning, failure to reformulate products to eliminate asbestos | Johns-Manville (US) | Subsidiary |
| Asbestos friction product and textile manufacture | Bombay, India | Numerous workplace hazards uncontrolled, failure to inform workers and tell them of medical exam findings | Turner & Newall, Ltd. (UK) | 74 percent ownership |
| Asbestos | Countries without labeling requirements | Failure to affix warning labels | Entire asbestos industry (Asbestos International Association) | — |

**Table 7.1** (Continued)

| Industry | Location | Type of hazard reported | Multinational affiliation | Type of affiliation |
|---|---|---|---|---|
| Asbestos cement manufacture | Ahmedabad, India | Water pollution, solid waste dumping, no warnings on products, lack of workplace dust controls | Johns-Manville (US) | Minority ownership, exclusive marketing of exports, raw material sales, plant design and construction supervision |
| Asbestos brake lining manufacture | Madras, India | Solid waste dumping | Cape Industries (UK) | 25 percent ownership |
| Asbestos brake shoe manufacture | South Korea | Substandard working conditions | Not known | — |
| Asbestos textiles | South Africa | — | German investors | Subsidiary |
| Asbestos milling | Quebec, Canada | Lack of workplace dust controls | Asbestos Corp. Ltd. of General Dynamics (US) | Subsidiary |
| Asbestos brake shoes | Cork, Ireland | Newly built brake shoe manufacturing plant utilizing asbestos as raw material | Raybestos-Manhattan (US) | Subsidiary |
| Asbestos mining | Northeastern Transvaal, South Africa | Abandonment of huge piles of uncovered asbestos ore wastes in an area of 200,000 residents | Turner & Newall, Ltd. (UK); U.S. Steel (US) | Subsidiary; less than 50 percent ownership, respectively |
| Battery manufacture | Indonesia | Hundreds of workers with kidney disease, | Union Carbide (US) | Subsidiary |

**Table 7.1**  (Continued)

| Industry | Location | Type of hazard reported | Multinational affiliation | Type of affiliation |
|---|---|---|---|---|
| | | pollution of drinking water with mercury | | |
| Epoxy spraying | Shipyards outside of Denmark | Eczema, cancer (?) | Not known | — |
| Chromate and dichromate manufacture | Lecheria, Mexico | Waste dumping, workplace exposures producing nasal septum perforation | Bayer (West Germany) | Partial ownership |
| Dye manufacture | Bombay, India | Water pollution | Montedison (Italy) | Partial ownership |
| Mercury cell chlorine plant | Managua, Nicaragua | Mercury poisoning, water pollution | Pennwalt Corp. (US) | 40 percent ownership and management of the plant |
| Steelmaking | Malaysia | Air pollution, workplace hazards | Nippon Steel (Japan) | Minority ownership and plant design |
| Polyvinyl chloride manufacture | Malaysia | High worker exposure to (carcinogen) vinyl chloride | "Japanese companies" | Partial ownership |
| Arsenical pesticides manufacture | Malaysia | Arsenic poisoning symptoms in workers, no monitoring of exposure | Diamond Shamrock (US) | Subsidiary |
| Polychlorinated biphenyls and other chemical wastes | Zacatecas, Mexico | Waste dumping | Diamond Shamrock, B.F. Goodrich, and Monochem (all US) | Waste disposal agent for large US firms |

**Table 7.1** (Continued)

| Industry | Location | Type of hazard reported | Multinational affiliation | Type of affiliation |
|---|---|---|---|---|
| Trichloro-benzene wastes contaminated with dioxin compounds | Belgium | Disposal of improperly labeled toxic wastes | Chemie Linz (Austria) | Wastes from producer |
| Pesticide manufacture | Bhopal, India | Grossly inade-quate safeguards in plant operation and design, bad history of injurious workplace and envi-ronmental expo-sures to phosgene and methyliso-cyanate preceding the catastrophic release in 1984 | Union Carbide (US) | 51 percent ownership |
| Extraction of rare earth com-pounds from monazite ore for use in electronics products | Papan, Malaysia | High exposure of workers to radio-active materials and open dumping of radioactive thorium wastes | Mitsubishi Chemical Co. (Japan) | At least 28 percent owner-ship and use of Mitsubishi technology |

*Source*: Except in the two cases noted, see Barry I. Castleman, "The Double Standard in Industrial Hazards," in Jane H. Ives, ed., *The Export of Hazard* (Boston: Routledge and Kegan Paul, 1985), 60-89; asbestos mining in South Africa from Phillip Van Niekirk, "U.S. Steel Holds Interest in Asbestos Dumps," *Rand Daily Mail* (Johannesburg), September 1, 1984; extraction of rare earth compounds from Yamaka Junko, "More Pollution Export by Japan," *AMPO: Japan-Asia Quarterly Review*, January–March 1985.

assumptions of full knowledge and economic constructs of "willingness to pay for safety" among the population victimized. But destroying poor people's health for an increment of profit is inescapably a moral issue, and narrow economic rationalizations fall short of justifying such predatory business conduct.

## Double Standards in Corporations' Liability for Harm Caused

In the United States substantial liability has been assessed in the wake of widespread public recognition of industrial health hazards. Claims for workers' compensation have predictably gone up with the rising incidence and recognition of occupational disease. In addition, little-noticed provisions in workers' compensation laws have lately been used in some cases to obtain the right to jury trial against the employer for full economic loss, pain and suffering, and even punitive damages. In Maryland, California, Illinois, and New Jersey, employers are being called to account for "intentional harm" to their workers. Since the filing of some of these suits, some companies such as Bethlehem Steel have dramatically changed domestic corporate policies on such matters as informing workers about the findings of periodic medical examinations.

Equally important are the mounting claims for product liability. U.S. workers in the trades, as well as industrial plant workers, are suing the manufacturers of harmful products. Typically, the products involved caused chronic, often irreversible conditions — such as sterility, cancer, or pulmonary fibrosis. The manufacturers are held by the courts to have had expert knowledge on the hazards of their products as well as a duty both to warn of known hazards and to test their product for nonobvious suspected hazards.

Many of the precedents in product liability for toxic injuries have arisen in suits against asbestos companies. These individual lawsuits, alleging asbestosis and cancer from exposure to asbestos, continue to be filed at the rate of 400 per month. After accumulating major liability in 16,500 cases, the largest U.S. asbestos company (Manville) sought refuge in federal bankruptcy court in 1982. By then, asbestos disease claims had cost defendants and their insurers over $1 billion, and ultimate costs were projected in the range of $10–30 billion. The bond ratings of many defendant companies have been lowered, and a $400-million GAF Corporation property deal fell through because of uncertainties over the company's liability for insulation once made by its Ruberoid Division.

The pressure of product liability and pollution liability lawsuits has changed the way business is conducted in the United States. Manufacturers are more keenly aware than ever of their duties to test products and warn consumers of product hazards, while insurers have grown extremely cautious about covering possible causes of long-latent forms of illness indefinitely.[13] Within the past year insurance coverage for liability from sudden and accidental pollution has become practically unavailable.[14]

But is there not a double standard here, too, if corporate policy on plant engineering safeguards, the use of warning labels, customer education, and even product formulation varies geographically, depending upon the potential liability? This has demonstrably been the case with asbestos, some pesticides, and many dangerous drugs.[15] Given the growing importance in the United States of product liability and pollution liability (for sudden as well as gradual releases, hazardous waste dumping, etc.), developing countries are sure to notice if U.S.-based multinationals restrict their improved business policies to their home country.

Du Pont states categorically that it does not have a double standard for U.S. versus foreign operations.[16] The Manville Corporation (formerly Johns-Manville) and Dow Chemical have stated policies of not selling potentially hazardous products to commercial customers who do not use proper safeguards. Unfortunately, Manville did not apply this policy to one of the company's own affiliates in India.[17] Yet such policies are already widely followed in the United States to limit potential corporate liabilities, and there is no technical reason why MNC's can't follow similar practices everywhere.

Developing countries are much less able to maintain legal systems that provide citizens with substantial access to civil courts for personal injuries. The expense of operating the courts in such a manner is formidable. It follows that this lack of capacity does not justify the deliberate use of such countries as testing and dumping grounds for hazardous chemicals. Multinational corporations cannot excuse their failure to warn employees or to compensate victims on the grounds that they "observed" local laws.

U.S. manufacturers of dangerous products also run the risk of being called to account by foreigners in U.S. courts. More than thirty banana-farm workers in Costa Rica who were sterilized by the nematocide dibromochloropropane (DBCP) are suing its manufacturers, Dow Chemical and Shell Oil, in Texas.[18] If such suits are successful, the liabilities could be substantial. In 1984 Dow settled a suit brought by six California workers sterilized by DBCP for roughly $2.2 million.[19]

In the wake of the chemical disaster in Bhopal, India, a number of lawsuits were filed against Union Carbide Corporation in U.S. courts in 1984 and 1985. The Indian plaintiffs, including the government of India, are demanding billions of dollars in damages. Union Carbide, which owns 51 percent of the plant where the gas release occurred, is accused of knowing, willful disregard for the public safety in the design and operation of the plant. Carbide operates a similar facility in the United States, but with many more safeguards than were applied in the Indian plant.[20]

### Public Impact of Double Standards

Multinational corporations will continue to face criticism over double standards in worker protection, environmental pollution, and related matters. To say that health abuses in developing countries merely follow local custom, that they are comparable to practices of indigenous industries, or that they violate no statutes is simply not enough. For MNC's a higher standard inescapably applies—not only because they have the expertise and resources, but even more because they observe the higher standard in major market centers and accept it as a cost of doing business in those home markets.

Media exposés of gross double standards can have worldwide effects on multinational corporations. Given the politically sensitive conditions in much of the world, multinationals involved in scandals may be pounced upon by everyone from communist trade unions to corrupt politicians and right-wing nationalist leaders looking for some good treatment in the press.

Certainly, reckless indifference to workers' health can lead to bitter labor-management disputes once the workers are informed. At Hindustan Ferodo, for example, a Bombay asbestos plant 74 percent owned by the British firm Turner and Newall, Ltd., worker health abuses were extreme and numerous in 1981. Following publicity in the British magazine *New Scientist*,[21] the *Times of India* conducted its own investigation. The company, it found, had fired employees whose medical examinations had shown they were suffering from asbestosis, and "at least 35 percent of those still on their jobs were afflicted and yet are neither discharged nor duly compensated."[22] Additional exposés were then published by *Business India, India Today,* and *Science Today.*[23] In the United States, Hindustan Ferodo was critically portrayed in *Newsday.*[24] And in 1982, Yorkshire Television in England berated Turner and Newall over conditions at the plant.[25]

At least one disabled former employee of Hindustan Ferodo has pressed the courts to get an honest medical evaluation of his asbestosis. The union, meanwhile, has turned to sympathetic professionals to learn about the dangers of asbestos and the technical and legal safeguards needed. It has also begun to obtain improved working conditions, although serious abuses of the Factories Act persist.[26] The Centre for Education and Documentation, based in Bombay, has examined reports of government inspections of asbestos plants and analyzed both the law and the controversies that arose at three asbestos manufacturing plants in 1983.

Another Indian asbestos company subject to publicity over bad working conditions was Shree Digvijay Cement Company in Ahmedabad. A local consumer group, the Consumer Education and Research Centre, is now negotiating with government and company officials to improve conditions inside and outside of the twenty-three-year-old plant. The Centre will take the company to court, if necessary, and the consumer group's lawyers have suggested that the company's failure to take prompt steps to improve the situation could cause Shree Digvijay the same problems its multinational parent, Manville Corporation, faces. Working conditions at Shree Digvijay will eventually cost the company substantial sums in future compensation claims: a government report shows concentrations of 216 million to 418 million fibers per cubic meter of air in the plant in 1980; the U.S. standard at that time was 2 million.[27] In India asbestosis has been a compensable occupational disease since 1976; workers' compensation is not yet provided there for cancer from asbestos, however.

Publicity is apt to be most intense in the countries where the multinationals are based, given the relatively advanced scale and freedom of operation of the media in industrial nations. For example, an Arizona paper and a Texas television station and newspaper all investigated the cross-border asbestos textile plants of a U.S. firm, Amatex.[28] The media not only uncovered much valuable material, but they also raised awareness and publicity in Mexican border towns and government offices. (Amatex has since closed the last of its asbestos-production facilities in the United States and sought refuge from damage suits in U.S. bankruptcy court.)

In Lecheria, an industrial area outside Mexico City, numerous multinational companies operate chemical plants. Among them until 1978 was a Bayer (West German) subsidiary, Cromatos de Mexico. The newspaper *Excelsior* wrote extensively about the deaths and illness among the workers and in the surrounding community and about chromate pollution inside this plant, where conditions were so bad that Mexican health authorities, under the pressure of publicity, shut down the operation.[29]

In Nicaragua the U.S.-based Pennwalt Corporation has operated a mercury-cell chlorine plant since 1967. In 1980 environmental health investigators found widespread mercury poisoning among the workers and documented not only gross contamination inside the plant but also tons of mercury pollution in Lake Managua.[30] The government ordered the firm to replace old, leaking pipelines and pumps and to shut down the plant every three months for maintenance. Many improved work practices have been introduced subsequently at the insistence of the workers and the government, and the site is now frequently inspected by physicians.[31] Widespread international publicity, strong public support in Nicaragua, and continued pressure by the Sandinista government have succeeded in inducing improvements by Pennwalt.

In Tokyo street demonstrations against Japanese companies charged with exporting pollution began over a decade ago. Protests focussed on Toyama Chemical (over closure of a Mercurochrome plant in Japan and plans to move to South Korea), Nihon Kagaku (over shifting a chromium refining and plating plant to South Korea, following a long history of severe air pollution and high worker lung-cancer rates in Japan), and Asahi Glass (over water pollution from its mercury-cell chlorine plant in Thailand).[32]

In 1977 Kawasaki Steel opened a sintering plant in Mindanao (the Philippines) to refine imported iron ore for its blast furnaces in the heavily polluted city of Chiba, Japan. Soon workers were being hospitalized with lung problems, but were told that "nothing was wrong" at the hospital designated by the company. Kawasaki had previously had an agreement with a hospital in Chiba to downplay work-related illnesses there, which was exposed in 1975. The Japanese "Stop the Pollution Export Committee" accused Kawasaki of similar tactics in Mindanao.[33] Kawasaki overcame opposition from local farmers and fishers in building the sintering plant at Mindanao. But the bitterness of these people over the severe social, economic, and environmental impact on their lives remains.

In 1982 Japan's Mitsubishi Chemical Co. and others (including a local firm in which Mitsubishi owned a 35 percent interest) opened a plant near the small town of Papan in Malaysia. Amid fish ponds, vegetable farms, and other industrial plants, and near Papan's water reservoir and a stream, the Asian-Rare Earth Company extracted compounds for electronic equipment from local monazite ore. Radioactive thorium wastes were dumped in the open, close to the plant, in plastic bags that easily broke up. When it became known that radioactive wastes were being wantonly dumped by an affiliate of a Japanese company, a public furor erupted in both Malaysia and Japan.[34]

The Papan Action Committee protested to various ministries of the Malaysia government, collecting 7,000 signatures on a petition. Citizens impeded access to the dump site and organized demonstrations, with up to 3,000 participants. In Japan a coalition of citizens' groups denounced the Mitsubishi Chemical Co., which replied that the plant was under the control of the Malaysians and which refused to answer questions. Japan's Foreign Ministry, fearing possible anti-Japanese sentiment, said it would investigate.

A Japanese genetics professor, Dr. Ichikawa Sadao, conducted radiation dosimetry measurements near the plant in late 1984 at the invitation of local residents and environmental groups. Dr. Ichikawa found that environmental radiation levels far exceeded international guidelines for community exposure issued by the International Committee for Radiation Protection (ICRP). His measurements on two plant workers also indicated that the ICRP-recommended permissible limit for occupational exposure was exceeded in the factory. Protests spread, and the Malaysian residents filed suit in the high court to halt operations and to demand cleanup of the existing contamination. A boycott of Mitsubishi products (Mitsubishi Chemical Co. is part of the huge Mitsubishi conglomerate) has begun in Malaysia, and critics in Japan have vowed to take strong action against Mitsubishi to set an example "so that similar cases can be exposed and 'pollution export' cleaned up."[35]

Probably the most extensive investigations of "hazard export" by multinational corporations have focussed on drugs and pesticides. The unrestrained promotion of drugs whose safety and efficacy have been officially doubted in some countries has been the subject of studies by governments, academic health scientists, international organizations, and the media. The strongest governmental action was taken by Bangladesh, which summarily condemned over 1,700 drugs that were not on the World Health Organization's list of about 200 "essential" drugs. The governments of Burundi, Kenya, Thailand, Mozambique, Greece, and India are also moving to ban numerous drugs as unsafe or ineffective.[36]

The story is similar with pesticides. Like drugs, their benefits are widely exaggerated. Given the casual way chemicals are stored and used in developing countries, and the large numbers of people exposed, pesticides consequently take an unknown but enormous toll in preventable death and disease.

Media interest in the promotion of drugs and pesticides in the Third World has been largely responsible for stimulating an international reaction. Outstanding exposés by filmmaker Robert Richter (*Nova*), by *Mother Jones* magazine, and by journalist Bob Wyrick (in *Newsday*) have been paralleled by major efforts by governments and consumer and environmental groups.

To confront the problem of international trade in banned hazardous products, the UN General Assembly first passed a resolution in 1979.

Then in December 1982 the UN General Assembly approved a resolution (no. 37/137) that said:

> Products which have been banned for domestic consumption and/or sale because they have been judged to endanger health and the environment should be sold abroad by companies, corporations, or individuals only when a request for such products is received from an importing country or when the consumption of such products is officially permitted in the importing country.

This resolution was adopted by 146 in favor, 1 against (the United States). In late 1983 the United Nations published its first *Consolidated List of Products Whose Consumption and/or Sale Have Been Banned, Withdrawn, Severely Restricted, or Not Approved by Governments*. This publication is regularly updated.

UN guidelines for consumer protection to provide governments with a common basis for regulating private companies were placed before the General Assembly in 1984. The guidelines were supported by the International Organization of Consumers Unions and opposed by "business interests in countries where these guidelines already exist as laws or regulations."[37] Pakistan led the battle for adoption of the guidelines, and over the opposition of the United States a somewhat weakened set of guidelines was adopted by the General Assembly.[38]

Churches have been highly effective in opposing health abuses by MNC's. The World Council of Churches has forcefully expressed its views:

> In general, global corporations have tended to aggravate, not to solve, the world's greatest problems. . . . Internationally, a system of cooperation between peoples and states should be created to replace the existing competitive relationships based on the [multinationals'] ethics of power, acquisition, profit and rampant materialism with cooperative relationships based on a new ethics of justice, equality, sharing, participation, and sustainability.[39]

Industry and its critics have meanwhile made some progress toward consensus. For instance, representatives of environmental and church groups have met with U.S. pesticide producers and worked out mutually acceptable guidelines for the advertising and labeling of pesticides sold in developing countries.[40] (U.S. exports of pesticides are rapidly increasing, in marked contrast to stabilized sales in the home market.) Similar action by European producers is expected to follow. The agreement to conclude the

Nestlé boycott (over infant formula promotion practices) is another example of how these health issues can ultimately be resolved.

Public interest groups and church organizations have developed functional networks over the pesticide, drug, and infant formula issues. They also work with trade unions to fight industrial double standards. Consciousness has been raised worldwide over the past five years, and the issue of double standards in workplace health protection is sure to receive increasing attention in the late 1980s. Industrial health double standards have been denounced by M. A. El Batawi (chief of occupational health at the World Health Organization), Herman Rebhan (Secretary of the International Metal Workers Federation), Charles Levinson (Secretary of the International Chemical, Energy, and General Workers Union), the scientific journal *Nature*, and the *Washington Post*.[41] The International Labour Office, which has expressed concern over this issue for years, held a symposium in 1981 where the topic was discussed at length.[42] In England the General, Municipal, Boilermakers, and Allied Trades Union has demonstrated a strong commitment to helping unions in developing countries gain expertise on health and safety and to use it for organizing purposes. Union health and safety leaders in Scandinavia take similar stands.

As these examples attest, interest groups likely to raise the issue of double standards in industrial hazards include trade unions, media, legislators, academics, environmental and consumer groups, medical clinicians, and others.

**The Role of International Organizations**

The problem of curtailing gross "double standards" in industry can be approached in numerous ways, including:

1. Providing information to governments, unions, and consumer and environmental protection organizations about known industrial hazards.
2. Publicizing abuses by multinational industrial corporations involving workplace and environmental health threats, both in the countries where the abuses occur and in the home countries of these companies, where such abuses would not be tolerated (or would be subject to prohibitive liability).
3. Developing the expertise and an appropriate body of law in all countries to confront such dangers, even before permits for new plant construction and expansion are granted.

The widespread double standards in industrial hygiene and environmental protection practiced by multinational corporations afford critics an easy target. But although some MNC's do take advantage of ignorance and nonregulation, indigenous companies and government-run industries are no better. Thus, while it may be initially useful to focus public attention on big foreign companies that definitely "know better," the ultimate goal should be to control extreme industrial health abuses—regardless of who owns the factories. Doing so requires raising public awareness and governmental commitment and educating workers about the hazards and control measures in the industries that employ them.

Several international organizations are working on these fronts. The International Metalworkers Federation in Geneva has frequently spoken up against double standards in industrial health and safety. The organization has also worked hard to train union shop-floor safety representatives around the world. The International Labour Office has programs for industrial hygiene and occupational health training—a service that has been in great demand in developing countries. ILO also issues alerts on health hazards as significant new discoveries are made, and it holds periodic conferences on health and safety issues and publishes practical materials in several languages. ILO collects and disseminates information on working conditions in member countries too, including control limits for toxic substances in workplace air.

The World Health Organization (WHO) is working with ILO and other concerned agencies toward meeting these goals by 1989:

1.  At least 50 percent of the countries will have developed occupational health programs to provide preventive health care to workers at their places of work, based on appropriate technology and workers' participation.
2.  A network of at least thirty occupational health institutions in developing countries (twenty more than in 1983) will by then be collaborating with WHO in research and information sharing.
3.  WHO will have developed guidelines on workplace inspection, exposure limits, and early detection and care for specific work-related diseases.[43]

Particular attention will be given to underserved sectors such as agriculture, small-scale industry, and construction. Carcinogenic and mutagenic hazards will be given special consideration. Research into the occupational health problems of developing countries (for example, organic dusts) and promotion of technologies suited to the needs of the developing countries are also planned.[44]

The United Nations Environment Programme (UNEP) provides a number of information services through its International Registry of Potentially Toxic Chemicals (IRPTC): IRPTC data profiles, legal data files for selected chemicals, scientific reviews of Soviet literature on toxicity and hazards of chemicals, and lists of environmentally dangerous chemical substances and processes of global impact. UNEP also has an International Referral System for Sources of Environmental Information and a directory of information sources on chemical safety.[45]

Activities of the UN Centre on Transnational Corporations include:

– Tabulation of Toxic or Hazardous Chemical Products (1982)
– Draft Code of Conduct for Transnational Corporations regarding Environmental Protection (1982)
– Working Group of Experts on International Standards of Accounting and Reporting Transnational Corporations: Environmental Measures[46]

The Pan American Health Organization (PAHO) also has advisory services and publications available on occupational health. PAHO functions as a regional WHO but retains its own identity as well.

The United Nations Industrial Development Organization (UNIDO) issues guidelines on the production and formulation of pesticides in developing countries. However, UNIDO has in general paid too little attention to the environmental and occupational health aspects of the projects it supports.

The World Bank for years has given some consideration to the potential environmental impacts of its projects. Occupational safety and health guidelines were first established in 1975, because it was clear that the most severe problems with toxic substances were in the workplace. In 1982 additional guidelines were issued for pesticide application, pesticide packaging and labeling, and pesticide transportation and distribution.

### U.S. Efforts to Control the Export of Workplace Hazards

In June 1983 U.S. Representatives Michael Barnes and Cecil Heftel introduced a bill (H.R. 3254) to enlarge current pre-export notification requirements for U.S. shippers of pesticides that are not registered for use in the United States. Barnes and Heftel would further amend the Federal Insecticide, Fungicide, and Rodenticide Act by requiring foreign importers of acutely toxic pesticides to state how they intend to assure safe handling, use, and disposal. The amended bill would apply to many pesticides approved for use under controlled conditions in the United States.

Members of the House Committee on Energy and Commerce who see foreign competition in industrial hazards as a threat to employment and industry in the United States are also active on this issue. They reason that if host countries allow foreign manufacturers to operate using substandard health and safety practices, the competition will be unfair and thus threaten American workers. In cases where U.S.-based interests profit from foreign activities that serve markets in the United States, these interests or foreign activities could be constrained by the government.

Proponents of this position include Sheldon Samuels, health and safety specialist for the AFL-CIO Industrial Union Department in Washington. Several years ago Samuels proposed that benzidine dye plants that export dyes to the United States be examined by U.S. inspectors to see that the industrial hygiene aspects of their operations came up to U.S. standards.[47] U.S. production of benzidine (a carcinogen) dwindled to one small dye manufacturer in 1977. But imports of benzidine-based dyes soared in the late 1970s, and the imported dyes contained substantially higher residues of unreacted benzidine than domestically produced dyes did.[48] Samuels reasoned that having U.S. inspectors examine the foreign dye plants is justified by the same logic that argues for U.S. health inspectors to examine foreign plants that can meat for the U.S. market. In 1985 Representative Don Peas introduced a bill to ban U.S. import of benzidine dyes altogether.[49]

There are precedents for U.S. unilateral action to prevent adverse consequences of business practices outside its borders including the Endangered Species Act and the Foreign Corrupt Practices Act. Both recognize that U.S. foreign policy interests are jeopardized when American multinational corporations engage in patently scandalous business practices around the world. More specifically dealing with a labor issue, the House Foreign Affairs Committee voted in 1983 to press for limited economic sanctions against those U.S. corporations doing business in South Africa that fail to offer equal opportunity to nonwhite employees.[50]

Congress clearly can affect abusive business practices by U.S. multinationals in other countries. The implications for the control of abhorrent labor practices by U.S. companies on foreign soil are profound. Is it worse to pay black employees less than whites for the same work than it is to expose a factory full of workers to gross levels of asbestos or lead dust? In addition to the health and safety abuses and racial discrimination, there are many unfair labor practices followed by U.S.-based companies in their foreign operations, especially in some so-called Free Trade Zones. These activities may be seen as a detriment to U.S. employment, the U.S. economy, and the foreign policy interests of the United States.

The U.S. government could institute several types of disincentives—none of them as yet embodied in law—against offending companies based in the United States or trading in U.S. markets. As with Trade Adjustment Assistance (in which the government pays workers laid off due to foreign competition, after a determination made by the Department of Labor), the Department of Labor could be authorized to investigate cases of U.S. job losses due to defined forms of "unfair foreign competition." U.S. inspectors might even be authorized to examine plants that export certain products to the United States, as suggested by Samuels of the AFL-CIO. Possible U.S. government actions also include:

1. Removal of most favored nation trade status with reimposition of higher tariffs for specific goods from specific countries.
2. A ban of imports from specific foreign plants, pending evidence of improved conditions.
3. Loss of foreign tax credits by U.S. owners who normally can deduct their foreign taxes from what the U.S. tax on their income from the foreign operations would otherwise be.

The Bhopal disaster has prompted U.S. environmentalists to call for export controls over the erection of potentially hazardous plants by U.S.-based firms. The U.S. government could assure that essential questions were asked and publicly answered prior to the construction of certain industrial projects.

The Union Carbide catastrophe in Bhopal has prompted concern over the appropriate use of U.S. courts by victims of corporate misconduct in countries where the bringing of personal injury suits is impossible. Case law on this class of issues is mixed, and Congress could define the conditions for the filing of such claims in U.S. courts. One admittedly limited possibility would be to allow such cases to go forward where the plaintiff can show that the U.S. multinational had a controlling interest in the foreign affiliate where the alleged harm occurred, and that the harm occurred as a result of substandard practices in worker and community protection compared with the standard of practice in the United States. Negligence should not have to be shown to obtain compensatory damages. However, if it could be shown that the U.S. multinational was actively involved in designing and operating its foreign business under substandard conditions, punitive damages could also be sought by the plaintiffs.

### Conclusion

Occupational diseases and injuries pose large problems that will grow as the Third World industrializes. Much of the responsibility for workplace hazards in developing countries arises from the sale of products and the management of manufacturing processes by multinational corporations. Where these hazards exceed the corresponding risks permitted in the home-based industries of the multinationals, a double standard exists.

The period since 1970 has seen the emergence of many independent professionals in occupational and environmental health, the environmental movement, and increased attention by trade unions to occupational health and safety. Workers and the general public now recognize health hazards long known to scientists. In turn, increased awareness has led to a massive and ongoing global effort to identify other health hazards. Given modern communication and the interdependence of people all over the world, information on industrial health hazards, on governmental control measures, and on trade unions' positions is rapidly made available in developing countries.

Multinational corporations in chemicals, drugs, and minerals have been harshly criticized over the past ten years for practicing double standards in public health protection. In the United Nations, the European Parliament, individual governments, the media, and the health professions, measures to enforce higher standards of business conduct in international trade have been demanded. These controversies have raised awareness and curtailed some extremely vicious promotional practices in recent years.

The growing industry in developing countries controlled by the multinational corporations can certainly be held to more than local standards of worker health protection. Many of the multinationals' production facilities are of recent vintage, and their design and performance can be measured against the state of the art from the time they were brought on stream. As these plants are in general larger and more highly unionized than indigenous industries, management will be correspondingly more pressed on health and safety issues. Government regulation will eventually apply a degree of uniform control to industrial hazards in general, as more countries develop that capability.

Forward-thinking multinationals will respond to this challenge by educating workers about potential hazards and how to minimize them. Initial plant designs can incorporate health and safety features that would cost much more if they had to be retrofitted later. Control equipment, once installed, must be maintained as carefully as process equipment—not allowed to fall into disrepair by complacency or ignorance. Management must be directed not to sacrifice safety and health by pushing workers or machinery to the breaking point to meet unrealistic production schedules. Suitable schedules of rest for employees and maintenance of equipment are necessary. Medical services trained to detect early signs of occupational illness and to inform workers fully are also very important.

In themselves, worker education and good work practices can go a long way toward controlling industrial hazards. Engineering controls unquestionably add more to fixed and operating costs; but there are offsetting benefits in labor relations, productivity, and long-term goodwill in the host community and country. Given the long-range investment objectives of the multinationals in locating industries in developing countries, it is plainly bad business to build a plant lacking vital safety features or to fail to provide workers in toxic dust occupations with separate lockers for their street and work clothes. The latter provisions were reportedly mandated "in most civilized countries sixty years ago."[51]

Some leaders in the chemical industry acknowledge the need to improve public perceptions about their industry's role in society. As explained by DuPont Executive Vice President William Simeral, the basis of such improvements cannot be just image advertising and business-as-usual. A willingness to face problems and solve them is called for. And the attitude that improvements in business conduct need only be conceded after all legal and political delays are used is, according to Simeral, highly counterproductive.[52] Multinationals that fail to heed such warnings may find that a notorious international reputation is more easily established than overcome.

Broad-based support for moderating double standards in industrial hazards is a reality today. The corporations that will find themselves most welcome and secure around the world in the 1990s will include those that take steps over the next five years to meet high standards in workplace and environmental health worldwide.

# IV Environmental Policy and Multinational Corporations: Country Case Studies

Few studies of environmental policies in developing countries exist and even fewer introduce foreign direct investment by MNC's into the analysis. One question is whether MNC's receive "national" or nondiscriminatory treatment with respect to environmental regulations. A second is the performance of foreign investors vis-à-vis domestic firms in complying with environmental policies. Perhaps the most important question is how host governments can exploit the data, technology, and management expertise of MNC's to improve environmental protection.

Turkey and Brazil were chosen as case studies in part because in these two countries industrial pollution is severe, as Engin Ural and João Carlos Pimenta document. Both authors find that there is no legal discrimination against foreign investors (as does Sung Hoon Kim in an unpublished study of South Korea), but both observe that the public may well expect a higher standard of performance by foreign firms. In fact the thrust of the argument in both chapters is that a study of MNC's must be imbedded in a larger framework for assessing the private sector and the development of national environmental policy more broadly, a finding similar to Goodman's in this volume. Except for their superiority as sources of environmental data and technology and their willingness to comply with regulations, MNC's are not so distinct in the industrial landscape of the Third World as observers in the United States might expect.

The more interesting stories in these two chapters concern domestic conflicts within developing countries. Turkey illustrates the ambivalence toward pollution control on the part of the powerful state planning and industry ministries, which have a mandate for economic growth. Brazil's environmental policies are strongly conditioned by its complicated federal structure, which allows considerable latitude for an energetic agency at the state level in São Paulo. Neither country has a vigorous tradition of private conservation organizations that pressure business and governments, but, supported by new media interest, some modest progress by such organizations is evident.

# CHAPTER EIGHT   Environmental Protection and

# Foreign Private Investment in Turkey

Engin Ural

## Environmental Problems[1]

Turkey has numerous and severe environmental problems, including air and water pollution, soil abuse, deterioration of flora and fauna, solid waste disposal, and noise.*

The two main causes of air pollution in Turkey are urbanization and industrialization. Urbanization is the more important. The influx of rural migrants and natural population growth in cities contribute to air pollution. Ankara is an extreme example, though air pollution is also increasing in Istanbul, Izmir, Eskisehir, Adana, and Gaziantep. Ankara's population is estimated to double every ten years. Sixty percent of the increase is due to immigration and 40 percent to natural growth. Urban growth without adequate controls results in air pollution.

The use of low-quality fuel and incorrect burning techniques contribute seriously to air pollution. Ankara and Erzurum represent the most striking examples. In January of 1982 the sulfur dioxide measurement was 698 micrograms per cubic meter in Ankara and 738 micrograms per cubic meter in Erzurum, where it rises as high as 1,057 micrograms per cubic meter on some days. This compares with a World Health Organization

*This chapter is the result of a team effort at the Environmental Problems Foundation of Turkey. I wish to thank EPFT staff members, especially Lale Uner and Mine Ozgun, who helped me with the work.

(WHO) primary standard of 80 micrograms per cubic meter. WHO states that 500 micrograms per cubic meter leads to excess mortality and hospital admissions.[2] Some 88 percent of the particles and 98 percent of sulfur dioxide in Ankara's polluted air are directly correlated with burning fuel for heat. The climate and topographical positions of Ankara and other Turkish cities also contribute to air pollution. Atmospheric inversions are frequent.

In Turkey's larger cities air pollution problems also arise from the increased number of motor vehicles and from inadequate waste disposal (burning). On average, 77 percent of the carbon dioxide in Ankara's polluted air comes from motor vehicles.

Industrial air pollution is due mainly to the incorrect selection of plant sites and to the emission of factories' waste gases into the air without adequate precautions. Only 6 percent of existing plants are pollution free. The Istanbul-Izmit area, Adapazari, Samsun, Murgul, Izmir, Hazar Lake, and the Adana-Tarsus region are most affected by industrial air pollution.

Water pollution in Turkey is a problem mainly in industrial and urban areas. Within industry chemical pollution is caused by the presence of organic and inorganic substances in factories' waste waters. Thermal pollution occurs when energy plants discharge heat that alters the color, clarity, and temperature of water. Biological pollution results from the presence of contagious and infectious disease vectors, including typhoid and cholera. In urban areas the major sources of water pollution are garbage and sewage, which affect drinking water, fisheries, and recreation.

Water pollution related to industry and to wastes in urban areas is mostly observed in Izmit and Gemlik bays in the Sea of Marmara and in the Golden Horn of Istanbul. Major lakes and streams such as Sapanca and Salt lakes, Sakarya and Porsuk rivers, and Ankara Stream are also polluted by industrial and settlement wastes. More than 120 industrial plants dump their wastes in the Bay of Izmit. Pollution is especially serious where the current is weakest and where industry and settlement are dense on the bay's northern shores.

The industries around the Bay of Izmit produce several kinds of pollution: biochemical oxygen demand and chemical oxygen demand—the most important indicators of pollution—and excessive pH. Discoloration and turbidity also exceed tolerable levels. In addition, unacceptable amounts of bacteria have been found in the wastewater of slaughterhouses, of such industrial establishments as Pirelli, Seka paper mills, Ipras, Petkim, Hereke Carpet Factory, Bayer Agriculture, Bayer Aspirin, and of plants producing food, superphosphates, and agricultural equipment. A complicating factor is that the floor of the Bay of Izmit is continually rising as industrial wastes and eroded soil carried by the rivers accumulate.

The Golden Horn has been filling up for centuries as erosion progresses. Since the Byzantine period, the Golden Horn has narrowed gradually by twenty to fifty meters on either side. With the buildup of organic material, the amount of oxygen in the depths of the inlet has dropped to 1 milligram per liter, accelerating the formation of hydrogen sulfide, a foul-smelling gas. The acid, oil, calcareous substances, various organic acids and substances, glycerine, soda, ammonia, tar, and similar compounds found in the Golden Horn all harm fish and shellfish. This process is exacerbated by pollution entering from the Mediterranean.

Turkey's foremost soil problem is erosion, often due to improper cultivation and grazing. Annual soil losses due to erosion equal an estimated 500 million tons—the equivalent of 20 million square meters of topsoil 20 centimeters deep. Other soil problems include the excessive or incorrect use of pesticides and fertilizers, waterborne industrial wastes that reduce soil quality and productivity, the use of valuable land for settlement or industry, and the use of high-quality agricultural soil to make construction materials. Agricultural pesticides are most widely used in the Mediterranean region, especially Cukurova. The types of pesticides widely used in the Cukurova region are chlorinated hydrocarbons, organophosphates, carbamates, and synthetic pyrethroids. These are used mostly for cotton, fruit olives, citrus fruits, vegetables, and feed grains.

Turkey's forests constitute 26 percent of the country's surface area. The Black Sea, Aegean, and Mediterranean regions are rich in forests. But wars, forest fires, landclearing for farming, illegal cutting of timber, unchecked grazing, and damages from factory smoke, railroads, highways, and settlements have all diminished this wealth. Every year close to 6,300 hectares of forests are destroyed as land is cleared for farming. Another 22,000 hectares are lost or damaged in forest fires. Overuse of forests decreases the variety of flora and fauna, destroys hydrological systems in river basins, increases the surface flow of rainwater, changes the local climate, erodes soils, and causes a decline in natural productivity.

Pastures and grasslands, which constitute 28 percent of Turkey's area, are found mostly in eastern, central, and southeast Anatolia. When these areas are converted into intensive pasture, serious problems arise: excessive grazing and an unsustainable increase in the number of domestic animals. Yet preserving grasslands and pastures is vital since they act as a buffer against pollution, produce oxygen, prevent floods, serve as water-collection basins, and provide food inexpensively. The annual value of the feed they provide, at no cost, is between 130 billion and 140 billion Turkish lira.

No other Middle Eastern or European country except the Soviet Union is as rich in wetlands as Turkey. These areas are economically, aesthetically, recreationally, and ecologically important in part because they produce more oxygen than the tropical forests of the same acreage. They also provide refuge and food for birds migrating throughout Asia, Europe, and Africa and are important for fisheries. Unfortunately, wetlands have diminished following programs for mosquito extermination and projects to obtain land for cultivation.

Turkey's energy sources are coal, oil and electricity, and noncommercial fuels (mainly wood), which provide 40 percent of the country's fuel needs. In Turkey as elsewhere energy production, conversion, and consumption affects the climate, the ecological balance, soil quality, landscape, and water quality. More specifically the use of animal dung as fuel in rural areas affects the economy negatively since it diverts an important resource from agriculture. Moreover, a large share (roughly 15.7 million tons) of the wood used in Turkey is obtained illegally. Coal and oil-fired utilities are an important source of air pollution.

Rapid urbanization, industrialization, changes in living conditions, and increasing consumerism have created a solid-waste problem for Turkey. High collection costs, budget difficulties, strikes, a lack of suitable dumping places, the failure to conform to technically correct disposal methods, and poor hygienic conditions add to the problem.

Of the major sources of solid waste—households, factories, and construction—household wastes pose the biggest problem in Istanbul, Ankara, and Izmir (Turkey's largest cities). An average of 82,230 tons of solid waste are collected every month in Istanbul. Given the city's 1979 population of four million, that equals an estimated 246 kilograms per person per year. In Ankara an average of 350 tons (or 0.27 kilograms per person) of solid waste were produced daily in 1972. By 1980 the total reached an estimated 1,163 tons per day—a difference attributed mainly to population increases. In Ankara's high-income areas the proportion of trash, paper, and similar substances in the waste is relatively higher; in other areas, ashes constitute the lion's share. In tourist centers such as Antalya solid-waste problems require additional attention when high temperatures combine with temporary population increases during the summer.

Turkey's large cities also suffer from excessive traffic-related noise. For example, noise produced by trains and highway traffic passing through Izmit far exceeds acceptable norms. Noise produced by street traffic reaches a level of 75 decibels during the day and rises to about 90 decibels (occasionally to 110) when trains pass. In Ankara, in shopping areas with many sidewalk vendors, the noise level reaches 90 to 92 decibels. According to a study conducted by Cukurova University, noise pollution in a large part of Adana constitutes a threat to healthy human life and work, exceeding the tolerable level of 40 decibels in much of the city. Within industry noise levels threaten workers' health. According to measurements taken in 26 factories, noise levels ranged between 80 and 139 decibels and exceeded 90 decibels in 31 percent of the cases.

### Foreign Private Investment

The flow of foreign capital into Turkey since it became a republic can be considered in two periods. Between 1923 and 1950 existing operations set up with foreign capital were nationalized, and no new foreign capital was allowed into Turkey. This ban on foreign investment reflected national sentiments and nationalistic trends born in the War of Liberation.

The second period began in 1950 when foreign capital was embraced as an important element in economic development, and legal and administrative measures for attracting foreign capital were taken. Despite these efforts there was no immediate large influx of foreign investment. To remedy this, Clarence Randall, then Chairman of the U.S. House of Representatives Commission on Foreign Trade Policy, was invited to Turkey. He drew up the text of Law 6224 for the Encouragement of Foreign Capital, which was put into effect on January 18, 1954.

Law 6224 is the major law controlling foreign investment in Turkey:

This Law shall apply to the foreign capital imported into Turkey and to loans made from abroad by the decision of the Foreign Capital Encouragement Committee and the approval of the Council of Ministers, provided that the enterprise in which the investment shall be made

a. will tend to promote the economic development of the country,

b. will operate in a field of activity open to Turkish private enterprises,

c. will entail no monopoly or a special privilege.

**Table 8.1** Foreign Private Investment in Turkey, 1982

| Sector | Number of firms | Percent of total investment |
|---|---|---|
| Chemicals | 25 | 10.2 |
| Electrical appliances and electronics | 16 | 6.4 |
| Petroleum | 14 | 12.0 |
| Machinery and metal goods | 14 | 6.2 |
| Motor vehicles | 14 | 9.2 |
| Food and beverages | 11 | 9.2 |
| Tourism | 9 | 2.2 |
| Paper and forest goods | 8 | 3.4 |
| Iron and steel | 8 | 9.2 |
| Banking | 8 | 6.2 |
| Textiles | 7 | 8.1 |
| Cement and mining | 5 | 3.0 |
| Agricultural industry | 4 | 3.1 |
| Transportation | 4 | 7.6 |
| Glass | 2 | 2.0 |
| Others | 13 | 2.0 |
| Totals | 162 | 100.0 |

Subsequent articles contain the rules regulating the reinvestment and transfer of profits, the guarantee of loans, and the import of foreign capital into Turkey. The Foreign Capital Encouragement Committee consists of representatives of the Central Bank, the Ministry of Finance, the Ministry of Commerce, the Ministry of Industry, and the Union of Chambers of Commerce and Industry.

The law focusses solely on the technical aspects of foreign private investment: the importation of foreign capital, the transfer of profits, etc. The social and economic effects of investment are not mentioned. Nor have the environmental aspects of foreign private investment been taken into consideration in the law or in the decrees.

Apart from the transfer of foreign capital, profit transfer, and some technical points, foreign private investments are governed by Turkey's general legal system. Companies are incorporated on terms set forth in the Commercial Code. Points not covered by codes are covered by regulations or by the decrees of the Council of Ministers. Environmental issues fall into this category, since none of the foreign investment laws cited here contains even a sentence about the environment.

Law 6224 remains in effect today and ranks among the world's most liberal foreign capital statutes, but it has not been very effective. Favorable general economic conditions are needed for both foreign and domestic investment. Economic instability; administrative, financial, and statutory limitations; exchange restrictions; market inadequacies; inadequate and inefficient economic and social infrastructure; low productivity; the effect of high indirect taxes on the efficiency and cost of operations—in short, conditions arising out of the structure of underdeveloped economies unfavorable to industrial investments—do not constitute an economic atmosphere attractive to investors, especially foreign capital.

Although general economic conditions have not been supportive of large-scale foreign investment in Turkey, some foreign investment has been made, and with the recent liberalization of the economic system, more is expected. As of late 1982 there were 162 foreign private investors operating in Turkey (see tables 8.1 and 8.2).[3] Eighty-seven percent of foreign private investment in Turkey has been in the industrial sector, while the remaining 13 percent has been in services. The amount invested by these 162 corporations totaled $2.5 billion at the end of 1982.

Twelve of these 162 corporations are completely foreign-owned (Bayer, Carlo-Erba, BP Touristic Investments, Pepsi Cola, Coca-Cola, Roche, Sandoz, Singer, Philips, Wyeth, American Express, and Citibank). The remaining 150 operate on a partnership basis with Turkish firms, with foreign equity ranging between 49 percent and 75 percent. Interestingly, the countries that lead the list on table 8.2 also dominate Turkey's foreign trade.

**Table 8.2** Home Base of Foreign Companies in Turkey

| Country | Number of firms |
| --- | --- |
| United States | 35 |
| Switzerland | 32 |
| West Germany | 31 |
| The Netherlands | 6 |
| United Kingdom | 6 |
| Italy | 5 |
| Others | 47 |
| Total | 162 |

As noted, permission for foreign investment in Turkey is granted in accordance with Law 6224. The Law for Protecting the Value of Turkish Currency (Law 1567, dated February 20, 1930) and its supplementary decrees regulate banking, shipping agencies and other services, licensing, and royalties. Oil drilling and related activities are regulated by Law 6326 (dated March 7, 1954). These laws differ only with respect to capital import and profit-transfer provisions. They do not vary significantly from one another from the standpoint of the environmental effects of investments.

Most industrial firms capitalized by foreign corporations are located in Istanbul, the largest metropolitan area and the commercial center of Turkey. Industry is concentrated in the area between Istanbul and Izmit (see figure 8.1). This ninety-kilometer strip covers the whole north coast of the Izmit Bay. The most advanced industries in the Istanbul-Izmit area are chemical processors. Crude oil drilling activities are carried on in southeast Anatolia. Oil refineries are located in Mersin on the Mediterranean coast, at the Bay of Izmit, and in Izmir, the largest Aegean port. Almost all of the service sector, including banking, is located in Istanbul.

Information on employment, revenues, shares in exports, and taxes paid in Turkey is gathered through research on the country's largest 500 industrial companies. These figures are available through late 1981, though they exclude foreign companies involved in oil drilling.

At the end of 1981 Turkey's 500 largest companies employed 519,533 people. Some 31,121 people, 5.9 percent of the total, work for foreign companies. Sales revenues of the 500 largest companies totaled $21 billion in 1981, while the total sales income of foreign companies came to $2 billion (10 percent).

Exports of these companies in 1980 totaled $480 million. Of that, $97 million (20 percent) represents the earnings of the foreign investors. Turkey's total export income for the same period was $2.9 billion, and foreign capital accounts for 3.3 percent of this income. Turkey's exports of manufactured goods totaled $1 billion. Companies operating with foreign capital account for 9.2 percent of this amount.

No studies have yet been done of the taxes paid by foreign capital firms compared with the total tax paid by domestic firms in Turkey. But the taxes paid by foreign companies in certain years afford a rough idea: in 1979, $120 million; in 1980, $174 million; and in 1981, $295 million.

In summary foreign direct investment plays a modest but significant role in the Turkish economy (especially in the chemical sector) and contributes importantly to Turkish manufactured exports.

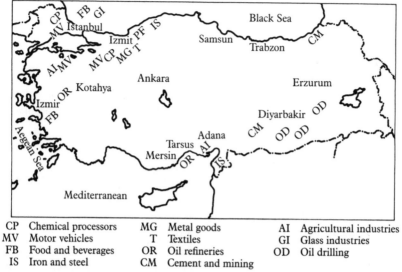

| CP | Chemical processors | MG | Metal goods | AI | Agricultural industries |
|----|---------------------|----|-------------|----|-----------------------|
| MV | Motor vehicles | T | Textiles | GI | Glass industries |
| FB | Food and beverages | OR | Oil refineries | OD | Oil drilling |
| IS | Iron and steel | CM | Cement and mining | | |

**Figure 8.1**  Foreign Enterprise in Turkey

### Environmental Management

Turkey's environmental policy has been governed by the fourth and fifth Five-Year Development Plans (1979–84; 1985–89) and the Environmental Law that became effective in August 1983.

Five-Year Development Plans. In Turkey general policies affecting all governmental and private-sector projects and investments are set forth in the Five-Year Development Plans. The excerpt cited below, related to environmental problems, is taken from the fourth such plan (1979–84).

Bringing solutions to environmental problems such as air, water, and soil pollution, and the deteriorating ecological balance endangering human life, caused by unplanned and uncontrolled settlement, industrialization, and agricultural activities, has been recognized as a basic policy in the Third Five-Year Development Plan. Necessary corrective measures will be taken against these problems, taking into account at the same time, the goals of industrialization and development. During the period of 1973–77, the environmental problems have been defined and a public awareness has been created. Today, the public is aware of the environmental problems resulting from settlement, industry and agricultural activities. However, the most effective methods of fighting against pollution, which could be adapted to fit our economic and social structure best, is not determined yet. It is also unknown to what degree the pollutants are absorbed and assimilated by the environment and what the capacity of the environment is to renew itself after such effects. No studies have been undertaken to establish environmental standards for different environmental regions.

Bringing solutions to the environmental problems, in conformity with the changing social structure, is a basic principle.

Additional consideration will be given to the preventive measures to be taken against the possible environmental problems that could be encountered in the course of developing industrialization, agricultural activities, and urbanization. Thus, in the long run, deterioration in the environment would be prevented by maintaining the ecological balance and preserving the natural resources.

After examining the alternative solution suggestions for environmental problems, the most fitting ones for our social, economic, and ecological structure will be adapted. The regional characteristics will be taken into account during the selection of preventive suggestions. The preventive measures will be put into application immediately in those regions where the human life is concerned.

In areas where the land use has not been planned, the ecological features of the region, and the environmental protection measures will be taken into consideration.

The local and central administrations will collaborate, in order to provide for establishing the local environmental policies and taking decisions on specific problems. The local administrations will be responsible for most of the decisions to be taken.

Legal, scientific, and technological innovations and developments taking place in the world, pertaining to environment, will be followed closely, and the necessary actions will be taken in adapting the fitting ones.[4]

The plan thus recognized a need for environmental management but contained no specific regulations governing the activities of private investment in relation to environment. Moreover, the State Planning Organization's prime concern is Turkey's rapid industrialization, so in its view conservation of environment should not impede growth. The State Planning Organization shows little support for environmental protection activities, fearing that such activities could constrain industrialization.

The Ministry of Industry (which is authorized to grant permission for private-sector investments) shares the convictions of the State Planning Organization.

The fifth Five-Year Development Plan, which was approved in 1984, also discusses environmental goals and strategies. A commitment is made to reduce or eliminate air and water pollution and protect natural resources. The section concerning social targets and policies calls for the liquidation of existing industrial plants in areas of excessive water pollution such as the Sea of Marmara and the Bay of Izmit. It also calls for systematic evaluation of environment during the prelicensing and project evaluation phases and during the licensing of establishments, and for emergency measures to control air pollution in Ankara and other urban centers. The unresolved issue, however, is the speed and vigor with which these laudable goals will be pursued.

*Environmental Law.* Law 2872, published on August 11, 1983, embraces several basic environmental protection and improvement principles.[5] As stated in article 1,

> The purpose of this law is to govern, according to definite legal and technical principles and in conformity with the goals of economic and social development, the arrangements to be made and the measures to be taken in order to protect and improve the environment, which is the common property of all citizens; to protect and make optimal use of land and natural resources in rural and urban areas; to prevent water, soil and air pollution; and to develop and guarantee the standard of health, civilization and living of the present generation and of future generations by preserving the nation's plant and animal life and its natural and historical wealth.

Two paragraphs in article 3 reveal the Turkish government's position on the environmental impacts of economic activities:

> In economic activities and in the choice of production methods, the most suitable technology and methods shall be selected and implemented with the purpose of preventing and limiting environmental problems.
>
> Those who pollute the environment or inflict damage on it shall be responsible, without assignment of fault, for the damage arising from the pollution and deterioration they cause. Such polluters, however,

may be excused from having to pay for the expenses of preventing and limiting pollution if they can prove that they took all possible measures necessary to prevent the said pollution.

Pollution prohibition is covered in article 8:

It is prohibited to introduce into, store in, transport to or remove from the receptor area any discharge or waste in such a way as to inflict damage on the environment or in a way directly or indirectly in contradiction with the standards and methods specified in the pertinent regulations, or to engage in similar activities.

In situations where there is a possibility of pollution, the parties involved are required to prevent that pollution; in situations where pollution is created, the polluter is required to take the measures necessary to stop the pollution or to eliminate or reduce its effects.

The Council of Ministers is authorized to enforce the Environment Law in accordance with article 34. The Supreme Environment Council

shall be under the chairmanship of the Prime Minister or some other State Minister to be appointed, and shall consist of the Ministers of Internal Affairs, Health and Social Welfare, Transport, Agriculture and Forestry, Industry and Technology, Energy and Natural Resources, Reconstruction and Housing, and Rural Affairs and Cooperatives, as well as the undersecretaries of the State Planning Organization and of the Environment Undersecretariat of the Prime Ministry. The secretarial functions of the Council shall be executed by the Environment Undersecretariat of the Prime Ministry.

The council has a variety of functions including examining pollution control plans and programs, determining the principles for land-use planning in urban and rural areas (including protected areas), formulating principles for cooperation and coordination among ministries and agencies with environmental protection responsibilities, and defining future environmental objectives.

As indicated, the principle that no corporate activities or products should cause any pollution is stated in article 8. In addition, article 10 asks any firm, corporation, or business to prepare an "Environmental Impact Assessment Report" about any activity with the potential to pollute the environment:

Firms, corporations and businesses which may pave the way to environmental problems as a result of the activities they plan to carry out shall prepare an "Environmental Impact Assessment Report." In this report, the manner of treatment of the discharge and waste that may cause environmental pollution as well as the measures to be taken in this regard shall be specified by keeping in mind all possible effects on the environment.

Principles regarding which type of projects will require an "Environmental Impact Assessment Report," the points to be included in it, and which authorities will approve it shall be stipulated by special regulations.

This article essentially alerts investors to proceed with caution. It requires any firm that could pollute to hire a capable expert to assess the impact and to take other measures to stop the pollution. Naturally, multinational corporations are covered by this law. The environmental impact assessments (EIA's) are potentially very powerful tools for controlling private-sector pollution and environmental abuse.

Another section of interest to investors is article 11, which states,

Firms, corporations and businesses, establishment of which is being planned, shall be required to set up, either independently or jointly, the purification plants or systems stipulated in the current regulations. Until such purification plants or systems are set up and put in working order, operating and usage licenses shall not be granted to firms, corporations or businesses.

Any firm, corporation or business which receives permission to operate and begins operations is required to inform of plans to modify its activities or enlarge its facilities. The official shall immediately inform the Environment Undersecretariat of the Prime Ministry and the relevant ministry of the situation.

Business concerns, which are responsible for purification, removal or treatment of discharge and waste of all kinds, shall also take precautions to ensure that no damage is inflicted on the environment through these measures.

The necessary technical methods to be implemented in introducing discharge and waste directly or indirectly into the receptor area shall be stipulated by special regulations, keeping in mind the nature of the receptor area and the possible ways of utilizing it.

Thus article 11 requires business to put purification plants or systems in working order before receiving an operating permit.

While introducing certain burdens on the citizens and industry, the law at the same time introduces a provision that may benefit firms producing or making investments in environment-protection-related technology. The law also introduces the "Environmental Fund," which will provide a twenty-year term credit to cover up to 45 percent of expenditures made for installation of purification plants to prevent environmental pollution.

Article 22 of the Environment Law establishes the legal penalty of fines for pollution. In addition, article 15 states that investors who do not fulfill the act's requirements and who repeat prohibited actions face a partial or complete shutdown of their businesses. The power to shut down plants rests with provincial governors or, in some cases, subgovernors.

Finally, article 28, covering collection of fines, requires firms and investors to compensate the administrative authorities for pollution abatement expenses and damages in those instances where the polluter failed to act, and the authorities incurred expenses for remedial pollution abatement.

Implementation of the law is uneven. Most investors are now preparing environmental impact assessments, which will be submitted to either the Ministry of Industry or the Provincial Governor's Office. The EIA's are not made public. Since August 1984 the Environmental Directorate General can accept or reject the EIA's, but the final decision rests with the Ministry of Industry. The procedure remains cloudy in part because the implementing regulations to the Environment Law have not yet been issued.

In general, investment (including foreign) and operating permits are issued by the Ministry of Industry, with construction and initial operating permits issued by the municipal governor's office. An explicit provision concerning pollution control and environmental protection in the investment agreement would be highly desirable, but it is not now customary.

Other laws of environmental importance include Public Health Law (no. 1593), the Municipalities Law (no. 1580), the Water Products Law (no. 1380), and the Forestry Law (no. 6831). None of these codes specifically addresses investors or investments, much less multinational corporations. Nor do they explicitly address environmental policy or environmental management. But the codes are important nonetheless since they make the central government or local administrations responsible for carrying out the law.

Environmental Standards and Regulations. The Environment Law provides Turkey's legal framework for dealing with the environment. Unfortunately, it does not establish standards of pollution or contain an annex that addresses standards. Moreover, article 3 of the law states that "the regulations that set the standards will be prepared and put in force within one year after this code is established." Thus the deadline for the regulations to be in force was August 11, 1984, but was not met.

Whether the regulations that will be set up for the Environment Law will consist of standards remains open to question. The public and the enforcing agencies assume that they will, however, and it is obvious that the Environment Law will be ineffective if pollution standards are not clarified in the regulations.

At the same time, the Office of Turkish Standards connected to the Prime Ministry is setting up the standards for air pollution and other environmental hazards. Article 3 of the Environment Law makes the Undersecretariat for Environment (since August 1984, called the Environmental General Directorate) responsible for setting up pollution standards, and that office has to coordinate with every other agency for this purpose. The Undersecretariat staff was about 80 during 1980–83, but when it changed into a Directorate General in 1984, there was a staff reduction of about 20 percent.

Apart from the few expected to be prepared soon, Turkey has no rules, regulations, or standards on environment. The only exception is the Water Products Law (no. 1380) of March 22, 1971, which contains a list of water-pollution standards. Since these standards have not been adequately enforced, the hope is that they will be revised when the new regulations are established.

Environmental Authorities. The Environmental General Directorate is the lead agency in environmental affairs. However, when pollution leads to human health problems, the Ministry of Health becomes involved, and under some circumstances such ministries as Agriculture and Forestry, or Industry, Reconstruction, and Housing have some authority. In addition, the State Planning Organization, which prepares the five-year development plans, concerns itself with environmental issues. The work of all these agencies is coordinated by the Supreme Environment Council set up for this purpose.

To most investors, the leading central government agency of interest is the Ministry of Industry. The ministry's chief interest is promoting new investments, including the granting of incentive and encouragement certificates. Nevertheless, by law it should be deeply concerned with whether the investments are polluting industries. Under article 29 of the Environment Law, the Ministry of Industry is also to encourage all economic investments or activities related to the prevention or elimination of pollution. In other words, Turkey is starting to encourage the use of environmental protection technologies and using disincentives—the revocation of "encouragement certificates"—with industries that pollute.

The local administrative bodies in Turkey are provincial local governments and municipalities. The Provincial General Assembly is the functioning body that coordinates public works and some social services. An elected body, it has little jurisdiction beyond the building of schools, roads, and other public works and education. In contrast the municipalities greatly influence the lives of citizens. (For every population of 2,000 or more and for all provincial and subprovincial capitals regardless of size, a municipality is established.)

Municipalities Law No. 1580 authorizes municipalities to oversee public health. Municipalities also issue construction and occupancy permits, monitor water quality, collect and dispose of garbage, clean the streets, and inspect food and food processing and distribution. However, while municipalities inspect and check up on these operations, they have no say over their creation.

Some conflict between the Provincial General Assembly and the governor of the municipality is unavoidable. A governor appointed by the central government and an elected mayor may have different political and economic beliefs. To forestall or manage conflicts born of these beliefs, article 6 of the Environment Law established Local Environment Councils, which are chaired by the governor and consist of the branch heads of the provincial administration, the mayor, the representative of the provincial board of education (where such a board exists), and the president of the local chamber of industry.

The functions of the Local Environment Councils include preparing and implementing environmental protection programs at the provincial level (and in accordance with decisions of the Supreme Environmental Council), coordinating environmental networks of agencies at the provincial level, identifying and reporting environmental problems to the Environment Undersecretariat, and organizing educational activities for environmental protection.

Each council is instructed to meet monthly, though the chairman (the governor) can convene unscheduled meetings too. It is hoped that these councils can effectively coordinate environmental activities at the top managerial level of the local administration. Certainly, including the president of the local chamber of industry indicates the involvement of the private sector.

Local Environment Councils have been established in most provinces; they tend to be active and effective when the governor is interested in environmental issues and in dealing with local problems of site selection, sewage, construction permits, etc. Once again, however, it is too early to say whether this central-provincial-municipal administrative structure is adequate to deal with environmental problems.

### Changing Attitudes on Environmental Problems

The recent developments in the Turkish legal system reflect an increasing concern for the environment. In particular article 56 of the constitution states that environmental protection is an important obligation of the citizens and the state. Given that few countries have environment protection articles in their constitutions, this is a big step for Turkey. The Environment Law described in detail in this chapter is further evidence that environmental protection has become important in the Turkish legal system.

Both these recent developments stem partly from public complaints about environmental pollution, especially in the big cities, and from press attention. At the same time, the publications and activities of the Environmental Problems Foundation of Turkey (EPFT)—including its role in getting the environmental protection article in the constitution—have accelerated this progress. The Environment Law Proposal prepared and submitted to related authorities by EPFT has also been accepted, and these two developments represent a turning point in the field of environment protection in Turkey. Among other things, EPFT's success as a private pressure group is unprecedented in Turkey and may be a new model for social change.

The need to get organized to comply with the Environment Law is now widely felt by the public and the private sectors. Speed and urgency may be lacking, but progress is occurring nonetheless. Abiding by the rules required by the law, preparing technical reports, setting up purification systems, and researching the effects of these on general operating costs have all engaged both the public and the private sector in environmental management issues.

The Public Sector. The Turkish government agencies that work on the environment have not had a trouble-free relationship during this period. The State Planning Organization's lack of support for environmental protection was made clear on several occasions. For its part, the Ministry of Industry has considered environmental protection efforts as obstacles to rapid industrialization. In fact, responding in the spring of 1983 to criticism of the decision to turn the most fertile agricultural lands in the south of Marmara region over to industry, the Minister of Industry stated emphatically that the growth of industrialization is far more vital than environmental protection — a comment strongly criticized by the press.

The Ministry of Finance's concern is that environmental protection activities represent an extra burden on Turkey's budget. Although it never publicly criticizes environmental protection activities, it is not very cooperative either — witness its refusal to allocate additional funds for environmental protection.

The Environment Undersecretariat became involved in conflicts with the Ministry of Health and the Ministry of Agriculture and Forestry over the division of responsibilities. The Environment Undersecretariat wanted a say in the Ministry of Agriculture and Forestry's efforts to preserve and protect forests and land and to participate in decisions involving pesticide use, which is also controlled by the Ministry of Agriculture and Forestry. In the case of air-pollution monitoring, the Ministry of Health has responsibility in Ankara as part of its public health mandate, but the Environment Undersecretariat also claimed responsibility for monitoring air quality. At times the water-pollution control activities represent another jurisdictional conflict, though the Ministry of Agriculture and Forestry is the responsible authority according to the Water Products Law (no. 1380).

All these disagreements stem from the Environment Undersecretariat's insistence that it is the governing authority over all matters related to the environment. In 1983 the Environment Secretariat signed protocols with the Ministry of Health and with the Ministry of Agriculture and Forestry that have helped settle the problems.

Since the inclusion of an environmental article in the constitution in 1982 and the enactment of the Environment Law in August of 1983, the public sector has been forced to bring all these environmental concerns to bear on its decisions and activities. A recent statement made by the State Planning Organization (SPO), the same agency that has expressed doubts about the relative importance of environmental protection and its potential as "an obstacle to industrialization," is quite interesting in this light. A group of SPO experts for the 1984 implementation program told a daily newspaper that the environmental factor should always be kept in mind and that the relation between rapid population growth and environmental problems deserved special emphasis.

Another influence on the public sector has been the attitude of the World Bank. In late 1982 World Bank President A. W. Clausen stated that environmental factors are to get special attention in each development project the Bank supports. This new policy will certainly affect Turkey, which receives substantial World Bank loans for public- and private-sector projects. Indeed, the effects registered immediately. For example the Industrial Development Bank and the State Investment Bank (two public organizations that coordinate Turkey's relations with the international agency) started educational programs and information and documentation centers about environmental issues for their personnel in 1983.

The regulations that the public expects to be prepared in conjunction with the Environment Law are very important to Turkey's long-term environmental prospects. For example, while the Law forbids excessive noise, it is the regulations that will set the noise threshold, thus determining when noise becomes "environmental pollution." Until these regulations are ready the article on noise in the law will not be put into effect. The same holds for other kinds of pollution too. Clearly, the preparation of technical details, regulations, and standards is a major issue facing Turkey. The problem is exacerbated by shortages of the knowledge and experience required to prepare technical details and standards. The Environment Law and the regulations that are going to be prepared soon will definitely create new business fields for the private sector. For fields where the experience and technology of the Turkish private sector are not sufficient, there will be a need and opportunity for international business, for commercial operations, and for technical help and advice.

The best long-term hope for change in the public sector lies with the Supreme Environment Council, described earlier. However, the council has met only once since August 1983 and thus far has not proved effective. Its effectiveness depends on the priorities of the political party in power, which since November 1983 has not favored environmental issues very strongly.

In general Turkey's municipalities are more sensitive to environmental problems than its central government since they are more aware of how environmental problems affect people where they live. Differences between the municipalities and the central government must be ironed out. The

Local Environment Councils may prove to be effective, providing unity and coordination.

Private Investors. Private-sector investors deeply affect environmental developments in Turkey. As indicated, they account for a large portion of total industrial investment in Turkey, and these investments are vitally important to the nation's economy. Yet from the mid-1970s until recently, many viewed environment protection as an unaffordable luxury that would prevent Turkey's industrialization—a view sometimes shared by the Ministry of Industry and by the State Planning Organization. In industry's view the funds set aside for environmental protection would be better spent on other investments. Behind such attitudes are the desire to keep business expenses to a minimum and the relative unfamiliarity of the concept of environment within business circles.

A case in point concerns the pollution standards found in the Water Products Law. Industry has responded negatively to this law on grounds that it unduly restricts its operations. At a press conference held on June 23, 1975, the president of the Izmir Chamber of Industry, speaking for the Aegean Chambers of Industry, asked for a one-year postponement of the application of the law. Although the Turkish government denied this request, many officials within the State Planning Organization shared investors' belief that concern for environmental protection will hamper the economy in general and industrial development in particular.

On the other hand, a more positive attitude toward the environment characterizes some industries. In 1982 the Eczacibasi Holding Company (which has no foreign capital) announced at the opening ceremony of a paper products plant on Izmit Bay that it had installed the most advanced waste purification devices available. Other plants located in the Izmit Bay have also, in accordance with the requirements set forth by the Environment Undersecretariat, started to survey their contributions to the pollution of the bay, following agreements made with TUBITAK (Scientific and Technical Research Institution of Turkey). The findings of these surveys are in the hands of the Environmental General Directorate, which has not yet disclosed them to the public. Multinational corporations such as Shell, Goodyear, and Pirelli, among others, have agreed to carry out similar studies.

Since mid-1983 companies specializing in developing technology for environmental protection have added a new dimension to environmental conservation efforts in Turkey. ALARKO and TEKSER, the major companies investing in this field, are designing devices for purifying polluted waters. The KAVALA Group is working on exhaust-filtering devices for motor vehicles. Moreover, the KAVALA Group has both supported the Environmental Protection Foundation of Turkey and has taken out newspaper advertisements announcing their commitment to and capabilities in the field of environmental protection.

The incorporation of environmental concerns into Turkey's constitution and law reduces opposition. Businesses that have realized the power of these two instruments have already begun working on ways to take environment into account in their activities. The protection measures called for by the Environment Law force investors to accept environmental restrictions on business operations.

The growth in public awareness of the environment since the late 1970s also affects investors. Mainly, industries that pollute the seas and lakes have been censured by people living along shorelines and in some neighboring municipalities. Nobody in Turkey blames private investors per se for all environmental pollution. But the public and the press do hold industry accountable for pollution, especially in such areas as Izmit, Izmir, and the Golden Horn, where industry is quite prevalent. In mid-1983 the subgovernor who stopped the work of the olive oil factories that were polluting the Aegean Sea received much support from the press, and the objections of the manufacturers were all in vain.

Business circles also began to realize that some extreme leftists who are against the private sector may use the weapon of environment against them, much as the Green Party has been doing in West Germany, and thus make potential investors wary of doing business in Turkey.

After passage of the Environment Law, businesses involved in environmental protection technology enjoyed a boom in Turkey since all new industries now have to set up purification systems. Some of these firms —among them ALARKO, TEKSER, and KAVALA—have become strong defenders of environment protection. (ALARKO and TEKSER produce factory-discharge and water-purification technology, while KAVALA works on emission-control technology for the automotive industry. None is affiliated with multinational corporations.)

It is likely that a conflict will arise between the local investors involved in environmental protection technology and the remaining local investors, as the former may push for strict standards and the latter for lax ones. Already, the Union of Chambers of Commerce and Industry of Turkey (UCCIT, the top-level organization of Turkish businesspeople) and the International Chamber of Commerce (ICC) (of which UCCIT is a member) are at loggerheads. While ICC has a very active Environment Committee, the Turkish group is not active in the environment committee of the ICC. Yet Turkish investors who sell environmental technology have now started lobbying in UCCIT and are trying to participate actively in ICC meetings in Paris.

Useful steps for local investors interested in environment would be to organize themselves, to exchange information on their experiences, and to import know-how, experience, and technology from abroad. Further, cooperating with private nonprofit organizations dealing with the environment will garner public support.

What role should multinational corporations play in environmental management in Turkey? First, they have to realize that concern for the environment is growing in Turkey. Before September 12, 1980, the extreme leftists used the "environment" as a tool to attack the private sector. Specifically, on several occasions they blamed the multinational corporations for polluting the environment. Today, however, criticism of the multinational corporations has subsided, though it could develop again. Clearly, the message to multinational corporations investing in Turkey is that public awareness of environmental issues is on the rise.

Second, since multinational corporations have more technical knowledge and experience with environmental management than local investors have, they should share this information to the fullest extent possible. Third, with this special knowledge and experience in environmental protection, multinational corporations can open a new area of business for themselves in Turkey, contributing to the host country's environmental protection efforts. Fourth, it follows that multinational corporations that contribute to environmental protection efforts in Turkey can create a better business atmosphere and receive the support of Turkish public opinion.

Fifth, the charitable organizations associated with most multinational corporations should be used for research, information dissemination, exhibits, publications, the awarding of prizes, and other activities, as well as to support Turkish organizations that sponsor similar activities. Finally, multinational corporations can cooperate with local investors, the public sector, and Turkish universities to cover the nation's need for personnel by bringing experts from abroad or by giving Turkish technicians a chance to train abroad.

Environmental protection in Turkey has had a late start. The elements of an effective program are now emerging, but success will require vision, commitment, and plain hard work on the part of government, domestic industry, and foreign investors. Multinational corporations are faced with a challenge and an opportunity. An effective partnership in environmental management is possible, but will require sustained and systematic effort.

## CHAPTER NINE   Multinational Corporations

## and Industrial Pollution Control in São Paulo, Brazil

João Carlos P. Pimenta

The original intention of this chapter was to examine the role of multinational corporations (MNC's) in industrial pollution in São Paulo, Brazil, and the positive contributions they might make to improve environmental management. As the research developed, it became clear that neither legislation nor government behavior separates MNC's from domestic firms, and the main issue is more effective industrial pollution control, regardless of business ownership. At the same time, however, MNC's have a potentially constructive role to play, and the research suggests some positive steps that could be taken. It also became clear that an understanding of the intricate web of relations and responsibilities for environment between the federal, state, and local government levels was necessary to evaluate industrial pollution control in São Paulo.

The structure of this chapter reflects these considerations. The first section analyzes federal, state, and local environmental responsibilities and policies. The second section considers the major problems and initiatives at the state and municipal level in São Paulo, and discusses the role of MNC's. The final section examines steps that might be taken to improve understanding and lead to more effective policy.

To research this issue, bibliographies and working papers were surveyed and interviews were held with pollution-control officials ranging from those at the very top to field inspectors. The views expressed here are not, consequently, mine, but mainly those of experts in the public sector.*

*The author is grateful for the cooperation of a large number of experts who assisted in this work, and especially for their patience in sometimes tiresome interviews.

## Governmental Protection of the Environment

The Federal Level.

*The constitutional framework.* Brazil is a federal republic in which union, state, and municipality all occupy definite places. Municipalities are not just state-delegated entities, but form local governments. Within limits they act on their own rights, with powers for self-determination, self-regulation, and self-administration. They have their own legislative and executive bodies, and the power to make laws concerning matters of local interest, to provide local public services, and to run their own administration. Generally speaking the union holds the powers expressly given to it by the constitution, while municipalities are empowered to deal with specific local interests. The states deal with whatever does not fall under the jurisdiction of the union or the municipality.

The Brazilian constitution does not mention pollution control as a responsibility of the union, but it does grant the union powers to defend and protect public health. States, too, have public-health responsibilities, though it is understood that state regulations must comply with union regulations and respect the powers of the municipality. Municipalities have the power to regulate all matters related to their "specific local interest."

This constitutional framework is very complex. Consequently, numerous legal and administrative disputes arise that only the courts can settle. A complicating factor is the recent creation, via federal legislation, of "metropolitan areas," including São Paulo. These do not constitute an autonomous level of government, only an administrative concept implemented by the states.

Distinguishing between "general" and "specific" regulations and between "local" or "regional" interests is difficult. From the early 1960s until recently the federal government has exercised so much power that state and municipal powers weakened accordingly. Indeed, the federal government chose the state governors, who in turn appointed the mayors of the state capitals. As a result the federal government position prevailed whenever opinion diverged. Thus state policy with respect to environment has not been distinct and independent of federal policy.

*National policy for protection of the environment.* At the 1972 UN Conference on the Human Environment in Stockholm, Brazil firmly rejected proposals for adopting international standards for environmental protection. The Brazilian delegate argued that this position did not reflect a "permissive" attitude toward environment problems, but rather that Brazil rejected any concerted effort by industrial countries to curb the industrial growth of developing nations.

R. V. Costa, a high government official, summarized Brazil's view at that time:

Their [the industrial countries'] central thesis was that the world marched towards chaos and that the only way to preserve the environment for future generations lay in stagnation, in the curtailment of economic development. Perhaps as a result of mere thoughtlessness, this could very well represent an easy solution for developed countries, since freezing per capita incomes at the level of five thousand dollars a year may not seem such an unbearable sacrifice. But for the underdeveloped two thirds of mankind, whose per capita income ranges from 100 to 300 dollars a year, such a solution was utterly unacceptable.

This explains the sometimes drastic position taken by the Brazilian Delegation during the preparatory meetings and, later, in Stockholm, to the effect that the solution to the problems of the environment should not be sought in the curtailment of economic development. In our view, the solution lies in directing development in such a way as to safeguard the environment and preserve those resources that cannot be replaced. On the other hand, we argued that the developing countries were not responsible for the present environmental crisis, as the pollution they caused derived from poverty. The main blame falls upon the developed countries, since today's poor environmental conditions stem from their high standards of consumption and their carelessness, in the last decades, in what concerns pollution problems. Consequently, it is the developed countries themselves which must pay the price of cleaning the environment, either directly, in their own territories, or contributing to such programs as the developing countries may launch with such a purpose. Our resources are already so scarce that it is not fair to ask us to divert any substantial amount of resources from economic development to the fight against pollution.[1]

Costa also lamented the defeat of the so-called additionality thesis put forth in Stockholm by Brazil. Under this principle some kinds of pollution would be fought in developing countries with technical and financial assistance from industrial countries supplementary and additional to aid received for development purposes. Unfortunately, the media in Stockholm depicted Brazil's position as irresponsible—an attempt to sacrifice the Amazon forests and to forgo pollution controls until economic growth could be achieved. According to Costa, Brazil's actual position was that economic development would generate the resources needed to control pollution and preserve the environment, even though at the time a few water pollution programs sponsored by the National Housing Bank were the only such national efforts under way.

Not surprisingly, after the Stockholm conference, measures to enforce environmental protection were taken rather slowly. After eight years, in 1980, Federal Law No. 6803 established the guidelines for industrial land-use zoning, which substantially enlarged the authority of the states over what had formerly been considered exclusively local matters. In 1981 the federal government enacted Law No. 6938, the Brazilian Environment Act, and in 1983 it enacted Executive Decree No. 88351, which regulates the application of the act.

The Brazilian Environment Act sets the objective of the national environment policy as "the preservation, improvement and recuperation of the environmental quality, adequate for life, assuring the country of conditions for socio-economic development, for the interests of national security, and for the protection of the dignity of human life." This legislation has introduced important conceptual improvements, mainly by focussing broadly on environmental protection instead of simply pollution. It also establishes the means for implementing the environment policy: use of standards for environmental quality; environmental zoning; evaluating environmental impact; licensing and reviewing of actual or potential polluting activities; granting incentives for producing and installing equipment to improve environmental quality; and imposing disciplinary or compensatory penalties on parties that fail to perform measures needed to protect the environment, among others. Today, by far the most effective of these instruments has been the licensing of activities.

The Environment Act also defines the set of institutions responsible for the protection and improvement of the environment. These are: (1) the National Environment Council, which "assist[s] the President of the Republic in formulating the guidelines of the National Policy for the Environment"; (2) the Special Secretariat for the Environment (SEMA, subordinate to the Ministry for Home Affairs), which exists to "promote, discipline and evaluate the implementation of the National Policy for the Environment"; (3) other federal agencies whose functions relate to environmental protection; (4) state agencies controlling all activities "bound to cause degradation of environmental quality"; and (5) local agencies, with the same functions as state agencies but limited to "local interests."

The National Environment Council (CONAMA) has the powers to help Brazil's president formulate the national environmental policy, establish general rules for licensing activities, require impact studies of large projects, establish national standards for controlling vehicular pollution, and determine which companies should receive funds or other fiscal benefits from official financing institutions, which in Brazil provide the lifeblood of most medium-sized and large private businesses. (Control over access to official sources of credit is a potentially powerful tool.) CONAMA's membership consists of the Minister for Home Affairs (acting as president of CONAMA); representatives from fourteen other ministries; the head of the Special Secretariat for the Environment; one representative from each state where the government has defined one or more "critical polluted areas"; one representative from each of the country's three designated "problem regions"; the chair of the National Commerce, Industry, and Agriculture Associations (private); the chair of the Brazilian Sanitation Engineering Association; the chair of the Brazilian Nature Protection Foundation (private); and the chairs of two associations for environmental protection, chosen by the president.

CONAMA has not yet been installed, which reveals the federal government's lack of firmness toward these objectives. Unlike CONAMA, the Special Secretariat for the Environment (SEMA) has existed since 1973. Its powers are to monitor environmental changes and act to correct adverse effects, to help environmental preservation agencies use natural resources rationally, to assist in the setting of norms and standards (by other bodies or agencies) that protect human health and foster economic and social development, to enforce regulations and standards established by law (as well as help other agencies do so), and to promote technical environmental training. With the enactment of the Environment Act, SEMA's role as CONAMA's executive and technical arm has been stressed.

The Environment Act also states that the Ministry for Home Affairs is in charge of "coordinating the actions of all federal agencies whose activities involve the preservation of the environment or the rational use of the environmental resources." These agencies include the National Housing Bank (responsible for basic sanitation), the National Department for Water and Energy, the National Department for Sanitation Works, the Northeast Region Development Authority, and the São Francisco Valley Development Company. Also included are the National Nuclear Energy Committee, the National Oil Council, the National Scientific and Technological Council, the Brazilian Institute for Forest Development, and the National Department for Human Ecology and Environmental Health.

*The national environmental policy in practice.* As mentioned, in the last two decades the federal government of Brazil has played a much stronger role than the constitution provides for, thus curbing open conflicts between federal and state or local officials. For example, when in 1976 the Mayor of Contagem moved to shut down a big cement plant because of air pollution, the federal government enacted legislation that reserved exclusively to itself the right to ask industries to take pollution-control measures. It also ruled that shutting down an industry of "high interest to the national development and security" was exclusively a federal prerogative. Further, according to the Executive Decree that regulated this law, "in setting criteria, norms and standards . . . consideration shall be given . . . to the need not to unduly restrain the country's social and economic development."

By comparison to the position taken in 1976, the Brazilian Environment Act has been largely positive and makes environmental protection a matter of high interest for the country rather than "unavoidable evil." The federal government's role today may be summarized broadly as both coordinating and supervising state and local agencies so as to avoid excesses that could unduly harm other interests. Still, the federal government has claimed to itself the sole authority for licensing establishments located in "petrochemical or chloride-chemical industrial special development areas" and nuclear power establishments. It also reserves to itself the power to set standards for vehicle pollutant emissions. Similarly, only the federal government can shut down an establishment for more than fifteen days. (Only Brazil's president can shut down a plant for more than thirty days, and an establishment shut down by a state governor can appeal to the Minister for Home Affairs.)

Despite this federal strength, state and local governments enjoy a wide field of action. They set most standards, provided that the standards are not less restrictive than federal ones, and, when there are no federal standards, are free to set their own. In addition, states (or municipalities, in states where there is no agency organized for this activity) are licensing agents. Thus any new establishment must apply to the state (or local) pollution-control agency, and such agency has powers to grant or deny the license, though the courts could repeal a decision. State and local levels can also impose fines, within the limits set by federal law. (Many have argued that federal limits are too low, although in theory an industry could be fined indefinitely at the daily rate of up to $7,300.)

In several respects the new law reveals that divergences between Brazil's federal agencies with environmental responsibilities still exist. The text of the Environment Act is typical of Brazilian laws. It spells out the institutional structure—the agencies within the system, their composition, and their fields—in great detail, only to define the subject of the "control powers" nebulously.

Moreover, the technical criteria that should be applied to controls are vague. The law itself, enacted in 1981, is not a "self-enforcing law." Thus the executive must enact a decree, defining and detailing several of its items, before it goes into effect. This decree was only enacted in 1983, almost two years after the act passed. As noted, the National Environment Council (CONAMA) has not yet been installed, indicating the government is implementing the system with utmost caution and the efficiency of the system has not been tested. In view of the powers reserved to CONAMA, this delay has hampered action of pollution-control agencies. For instance, the council has not yet determined in which cases impact studies are required, nor has it set vehicle emissions standards.

As CONAMA is not installed, the powers of SEMA remain essentially unaltered and still very limited, partly because its original charter is not strong enough and its technical staff is too small. Until now, SEMA's achievements—far beyond what could be expected, considering such limitations—have been based on the personal prestige and dedication of its chairman. The question, of course, is whether a "one-man show" can survive over the long run.

As for the Ministry for Home Affairs' coordination of the activities of other federal agencies, it is more a formality than a practice—as the law intended.

One conclusion is that despite the elaborate structure of the Environment Act, federal government actions (and omissions) still show a strong preoccupation with the idea that environmental protection may hinder economic development.

*MNC's and the national environmental policy.* Nowhere in Brazil's environmental protection laws and decrees enacted during the past two decades is any mention made of the national or foreign ownership of an enterprise; much less is any distinction made between them. Accordingly all the officials interviewed during this research say that, in practice, no such distinction is ever drawn.

This is an important finding. It shows that there is no discrimination between foreign and local firms with respect to environmental regulations either in the legislation or in the practice. MNC's are held to the same standards, neither higher nor lower, than domestic firms, and the issue of discrimination treatment apparently does not arise, although, as noted below, MNC's are subject to closer public scrutiny. Environmental disputes between business and government are not unique to MNC's, but reflect issues that divide the business sector (foreign and domestic) from the government.

The Law of the State of São Paulo. São Paulo state's Environment Act was enacted in 1976, five years before the federal government's act. Consequently it is less comprehensive, and it focusses almost exclusively on pollution control. Nevertheless, the state act makes the state executive arm (the Environmental Sanitation Technology Company, or CETESB) Brazil's most effective environmental protection agency. Chartered as a state-owned company in 1973, CETESB is the direct descendant of a line of state pollution-control agencies, though its powers were initially restricted to water pollution matters. (In Brazil the three levels of government own or control many organizations chartered as private companies. CETESB was chartered as such, mainly to allow for a larger degree of administration flexibility, especially in regard to personnel management.) Later these powers were widened. Today they are defined by state legislation as the "control of the environment quality—water, air and soil—in the State, as well as the related research and services of scientific and technological character."

CETESB's powers cover the installation, construction, expansion, and operation of any pollution source—be it industrial, agricultural, or commercial establishments, equipment and machinery, or open-air combustion and self-propelled vehicles. The Brazilian Environment Act has confirmed most of these powers. Specifically, it has settled CETESB's role as the actual controlling agency for the state of São Paulo. Accordingly it is empowered to appraise projects and grant licenses, to check business sites, to impose fines and restrict activities, and (with the governor's approval) to shut down operations for up to fifteen days (more, if the order is renewed). CETESB's revenues come from licensing fees, the rendering of technical services to other Brazilian institutions, and state grants.

In Brazil local governments usually try to replicate federal institutional models. Thus, in 1983, São Paulo state government created its own Environment Protection Council. It is too early to know if this will have real impact.

Since local governments (which theoretically have the power to fight pollution) are loath to do anything to drive local industry from their territory, the state government has intervened in the industrial zoning of the São Paulo Metropolitan Area. It is involved in general industrial zoning for the whole area (based on federal legislation designating "critical polluted areas") and (through a second law) in designating "water supply protection areas." It is also regulating residential use in these zones.

The entity in charge of applying these zoning laws is the state's Department (Secretariat) for Metropolitan Affairs, which acts through another state-owned company, EMPLASA. All new industrial projects in the area, as well as all land developments in the "water supply protection areas," have to be submitted to EMPLASA before they can be licensed by the municipality.

In the state environmental protection legislation, an enterprise's ownership is not mentioned. Similarly, no distinction is made in municipal legislation. Thus, as at the federal level there is no evidence that MNC's are treated differently from local firms.

**Industrial Pollution and Control Activities in the State of São Paulo**

General Background. São Paulo is by far the most industrialized state in Brazil. Located in the southeastern part of the country, it occupies 248,600 square kilometers, which is only 2.9 percent of Brazil. In 1980 the state's population was 25 million, 11 million of whom were economically active (21 and 23 percent of the country's total population, respectively). These 25 million people generate approximately 49 percent of Brazil's industrial revenue. The state's per capita income is about $4,000 (1982), which is 1.7 times the national average. In 1980, from a total of 97,000 businesses in Brazil, the 46,000 located in São Paulo state employed more than 6 million workers, half the nation's workers who had fixed jobs.

Spanning nearly ten municipalities, including São Paulo (the state capital and most important city), is the greater São Paulo metropolitan area. With a population of more than 13 million in 1980, greater São Paulo covers 8,000 square kilometers. The area's population growth rate is 4 percent per year, compared to 2.5 percent annually for all Brazil indicating increasing concentration in São Paulo. The metropolitan area generates 65 percent of the state's industrial revenue and more than 30 percent of that of the nation. Per capita income is nearly 2.5 times the national average.

Approximately 25,000 business firms are established in greater São Paulo and together they employ more than 35 percent of the country's labor force. Multinational corporations have a substantial share in this business. Although data are not available for São Paulo, in Brazil as a whole 154 MNC's are among the 500 largest private companies (excluding banks and other financial companies) operating in the country, and they claimed gross sales of an estimated 45 percent of total national sales. (When government-owned companies were taken into account, the MNCs' share was still around 30 percent.)

Major Problems—Polluted Water and Polluted Air. Industrial concentration in the state has created critical water, air, and soil pollution, especially in greater São Paulo. Another city, Cubatão, is in an especially critical situation with respect to pollution, as explained below. Analyzing pollution is difficult, however, since there are few reliable data despite the remarkable improvements in control achieved in the last few years by the state environmental control agency. This data shortage notwithstanding, water pollution is the most extensive environmental problem in the state of São Paulo, and industry is a significant contributor. Most cities in the state lack the funds to collect sewage, and only a few of these treat it before releasing it into the rivers. Where present, industry uses municipal sewage facilities.

In the state's interior the problem is relatively mild since neither population nor industrial density is high. But some basins have serious problems. By far the worst case is the basin of the Paraíba do Sul. The Paraíba Valley, strategically located between Brazil's two most important cities, has attracted numerous industries including many MNC's, mainly as a spill-over from greater São Paulo. The federal government has declared Paraíba a "critical pollution area," and a special committee—which developed the first environmental-based industrial zoning model to be used in the country—is planning pollution control activities in the area.

Other areas also present difficult problems, especially those where agroindustry is concentrated. In the city of Cubatão, a serious mercury discharge into lake waters by a national petrochemical industry was detected a few years ago. Emission has been controlled, and research is now being done to establish the long-term effects on the environment.

The biggest water-pollution problem, however, is in greater São Paulo itself, where only 5 percent of all sewage generated is treated before being released to the rivers, lakes, and septic tanks. Because the waters of these rivers are used not only for domestic and industrial supply, but also for electric power generation, conflicts of interest among users have delayed the implementation of treatment systems. The sewage treatment and disposal master plan officially adopted up to 1974 provided for pumping all the discharges upstream in order not to disturb—in fact in order to benefit

—electric power generation. Since then there has been a great deal of debate, with no practical results.

Evaluations performed in 1978 for the sewage master plan showed that, for the whole area, industry was responsible for 44 percent of the biological oxygen demand (BOD) load discharged into local waters. In most waters, the capacity for self-purification had been far exceeded. In that year average BOD concentration for the urbanized area was estimated at 80 milligrams per liter. The most polluted river averaged 140 milligrams per liter, which is around half that of raw sewage. In 1978 the average dilution index was already very low—under 3.0—and decreasing. By 1985 it was estimated that the index would be around 1.5 and the average BOD concentration would reach 150 milligrams per liter.

Air pollution, the other critical problem, is visible to all in greater São Paulo. The concentration of particulate matter annually averaged up to 139 micrograms per cubic meter in 1982, compared with the safety limit of 80. In that year the maximum daily standard was exceeded sixty-five times on thirty-three different days. Once, the daily concentration reached 409 micrograms per cubic meter.

In 1982 total particulate emissions in greater São Paulo were estimated at 320 metric tons per day. Of these, stationary sources contributed 194 tons (61 percent), while vehicles were responsible for 69 tons (22 percent). Estimates for 1983 show a decrease for those figures as a result of control measures.

For sulfur dioxide the picture is not much better. The annual standard of 80 micrograms per cubic meter was far exceeded: 172 micrograms per cubic meter at one monitoring station. Daily concentration standards were exceeded ten times in 1982, with a maximum value as high as 639 micrograms per cubic meter.

Total emissions of sulfur dioxide amounted to an estimated 800 tons per day with 660 tons from industry. From these, 630 tons result from fuel burning. Vehicles contributed 145 tons per day.

Carbon monoxide concentration is also very high in the greater São Paulo atmosphere. In 1982 the monitoring station with the highest annual concentration read 11 parts per million. For reference, the maximum *daily* standard—9 parts per million—should not be exceeded more than once in a year. In fact, it was exceeded 256 times. Vehicles are the major source of carbon monoxide in this area, contributing more than 95 percent. By comparison the average carbon monoxide emission of gasoline-powered automobiles in Brazil is roughly five times the maximum level accepted in the United States in 1975.

Photochemical oxidants are also present in greater São Paulo's air. In 1981 the standard (maximum hourly average: 82 parts per million, not to be exceeded more than once a year) for these pollutants was exceeded ninety-three times, on forty-one days in the most polluted area. The maximum detected was 323 parts per million. Greater São Paulo's air quality is worse during the winter, when thermal inversions of several days are frequent.

Today, the most acute industrial pollution problems are in the city of Cubatão, some kilometers from São Paulo. There, a heavy industrial concentration has created a critical condition: the population suffers serious health problems as result of exposure to levels of pollution far above any acceptable standards. Operating in a relatively small area, twenty-three large industrial plants (plus dozens of smaller ones) are the major source of environment degradation. These include a steel plant, a paper plant, a rubber plant, several nonmetallic manufacturing plants and assorted chemical plants. Five of these plants are federally owned and four are owned by multinational corporations.

CETESB Activities. By late 1983 CETESB, the state pollution-control agency, had more than 2,000 employees, of which about 600 were university graduates, and 300 were intermediate-level technicians. Total operational revenue from fees and services was $12.5 million. Total operational expenses (including overhead) amounted to $12 million. When other items are considered, mainly the effect of foreign currency exchange rate variations on CETESB's sizable foreign debt, the agency's annual losses amount to $8.6 million. The difference was supplied by the state and by long-term loans.

One of CETESB's most efficient tools is the power to license the installation and operation of any new source of pollution in the state. A permit is needed to build or expand any nonresidential establishment. In case of large projects, CETESB usually asks to see a detailed engineering design before granting such an "installation permit." Disagreements frequently arise at this point since some companies argue that detailed designs may reveal industrial secrets.

Evaluation criteria at this stage depend on the location. If the area has been designated by CETESB as "saturated" with relation to a specific pollutant (based on established ambient standards), a permit will be granted only if emissions of that pollutant are anticipated as insignificant. Emissions for nonsaturated pollutants are allowed if they are within limits set according to the type of industrial process involved and the project will use the "best feasible technology available" for control. In addition, before the actual start of operations, the company must apply for an operating permit, which CETESB will grant only after it has checked the plant's compliance with conditions and requirements set forth on its installation permit. (For big units CETESB usually issues a ninety-day operating permit. Once that first period elapses, the unit will again be checked before final permit is granted.) In 1982 CETESB issued over 9,000 installation permits and 7,000 operation permits in the state.

The control of existing establishments is more complex. In general action is taken when CETESB receives complaints or when officials detect high pollutant emissions during routine inspections. For areas designated as saturated CETESB sets environmental quality standards in terms of individual maximum pollutant contents. When standards are exceeded CETESB then develops specific mathematical models to determine which reductions are required. Sources are ranked according to the effect on the ambient pollution of the reductions they can achieve. The first group, whose emissions sum up 80 percent of total, is assigned to class A. The second group belongs to class B. Remaining sources are included in class C, over which no action is taken unless CETESB receives complaints from neighbors. Action is taken starting with the unit whose control will represent the most improvement.

An important fact is that CETESB does not require an environmental impact assessment from the investor. Officials say that because federal law has not yet set all criteria for such assessments, legal problems could arise. It seems, however, that the agency's tradition is heavily biased towards the pollution-control approach.

The use of land zoning based on environmental protection modeling to control water pollution has been applied just once in the state, in the Paraíba Valley, with excellent results, and other basins are now under study.

In general CETESB sets standards for effluents based on the classification assigned to the receiving water body. Four classes are provided for by federal regulations, based on water quality objectives. These range from water suitable for domestic use without prior treatment (class 1) to water suitable for boating, some industrial uses, irrigation of nonfood crops, and other, less demanding uses (class 4). A set of standards is then established for the discharges allowed on the water bodies of each class. On class I water bodies, for instance, no discharge whatsoever is allowed.

In greater São Paulo all water bodies (or parts of them) located within the urbanized area are designated as class 4. The sewage collection and treatment system being constructed by the state government is designed to take care of all effluents generated, be they domestic or from business establishments. Standards are set to meet the capacity of that system.

In October of 1983 CETESB's survey of water bodies of the greater São Paulo area showed an estimated BOD potential load (that is, BOD load present if all industries were discharging their effluents with no treatment) of 92,000 kilograms per day, against an actual load of 54,000 kilograms per day. Among the firms discharging into these waters are a few MNC's, including Hoechst, SKOL, NEC, ASEA, ELCLOR, Philips, Lucas, and Levi Strauss. But many other MNC's that generate high volumes of pollutants (such as White Martins, Corning, Vulcan, again Philips, and Perkins) treat their effluents highly effectively and are classified on the class C portion of the ABC curve.

As for air pollution, programs are under way in greater São Paulo to reduce particulate matter and industrial emissions of sulfur dioxide. The particulate matter program covers 162 industries. Together they account for 97.5 percent of the area's total emissions. Fourteen of the 162 firms are multinationals that are together responsible for 6 percent of total emissions. Another 560 industries are being acted upon by CETESB in response to complaints made by neighbors.

CETESB's sulfur-dioxide control program lists 342 establishments. Together these firms discharged an estimated 132 tons per day in greater São Paulo's atmosphere as of October 1983 (22 percent below the total potential emissions of this group). The sulfur-dioxide control program is not as advanced as the particulate matter program. Only 46 establishments in this program are considered as controlled, while 122 have presented detailed plans to CETESB and 172 others are conducting studies on the polluting emissions.

In winter CETESB oversees a program known as Operation Winter, to counter episodes of air pollution caused by frequent thermal inversions. In Cubatão, CETESB is launching a three-year program to bring average pollutant concentrations to about half their current levels. Following the deadline for submitting control plans (July 1984), CETESB plans to take action against those industries that have not submitted plans. Meanwhile, CETESB is initiating eleven research projects (besides five already under way) to fine-tune the new control requirements.

A program to help Cubatão face episodes of winter pollution has also been implemented. Under this schedule, open-air waste burning and fire-fighting drills are strictly prohibited. Boiler and other equipment cleaning is restricted, as is the loading and unloading of phosphatic rock and other powdered materials. Any processing is closely regulated, and use of low-sulfur fuel oil and phosphatic rock with 1 to 1.5 percent moisture is mandatory.

To support its control programs, CETESB is extending and improving its environment quality monitoring. In greater São Paulo a network of forty-one stations (of which twenty-seven are automated) monitors particulate matter, sulfur dioxide, carbon monoxide, and photochemical oxidants in the air. In Cubatão air quality is monitored by two automated stations. And CETESB monitors water quality in São Paulo's more than eighty beaches and twenty-nine rivers.

CETESB also helps municipalities operate and maintain their water supply and sewage-treatment systems. CETESB's technical teams conduct extensive research programs. Recent major projects include the development of technology for reducing emissions in certain industries such as producing alcohol from sugar cane.

Some 2,500 people from public and private institutions attended training courses offered by CETESB in 1982. In addition to the World Health Organization, the Pan American Health Organization, and the United Nations Development Program, CETESB maintains permanent technical cooperation agreements with a dozen foreign environmental institutions. In 1982 CETESB used the services of thirty-seven foreign consultants and granted financial support to forty-one of its technical staff to attend courses abroad.

Efficiency of Control. The licensing system has proved highly effective in São Paulo. Expansion is also controlled by municipal building inspectors who will not grant permits in the absence of environment control licenses. Even expansion involving simple equipment installation or increased production will soon be monitored through the state value-added tax system. Conscious of these restraints, firms begin consulting with CETESB in the early stages of their projects. CETESB offers technical assistance and indicates alternate locations where regulations are less strict, even before a project is formally submitted. Not surprisingly, in view of close prior consultations, the number of formal applications rejected is low.

For existing businesses, the problem is more complex. Save for acute cases, CETESB will ask a company to submit a plan to reduce its pollutant emissions within a reasonable period, say ninety days. If the plant is large and emits several pollutants, the plan may demand multi-staged implementation. After the plan is approved the company is asked to prepare detailed designs, which CETESB also analyses. After approval a construction time schedule is agreed upon.

If a company does not answer or fails to comply with the conditions and deadlines, CETESB then has, at least in theory, several means of enforcement. First, it may fine the company. Fines range from 82,000 to 8.2 million cruzeiros (currently equivalent to U.S. $73 and $7,300, respectively). If pollution persists, fines may be imposed on a daily basis, amounting to as much as $220,000 a month. In 1982 CETESB exacted 771 fines in the state of São Paulo. CETESB may also request the state governor to halt operations of an establishment for a maximum period of fifteen days. Interruption longer than fifteen days must be approved by the Minister of Home Affairs. Only the president can authorize shut-downs exceeding thirty days.

Virtually all standards (both ambient and effluent) adopted in São Paulo are based on those of the U.S. Environmental Protection Agency. This fact has accelerated control implementation, but has also caused a number of pitfalls due to lack of experience on the part of local officials and consultants. In the case of the water-bodies quality classification system, for instance, problems arise when regulations do not impose a minimum distance from discharge to sample collecting points. Control of sulfur oxides in greater São Paulo's air is another case in point. Although CETESB has significantly reduced industrial emissions, until recently considered the main source of this pollutant, monitoring data show that sulfur content in the air has not decreased, and the program is undergoing reappraisal.

Pressure Group Activities. The authoritarian regime that prevailed until a few years ago in Brazil was not fertile ground for private groups to exert pressure over the establishment, partly because the press suffered periods of censorship. Today the move is toward liberalization and full recognition of civil rights. Community organization is nevertheless a slow process.

An exception is a group reclaiming the Billings Reservoir—a lake south of São Paulo that is today almost totally unusable because it contains so much sewage. The sewage could be released downstream if a hydropower plant near the shore did not require the water to be diverted through the lake. The group fighting for the Billings Reservoir revival has drawn attention to the problem, mobilizing the press, politicians, and officials, and has achieved some success. And in the city of Cubatão, community groups have formed and succeeded in attracting attention. These are exceptions, however. Generally, the public, government officials, and technicians are unaccustomed to such activity.

The Role of MNC's. Among the cases generating public debate in the state of São Paulo, few have involved MNC's. The two most widely publicized issues involve accidents rather than sustained pollution. The first occurred in 1976, when the Champion paper plant located in Mogi Guacu (roughly 100 miles from São Paulo), released thousands of tons of toxic liquid into a nearby river. The problem arose because the installation of a black liquor furnace had been delayed and waste black liquor was stored in ponds. heavy rains flooded the ponds and river, leading to release into the river. Most of the river life died and pressure against the company rose. CETESB merely admonished the company at the time. Subsequently the restoration of river life at the company's expense became an issue. Eventually Champion paid CETESB for a study on the restoration of river life. The study itself remains unfinished and plant and animal life in the river was never completely restored.

The second case involved AJI-NO-MO-TO, a Japanese food additive manufacturer located in Limeira, about 100 miles from São Paulo. CETESB denied the company's original request to use the river for waste disposal, but this decision was later overruled by the central office, which granted the company a "temporary permit." Soon after the plant began operations the domestic water treatment unit for the town of Americana, four miles downstream, started having problems. The concentration of ammonia in the water was so high that city authorities curtailed the water supply, creating an uproar against the company. Eventually CETESB withdrew the temporary license, and production was stopped for forty-five days. The company was compelled to build security tanks and install complementary equipment. Later the Americana District Attorney prosecuted four of the company managers, who were sentenced to prison (the same court decision that found the accused guilty also declared their crime not punishable, on the grounds that the time limitation set by law had already been exceeded).

Thanks to the recent legislation, the AJI-NO-MO-TO incident was the first

Brazilian case of criminal conviction as a result of industrial negligence toward the environment.

No evidence indicates that domestic companies are treated differently from foreign firms. However, when a foreign-controlled company has caused the pollution problem, the press and the public examine the situation more closely. Thus foreign-owned firms may be held to a higher standard in the public's mind, even if the legislation is nondiscriminatory.

Differences with respect to financing pollution control are also an issue. In 1978 the state of São Paulo government put forward a bill aimed at creating a revolving fund to finance anti-pollution projects, at subsidized rates, using money from the state and a World Bank loan. A group of (then) opposition party members objected on the grounds that MNC's would benefit from what amounted to state subsidies. But when the administration stated that multinationals would not have access to the fund, the opposition party found—as part of a political maneuver—other reasons to reject the proposition. Later the administration established the fund without congressional approval. The state's by-laws still do not allow foreign-controlled firms to become borrowers.

Agreements made in 1980 between the World Bank, the federal government, the state government, and several agencies allow a $58-million loan to be used for pollution-control projects. The loan is to be relent to private industry for pollution control at subsidized rates. But this project's industrial financing component has turned up few candidates for loans. The reasons cited for this poor performance include the Brazilian economic crisis; the delay of the greater São Paulo sewage treatment system (and the consequent postponement of more vigorous state action for water pollution control); the complexity of contractual and operational arrangements; a failure to appropriate federal funds; red tape; the fact that major industrial particulate matter sources are already under control; and constraints on loan applications for projects that "include a substantial change in the technological or production process" (which bans the substitution of oil-burning boilers for electric power production, a significant sulfur source).

The World Bank proposed to amend the agreement to allocate 28 percent of the loan to "general financing." The proposal would sacrifice pollution-control objectives on grounds that improving the Brazilian economy is a higher priority. Both the Brazilian and the state governments accepted this proposal, but it was later rejected at the World Bank's higher echelons. Although amendments have not yet been signed, the bank has permitted some changes, including the use of funds to finance boiler electric power and joint solid wastes treatment. One conclusion from this experience is that progress in industrial pollution abatement may be hostage to the general economic conditions. A second conclusion is that even cheap money may not always be enough inducement to industry for pollution control.

### Steps for Better Cooperation

This section identifies positive steps that MNC's and government might take to improve pollution-control management in their Brazilian operations. Several factors must be kept in mind.

São Paulo is already an industrialized area. Industrial pollution is not a disagreeable prospect but a present reality. Thus, action must be remedial as well as preventive. Also, pollution control is still in the early stages of development, even though progress since the first state agency was established two decades ago has been considerable. Between 1960 and 1975 the pioneer pollution-control agency in São Paulo was a joint committee comprised of delegates from three of the country's most industrialized municipalities and eleven of the area's largest industries. Among these, several MNC's were the major financial supporters of committee activities. When the state absorbed the committee in 1975 it dispensed with both municipal and industrial participants—a decision some observers regret today. Mutual collaboration and joint efforts by business and government can have a high payoff.

Allowing greater industry participation seems to be the most positive step governments can take in anti-pollution regulations. Industry's participation inevitably implies the participation of MNC's. Today although MNC's are not discriminated against by law as far as pollution control is concerned, their foreign ownership leaves them open to close scrutiny by national politicians and journalists. As a result MNC's tend to respond faster when asked to correct environmental problems.

In this connection, during the military government period, large state enterprises frequently resisted environmental controls. With the new political situation, pollution-control officials have detected a radical change in attitudes, and the prospects for effective environmental controls are better.

Also influencing MNCs' favorable response are internal corporate policies, protection-minded managers, and technical and financial capabilities. Somewhat surprisingly Brazil's pollution-control officials, both state and federal, frankly favor MNC's: "They have the know-how and the capital to control their effluents; moreover, they are usually conscious of their social responsibilities regarding the environment. They are also more responsive to government and public disapproval." Pollution officials recognize that bigger concerns are bound to provoke bigger accidents, but that big national companies have provoked serious accidents, too. In general, MNC's stick to their commitments, while nationals tend to "slide" on their agreed schedules and projects.

On the other hand numerous MNC plants in São Paulo are classified as "non-complying" with pollutant-emission standards set by CETESB. New pollution-control regulations were recently established in São Paulo, and many older plants were built before the standards existed. Many MNC's were loath to follow even the same standards they might face in their own countries, and many found themselves exceeding maximum emission levels once they replaced imported fuel oil with domestically produced high-sulfur content fuel. Since oil production, oil imports, and industrial distribution are government monopolies, it is almost impossible to burn the fuel oil presently available and comply with CETESB standards. Nevertheless, most MNC plants located in the state of São Paulo do not present special problems to pollution-control authorities that go beyond the general problem of compliance.

*Better Compliance.* These considerations lead all pollution-control officials interviewed to suggest that the most important action MNC's can take is to comply with pollution-control standards. National entrepreneurs frequently ask officials "why should we comply with standards if our American (or German, or French, or whatever) neighbors are not?" This rationale appeals to some politicians, so if MNC's were off the noncompliance list, CETESB would be rid of a big problem. MNC's can have a positive demonstration effect.

*Control of Vehicle Pollution.* Motor vehicles, all made by MNC's, are the major source of air pollution in greater São Paulo, and only the federal government can legally enact vehicle emissions standards. While a thorough analysis of every aspect of vehicle emissions regulation is beyond the scope of this chapter, it should be mentioned that São Paulo's pollution-control officials—both state and local—feel auto manufacturers could and should (in conjunction with local control agencies) try to tackle the problem. This is not being done.

Knowledge of Local Conditions. Another common complaint among officials is that newly arrived MNC's frequently have little knowledge of the country, its legislation, procedures, and habits. Often such firms apply experience acquired in other developing countries to Brazil, only to meet with poor results. To get a better feel for the local situation, new firms could get information from veteran companies. Thus it seems worthwhile to investigate how established companies could collaborate with newcomers, either directly or through associations such as Chambers of Commerce (which already provide information, albeit formal and superficial). This recommendation applies to all aspects of MNC activities, including environmental performance.

Permanent Channels of Communication. Brazilian environmental officials find it easier to confer with MNC's than with national companies. Not only are MNC managers more receptive to working out communications problems, but they also frequently have home-office support, either through permanent personnel or outside consultants. Indeed, maintaining a permanent corporate environment department as a counterpart to CETESB's technical body makes negotiations infinitely easier. This is true since most industrial pollution problems are not solved once and for all, especially in a developing region such as São Paulo, in which the environmental protection system is not yet completed and external conditions may change (as in the case of the sulfur content of the available fuel oil in São Paulo). The conclusion is that MNC's should maintain permanent environmental technicians and experts in the field as well as in the home office.

During the studies leading to the zoning of the Paraíba Valley, CETESB officials collaborated often with those companies—among them MNC's —that maintain permanent environmental personnel. Not only are technical discussions facilitated as knowledgeable people sit on the other side of the table, but also managers tend to be more receptive, having had contact with the internal environmental department. Education and training programs *within* the corporation are also valuable in promoting environmental responsibilities and minimizing emissions and accidents.

In the Cubatão area, where industries are the target of widespread antipathy, Union Carbide had been mentioned by CETESB officials as an outstanding example of good behavior, though whether this reputation changes after the tragedy at Bhopal remains to be seen. Besides keeping pollutant emissions well below legal limits, the company has developed an internal environmental program at all corporate levels. With the support of

CETESB and the State Industries Association, the idea of an internal environmental department is being introduced into other plants in the area.

Training and Research. In Brazil training and research are badly in need of technical and financial support. Unlike other countries Brazil has no tradition of the private sector directly supporting courses, students, or government agencies. As a result university staff and professors, as well as officials responsible for research, have reacted favorably to the prospect of additional support from MNC's. This support would be gladly accepted provided mechanisms exist (or are created) that could satisfactorily keep both institutions and individuals above suspicion of co-option by the industrial establishment. Mechanisms could easily be developed (for example, support for academic research in pollution engineering departments) and it is surprising that little has been done thus far in this area.

Community Involvement. Examples of community involvement in environmental protection among industries in the state of São Paulo cannot be identified. But public pressures do affect corporate actions. In the wake of the accident provoked by Champion, the company has developed some protection programs. In general corporate managers regret their own previous inaction, though they fear that community involvement may get out of control and become grounds for political exploitation. In one case of such inaction a large paper plant with a project in the state was forced to look for a location in a neighboring state due to public pressure. Similarly a plant that had been a severe lead polluter moved from greater São Paulo to the Paraíba Valley, there installing brand new and sophisticated equipment with emissions well within standards. With its project and installation approved by CETESB, community pressure is so high that the company is operating under the protection of a judicial mandate.

## Conclusions

The federal structure of Brazil has in some ways helped improve pollution control in São Paulo. When the federal government assigned a low priority to pollution control, the municipalities and, later, the states used their autonomous powers to improve conditions at the state level and to force the federal government to take action.

Today the federal government supports pollution abatement more strongly. Mixed feelings remain, however. For example, the federal Special Secretariat for the Environment (SEMA) badly needs strengthening. And the hesitation to tackle vehicle pollution shows a widely held view that pollution control works against economic development.

There is no evidence that other states in Brazil have weak anti-pollution regulations to attract industries that otherwise would be located in São Paulo. Other advantages seem to make up for any losses incurred by complying with pollution standards, since restrictions imposed in São Paulo have not driven MNC's away. At the federal level and in the state of São Paulo, no discrimination against foreign enterprises in pollution control has been detected.

São Paulo enjoyed remarkable collaboration between local government and private industries (including MNC's). This spirit of collaboration waned when the state government took over the control agency, but the time may be ripe for its revival.

MNC's, on the whole, have a better record than local and national firms in pollution abatement. Consequently pollution officials prefer to deal with MNC's. Notwithstanding this good record, state pollution officials resent the fact that auto manufacturers won't take responsibility for exhaust-emissions control.

The status of compliance of MNC's is very important for the effectiveness of pollution-control officials. Officials feel that a publicly known case of a noncomplying MNC may seriously affect the system's credibility. Newly arrived MNC's should strive to acquire knowledge of local conditions, including environmental policy, before dealing with the government. Corporations should maintain in the host country an organizational unit of pollution-control experts. Control officials believe this is one of the most important ways to improve communications.

Managers in general fear that community activities related to environmental protection may get out of control and exert political pressure. Technical and financial support from the private sector for training and research would be welcomed by universities and agencies. There are ways to avoid possible objections of conflicts of interest in the case of such support.

# V  Analysis and Lessons from
an Industrial Accident: Bhopal

The disaster in Bhopal, India, in 1984 has special features that set it apart
from many environmental problems. Most notably it was an accident, both
sudden and unanticipated. Many instances of pollution and environmental
deterioration—as for example from auto emission standards set at less
than 100 percent abatement—are anticipated and stem from decisions to
tolerate some decline in environmental quality. Also, environmental damages are often gradual and cumulative, as for example the hypothesized
effects of chlorofluorocarbons on the ozone layer. Indeed, the release of
methyl isocyanate gas at Bhopal is perhaps more typical of industrial accidents such as natural gas explosions or mine cave-ins than of most instances
of environmental damages.

Nevertheless other features of Bhopal tie it closely to this book's main
themes. A principal issue is *why* the explosion was unanticipated, a question that also occurs in some environmental problems. Thomas Gladwin,
in his case study, investigates the two cycles of management failures: by the
foreign investor, Union Carbide, and by the Indian government authorities.

So doing, he casts light on the broader question raised in this volume—the adequacy of corporate and government response to environmental concerns in the Third World. His analysis also returns us to other threads: the control of hazardous products (investigated by Goodman and by Scherr), the question of adapting MNC behavior to developing country conditions (examined by Castleman), and overlapping and sometimes conflicting host-country regulatory structures (described by Gillis, Goodman, Pimenta, and Ural).

Wil Lepkowski, in the final chapter, also identifies management and regulatory failures, but moves beyond the immediate circumstances of Bhopal to speculate on the larger questions of chemical industrialization and industrial safety throughout developing countries. He concludes that a "safety ethic" must be melded to the "efficiency ethic" that has already taken root among Third World industrial leaders.

## CHAPTER TEN  A Case Study of the Bhopal Tragedy

Thomas N. Gladwin

"The worst industrial accident in history" . . . "The seminal environmental event of the decade" . . . "The chemical industry's Three Mile Island" . . . The most "wretchedly undignified hideously helpless form of mega-death after Hiroshima and Nagasaki."[1] Each phrase has been used to describe the tragedy that occurred in the central Indian city of Bhopal during the early morning hours of December 3, 1984. That is when some forty tons of highly toxic, vaporized methyl isocyanate (MIC) escaped from a storage tank at a pesticide plant 50.9 percent owned by Union Carbide. The gas cloud enveloped half the city, killing more than 2,000 people (by some estimates more than 5,000) and injuring as many as 200,000, mainly causing lung and eye damage.[2] The tidal wave of human suffering stunned both India and the entire world. "Could it happen here?" many asked.

The Bhopal catastrophe variously triggered widespread "chemophobia" around the world, a proliferation of legislative proposals dealing with toxic air pollutants and community right-to-know rules, an almost total curtailment in the availability of liability insurance covering "sudden and accidental" pollution, and calls for international codes of conduct and safety assistance programs for developing nations. Union Carbide saw its stock plummet, its debt ratings were downgraded, and ownership was challenged by a hostile takeover bid by the GAF Corporation. These financial consequences could be traced to the accumulation of about 100 lawsuits filed against the company in the United States seeking more than $50 billion in damages (an additional 1,200 suits were filed against Union Carbide in India).[3] Beyond Union Carbide, the accident confronted the entire chemical industry worldwide with some of the most profound ethical, legal, social, and technical questions ever encountered.

The company, in a highly technical report on its own investigation of the disaster, asserted that the accident resulted from a large amount of water "inadvertently or deliberately" entering the storage tank (Union Carbide's attorney later asserted that the company had "all but ruled out everything but sabotage").[4] The accident occurred in the context of "a unique combination of unusual events," according to the report, and was traceable to numerous errors and violations by the Indian subsidiary. Union Carbide's top U.S. management also asserted that responsibility for plant safety rested entirely with Union Carbide India, Ltd., and that the parent company would not accept legal responsibility for the accident.[5]

The Indian government criticized the company's report for containing "unjustified and unacceptable" assertions and on April 8, 1985 filed suit against the parent Union Carbide Corporation in federal court in New York seeking an unspecified amount of compensatory damages on behalf of Bhopal victims, along with punitive damages "in an amount sufficient to deter Union Carbide and any other multinational corporation from the willful, malicious and wanton disregard of the rights and safety of the citizens of those countries in which they do business." Setting forth a novel legal theory of "multinational enterprise liability," the suit said that defendant Union Carbide was "primarily and absolutely liable for any and all damages" arising from the poison-gas leak because

> key management personnel of multinationals exercise a closely-held power which is neither restricted by national boundaries nor effectively controlled by international law. The complex corporate structure of the multinational, with networks of subsidiaries and divisions, makes it exceedingly difficult or even impossible to pinpoint responsibility for the damage caused by the enterprise to discrete corporate units or individuals. In reality, there is but one entity, the monolithic multinational, which is responsible for the design, development and dissemination of information and technology worldwide, acting through a forged network of interlocking directors, common operating systems, global distribution and marketing systems, financial and other controls. In this manner, the multinational carries out its global purpose through thousands of daily actions, by a multitude of employees and agents.

Persons harmed by the acts of a multinational corporation are not in a position to isolate which unit of the enterprise caused the harm, yet it is evident that the multinational enterprise that caused the harm is liable for such harm. The multinational must necessarily assume this responsibility, for it alone has the resources to discover and guard against hazards and to provide warnings of potential hazards. . . .[6]

During the fifteen months following the accident—while the medical and financial plight of the dependents and injured in Bhopal reportedly worsened (less than $75 million in emergency relief had made its way to the victims)—the primary focus of activity centered on dozens of investigations, consolidation of U.S. lawsuits, intensive pretrial maneuvering and discovery, and efforts to reach an out-of-court settlement.[7] Union Carbide's major legal aim during this period was to have all Bhopal-related claims filed against it in the U.S. dismissed on the ground of *forum non conveniens*, arguing that the plaintiffs, along with key witnesses, medical records, documents, standards, facilities, contractors, and such were all in India.[8] Damage awards to victims made by an Indian court would, by all consensus, be considerably lower than those made by an American one.

Out-of-court, Union Carbide in April 1985 proposed spending $240 million spread over a 30-year period (present value of the offer equal to about $100 million) in compensation, which the company considered to be double the maximum liability that Indian courts would levy based on research on the value of human life in India.[9] This initial offer was described as "ridiculously low" by an Indian government official, with knowledgeable sources saying privately that the government was seeking between $1 and $5 billion.[10] Nine months later, under the prodding of the U.S. federal judge in charge of the case prior to his deciding on the issue of forum, attorneys for Union Carbide and the government resumed active work on an out-of-court accord, with Union Carbide reportedly boosting its initial offer by some $50 to $100 million.[11] As of March 1986 (time of this writing) the revised offer had not been accepted by the government; most legal and financial analysts were projecting that an acceptable out-of-court settlement would need to fall in the $400 to $600 million range.[12] Otherwise the outlook was for a long and bitter litigation.

Although it will probably be some time before a truly definitive account emerges as to exactly why and how the gassing occurred, a tentative identification of lessons of the Bhopal disaster is possible. Based on a distillation of the results of various investigations that have been released,

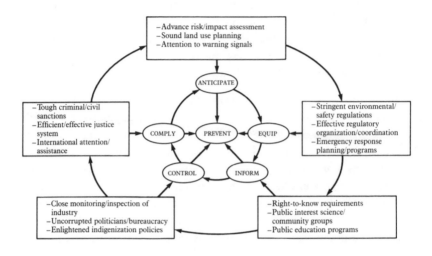

**Figure 10.1** Corporate and Public Policy Variables Bearing upon Accident Prevention

along with massive media coverage of the tragedy, the evidence indicates that, at all levels, both Union Carbide and the Indian government failed to ensure adequate environmental and industrial safety at Bhopal.[13] As shown in figure 10.1, an explanation of why the accident was not prevented can be traced to an interaction between two cycles of management failures, one corporate and the other governmental. On the inner ring, apparent failures by Union Carbide to adequately anticipate, equip, inform, control, and comply with standards can be pinpointed. This cycle of multinational corporate failure can be explained, in large measure, by a closely related cycle of governmental failure at work in the external setting in which Union Carbide operated. As will be hypothesized in this chapter, none of the government control or leverage points shown in the outer ring of figure 10.1 were working effectively to prevent accidents in the case of Bhopal. The public policy environment, in other words, may have worked to reduce both Union Carbide's motivation and its capacity to ensure adequate safety at the Bhopal location.[14]

## Corporate Failures

Failure to Anticipate. The available evidence bearing upon the question of whether Union Carbide failed to anticipate the potential risks and health/environmental consequences of its MIC operations at Bhopal is mixed. It appears, for example, that very little was known about the health effects of the chemical being produced, particularly with regard to the long-term effects on human health of large-scale exposures, which a company spokesman had to admit were "beyond our experience."[15] The issue of storing large quantities of MIC in huge tanks at Bhopal was apparently disputed within Union Carbide during the early 1970s, with local management reportedly arguing against it for both "economic and safety considerations."[16] A 1982 safety study of the plant uncovered problems that presented "serious potential for sizeable releases of toxic materials" in the phosgene/MIC unit and storage areas, "either due to equipment failure, operating problems or maintenance problems."[17] Union Carbide's manual on methyl isocyanate, issued in 1976, warned that it could "undergo a runaway reaction if contaminated."[18] In September of 1984 an internal report regarding the company's MIC unit in Institute, West Virginia, further warned that a "runaway reaction" in the tank containing the substance was possible if it were contaminated by water from a cooling system or catalytic materials from a flare system, and that it could have "catastrophic" consequences. Corrective actions were apparently taken at Institute, but the company never forwarded the warnings to engineers at the sister plant in Bhopal because "there was not reason to share," given differences in the cooling systems employed, according to a Union Carbide spokesman.[19]

Thus it appears that risks associated with large-scale storage, runaway chemical reactions, and toxic gas releases had been identified and specified, at least within the U.S. operations of Union Carbide. The failure of anticipation, therefore, may lie more with assessments of whether those risks could be effectively managed or mitigated. Consider the following list of factors operating in the Bhopal and Indian environment that may have augmented the probability of an accident or the severity of adverse consequence in the event of such an accident:

1. Encroachment of densely populated shantytowns composed of poor, illiterate people right near the boundary of the plant.
2. Absence of a highly educated pool of workers and high turnover among employees.

3. Weak enforcement of relatively lax health, safety, and environmental laws.

4. Nepotism and cozy ties between plant management and local politicians.

5. Import controls that could block or delay the procurement of key parts and equipment.

6. Absence of a deep commitment among workers to the importance of preventive maintenance.

7. Regulations mandating labor-intensive rather than capital-intensive operations, making safety dependent on proactive manual rather than passive mechanical actions.

8. Regulations requiring significant participation of local owners and partners whose regard for safety and environment protection could be different from that of the foreign enterprise.

9. Regulations constraining the firm's ability to lay off workers and close the plant if it became uneconomical.

10. Public transportation, communication, health, and safety systems that could inhibit proper emergency evacuation and relief efforts.

The point of the above list is that a hazardous chemical operation may be manageable in one location, but not so in another. What Union Carbide may have done was to site a hazardous operation in a rather hazard-prone environment, perhaps thus exponentially raising the probability of disaster. As one prominent Indian observer recently noted about the tragedy, "Western technology came to this country, but not the infrastructure for that technology."[20] The technological reach, in other words, may have exceeded the managerial, cultural, and institutional grasp.

A more ominous interpretation could be that the risks of both the technology and the environment were generally understood, and that the perceived interaction of these risks (conceptualized in terms of economic costs and benefits) was deemed *acceptable*, both on the part of the company and the government. Such would be consistent with the frequent admissions by Indian scientists and industrialists of gross complacency regarding human safety.[21] And as V. P. Gokhale, Chief Operating Officer of Union Carbide Ltd., told the *New York Times*, "There were no indications of problems. . . . [W]e had no reason to believe there were any grounds for such an accident."[22] Following from a brilliant new analysis of the generic problem by sociologist Charles Perrow, perhaps what happened in Bhopal was merely a "normal accident," that is, one that should have been expected given the

apparent widespread acceptance of living with a complex high-risk technological system that could operate and indeed "go out of control" in ways
beyond the comprehension of those who designed, managed, operated,
monitored, and chose to live next door to that system.[23]

*Failure to Equip.* No matter what the final judgments turn out to be regarding risk anticipation and perception, it appears from the efforts of investi-
gative reports that Union Carbide clearly failed to equip its workers, its
management, its community, and the plant itself at Bhopal with adequate
safety "software and hardware" commensurate with any rational assessment
of the objective risks involved. A seven-week inquiry by reporters of the *New
York Times*, for example, concluded that the disaster "resulted from operating errors, design flaws, maintenance failures, training deficiencies and
economy measures that endangered safety."[24] Similar conclusions were
reached in detailed reports issued, for example, by the Council of Scientific and Industrial Research (the Indian government's central research
organization) and the International Confederation of Free Trade Unions.[25]

In December 1984, after the accident, a Union Carbide spokesman at
headquarters stated that the company "regards safety as a top priority. We
take great steps to insure that the plants of our affiliates, as well as our own
plants, are properly equipped with safeguards and that employees are
properly trained."[26] Unfortunately, this statement does not mesh with testimony of workers at, and inspectors of, the Bhopal plant. The general
secretary of the union at the plant, along with other workers, for example,
reported that plant management had drastically reduced staffing levels at
the MIC unit, had cut back on training programs, had lowered the
qualifications required for supervisors, and had not induced much in the
way of safety-mindedness—"internal leaks never bothered us" is how one
employee put it.[27] The 1982 safety audit of the plant by U.S.-based Union
Carbide inspectors found that training comprised "rote memorization"
without "a basic understanding of the reasoning behind procedures" or
much in the way of "what if" thinking, that maintenance people had been
signing work permits they could not read, that there was a high turnover
rate, and that "personnel were being released for independent operation
without having gained sufficient understanding of safe operating procedures." As a result of such deficiencies, the report concluded that "the
plant represented either a higher potential for a serious accident or more
serious consequences if an accident should occur."[28] Union Carbide has
reported that most of the defects discovered in 1982 had supposedly been

put right by June of 1984, but no on-site inspection to confirm the corrections was ever carried out. Union activists have reported that not one of the recommendations of the American audit team was ever implemented.[29]

The most damning allegations of this "equip" hypothesis relate to the plant's hardware. Union Carbide's own investigation found that safety conditions were so poor at the time of the disaster that the plant "shouldn't have been operating."[30] The company's investigation had substantially confirmed earlier reports that at least five elaborate fail-safe systems designed to prevent or contain the type of gas leak that occurred all failed just when they were most needed. The magazine *India Today*, which conducted its own investigation, concluded, "had the systems been working, had the employees kept their wits about them and reacted the way they had been taught in emergency drills, most of the methyl isocyanate escaping into the air could have been rendered harmless."[31]

What explains this reported pattern of multiple system failures and neglect of safety, maintenance, and training? The role of lax worker, public, and governmental pressure will be explored later. But another painful hypothesis must also be raised here. Some of these lapses and inadequacies may have been consciously ordered or condoned by plant management as part of a cost-cutting program. The $31 million Bhopal plant had reportedly lost $7.5 million from 1978 to 1983; had lately been running at only 30 percent of capacity due to drought and competition-induced declines in demand for Union Carbide's pesticides in India; and with the approval of U.S. headquarters, was on the auction block and would perhaps soon be closed down.[32] As a former project engineer at the Bhopal plant told the *New York Times*, "the whole industrial culture of Union Carbide at Bhopal went down the drain. . . . The plant was losing money, and top management decided that saving money was more important than safety. Maintenance practices became poor, and things generally got sloppy. The plant didn't seem to have a future, and a lot of skilled people became depressed and left as a result."[33]

Failure to Inform. Given the above it is not hard to understand that Union Carbide also apparently failed to warn adequately its workers, the authorities, and its neighbors in Bhopal about the hazardous nature of MIC and its storage. Interviews with current and former plant employees indicate that most workers knew that the substance was dangerous, but not the extent of the danger. Because of rapid turnover and reduced training, most workers had "neither read nor understood" the company's technical manual for MIC.[34]

Many government officials at the local, state, and national levels in India have asserted that they were unaware of the risks. The Mayor of Bhopal has charged that the local Union Carbide management kept "everything secret."[35] Most government agencies, according to their own admissions, were unprepared to cope with the disaster. As noted by the chairman of the Central Water and Air Pollution Board, "we had no inkling of what kind of emergency steps should be taken" in such a situation.[36] No evidence has emerged that either the company or the local government had drawn up any contingency plans to handle a potential gas leak at the plant. And a shocking lack of coordination evidenced itself during the actual accident —the police superintendent was not informed, for example, and rescue workers didn't arrive on the scene until about four hours after the leak began. Many lives might have been saved if evacuation efforts had gotten under way during those critical early hours.

As for the community, almost all reports indicate that virtually no one in the shantytowns surrounding the plant fully understood the hazards posed by the plant. Neither the company nor the government had made an effort to educate the public as to what to do in the event of an emergency. Even during the accident there was no effective public warning of the disaster —the factory's emergency alarm evidently sounded two hours after the leak began but could not be differentiated from other sirens that sounded for a variety of reasons many times during a typical week. The extent of community ignorance is summed up by the fact that even a few days after the accident, many Bhopal residents still didn't understand what had hit them. As one of Mother Theresa's Missionaries of Charity put it at the time, "These are poor, illiterate people. They don't understand what happened. Many are still asking me to explain what came in the night and blinded them and killed their families."[37]

Failure to Control. Since the accident, there has been considerable self-serving self-exculpatory behavior that can be traced to what appear to have been woefully inadequate control systems in operation all the way down the chain of responsibility. For cost-cutting reasons, the amount of supervision had been reduced at the Bhopal plant. Whereas the MIC unit had reportedly in earlier years been staffed by a dozen operators, three supervisors, and one superintendent on each shift, at the time of the accident the number had been cut to six operators on each shift with one supervisor.[38] Going a bit further up the line, it should be noted that the head of Union Carbide India, Ltd. (UCIL) stated in an interview that the Bhopal plant was responsible for its own safety, with little in the way of outside scrutiny.[39] At its headquarters in Bombay, UCIL had only one safety officer, whose job was not that of monitoring the safety of the plants in India, but rather simply keeping the safety manuals supposedly to be used in those plants up-to-date. The senior management of UCIL was reportedly unfamiliar with pesticide plant processes—the production supervisor on duty at the Bhopal plant at the time of the accident had reportedly been transferred from a Union Carbide battery plant only a month earlier and "was not fully familiar with either operating or maintenance procedures [at Bhopal]."[40]

The most controversial question regarding control has centered on the relationship between the parent corporation in the United States and its 50.9 percent owned Indian affiliate. Although posturing for the sake of legal and public relations reasons has clouded the issue, most of the available evidence appears to indicate that although Union Carbide U.S.A. possessed the legal right—many say the obligation—to closely control matters of plant safety and environmental protection in its Indian operations, it essentially chose not to.

Evidence of the weak authority links between parent and subsidiary in regard to safety takes many forms. To many observers during the first two weeks after the accident, for example, it was clear that executives at Union Carbide headquarters had little substantive knowledge of what was really going on in India. No detailed knowledge of the safety standards, safety systems, or evacuation plans in existence at the Bhopal plant, or even blueprints of the facility, could apparently be found at Union Carbide headquarters. The Bhopal plant had gone totally indigenous after 1982 following the departure of the last American supervisor. Local management determined the frequency of safety audits, and the last "operational safety survey" conducted by parent auditors had been conducted thirty-one months before the accident. That survey had found ten "major" deficiencies, but Union Carbide has admitted that no safety experts from the parent company ever returned to Bhopal to follow up on the critical 1982 study.

All of this seems to reflect a pattern of "local adaptation," in which UCIL apparently was allowed to follow its own course, without much in the way of active and coherent headquarters intervention, monitoring, control, and sanctioning on matters of plant safety and environmental protection.[41] Warren M. Anderson, Union Carbide's chairman, conceded that "the appropriate people" at the company in the United States "should have known" about the problems at the Bhopal plant. He attributed their lack of knowledge to "broken lines of communication."[42] What headquarters knew or did not know emerged in 1985 and 1986 as the central issue in the Bhopal litigation.

Failure to Comply. Numerous reports have concluded that Union Carbide's operation at Bhopal failed to comply with important safety standards, particularly its own internal standards.[43] A senior Union Carbide spokesperson, in fact, recently said that the Indian subsidiary operation of that plant was "not in conformance with a whole series of operating procedures."[44]

It is now clear that the safety systems at the Bhopal plant differed from those at its sister plant in Institute, West Virginia. A few days after the disaster, Union Carbide headquarters issued a news release stating that the two facilities were "essentially the same" and that "safety precautions for working with MIC at both facilities are the same."[45] The company later retreated from this position.

Later investigations indicated that a computerized data-logging/early warning system to detect temperature and pressure irregularities had been installed at Institute, but not in Bhopal. There were fewer control instruments in general at the Bhopal plant, and different technologies were used in certain safety systems. Devices to clean and burn off escaping MIC at Institute were automatic. In Bhopal the devices were manually operated. According to Union Carbide's vice president for health and safety, a Bhopal-type accident "couldn't happen" at Institute, given its sophisticated safeguards.[46] Unfortunately, however, one did happen there on August 11, 1985, when a large plume of toxic aldicarb oxime (a compound that is combined with MIC to produce aldicarb, a pesticide ingredient) was accidentally released from the company's plant at which $5 million had recently been spent on safety improvements; the gas cloud injured 135 nearby residents and severely eroded Union Carbide's credibility.[47] As for Bhopal, one member of the Union Carbide team that had performed the 1982 operational safety survey at Bhopal admitted to the press that the safety systems of the Indian plant had not been "up to American standards. . . . [I]t is an entirely different set up. . . . [T]he demand is on the human out there."[48]

Is the tragedy, then, a case of a multinational company having a double standard on health and safety at home and abroad? The safety criteria established for Institute and Bhopal may have been identical on paper, but the extent to which they were actually enforced differed greatly. The "safety hardware" may have been functionally equivalent, but the "safety software" —worker training and skill and skill qualifications, safety and maintenance consciousness, contingency planning for emergencies—was obviously radically deficient at Bhopal.

### Governmental Failures

Union Carbide has been lauded in the United States as one of the most technically competent and safety-conscious companies in the industry. In India, too, its reputation for safety was among the best. Why the long list of apparently life-threatening design flaws, operating errors, defective systems, and managerial mistakes?

The major focus in this chapter so far has been on the internal Union Carbide setting, noting how failures to adequately anticipate, equip, inform, control, and comply may have directly or indirectly raised the probability of the disaster occurring. Various potential internal causes of those failures have also been pinpointed (for example, cost-cutting necessitated by financial losses, high turnover of workers, etc.). But this assessment goes only so far. To attempt a fuller explanation of the corporate failure cycle it is essential to turn to the external setting in which Union Carbide was operating. A quick tour of this (see figure 10.1) reveals that it was accident-facilitating in nature. The public policy environment, in other words, must bear partial responsibility for the tragedy.

Anticipation. Prime Minister Rajiv Gandhi has acknowledged that the disaster was "a result of planning in an uncontrolled manner."[49] The scrutiny given by Indian officials to the potential hazards of Union Carbide's pesticide production facility during the formal governmental approval process was reportedly "shallow and superficial"; the decision was primarily made on the basis of employment, foreign exchange, and industrial self-sufficiency.[50] The anticipation of hazards during plant operation was given short shrift by local and state politicians, who allowed a densely populated squatter's colony to be built right up against the plant.

The motivation of a firm to anticipate the risks and consequences of its operations is not likely to be fostered by a track record of regulatory/political inattention to warning signals. An attempt by a local official to get the pesticide plant moved beyond city limits in 1975 was apparently squelched by higher government officials.[51] At least three significant chemical and gas leaks, including one that killed a plant operator, occurred during 1982 and 1983.[52] A local journalist published articles at this time entitled "Save, please save this city," "Bhopal on the mouth of a volcano," and "If you don't understand, you will be wiped out."[53] All of this led a news bureau chief in Bhopal after the accident to conclude, "It is the bureaucrats who are responsible for all this."[54]

Equipment. The massive fail-safe failure described earlier becomes easier to understand when one acknowledges the very low standards of the Indian government's poorly financed and poorly staffed regulatory apparatus for health, safety, and environmental protection. It is not that India is without occupational health, safety, and environmental laws, but rather, according to an Industry Ministry official, "where things go wrong is in the implementation of the laws."[55] Union Carbide's Bhopal plant, in fact, had been granted an "environmental clearance certificate" by the state pollution-control board just a few weeks prior to the accident. The problem is that the certificate was granted on the basis of "terribly outdated" laws and procedures. As admitted by the Chief Minister of the state government, "Most of these rules were framed quite a long way back . . . they certainly need updating in view of new processes."[56] This is a telling statement, especially considering the pollution-control board possessed no instruments to measure air pollution, and no regulations or enforcement of any kind was in existence with regard to the storage of highly toxic substances. In sum, India does not appear to have worked out an environmental ethic applying to hazardous production processes. As indicated by the absence of automated safety systems at the plant and emergency response systems in the community, the reality of environmental safety, as Union Carbide probably perceived it, was that environmental safety in the setting of Bhopal was a discretionary "luxury good."

Information. A year after the accident, the newly appointed secretary of a beefed-up Environment Ministry in India declared, "If there is a lesson to learn [from Bhopal], it is when we buy black boxes, we must know the entire consequences."[57] The failure of Union Carbide to share fully information on the hazards of its pesticide operation with its own workers, with local officials, and with the general Bhopal community can probably be simply traced to the fact that the notion of "right-to-know" had not yet emerged as a popular notion or demand in India (nor in most other nations). The power balance in most developing nations is still such that workers and plant neighbors have not formally or informally acquired the right to know the risks to which they are being exposed. Environmental pressure groups and independent public interest science organizations are in a very early stage of their evolution in societies such as India. General public education on technology, health, and environment is likewise just beginning. As explained to the *New York Times* by Rashmi Mayur, a founder of the Urban Development Institute in India, "Three-quarters of the population of India doesn't know what ecology means and has no understanding of the concept of hazardous chemicals. There is no continuum of intelligence, as in the United States. There are only two layers: a thin veneer of highly skilled people at the top and hundreds of millions of people who don't have a basic understanding of industrialization at the bottom."[58]

Control. What motivation can there be to carefully control your own operation when virtually no one else is monitoring what you do or do not do? As the Director of the Delhi Science Forum summed it up, "inspection in India is a farce."[59] Factory inspectors in the state of Madhya Pradesh, in which Bhopal is located, (an area almost twice the size of Great Britain) numbered only fifteen, and this small group of poorly paid people had 8,000 plants to cover during 1984 in this largest state of the nation. And this had to be done without the benefit of such basics as department vehicles, telephones, chemical hazards training, or much in the way of status.[60]

It is not clear when the last in-depth government inspection of the Bhopal plant took place. The chief inspector of factories, however, stands accused of having renewed the Union Carbide factory license annually without considering earlier safety lapses. The secretary of the Indian National Trade Union Congress told the press that inspections of the plant by local officials were rather irregular and superficial, with the consequence that "complicity of government officers" in the tragedy is a distinct possibility.[61] The Indian press has also been full of allegations of corruption in the factory inspectorate, with the acceptance of payoffs in exchange for permits, licenses, and clearances apparently being a fairly standard practice.[62] Going beyond the inspectorate, other reports have noted a pattern of apparent cronyism between Union Carbide and the local political establishment, with some key posts going to relatives of local politicians.[63]

And an opposition political leader has called for a formal investigation into the possible role of nepotism in the Bhopal plant management.[64]

Along with lax monitoring, one must also examine the possibility that governmental regulations driven by nationalism may have reduced Union Carbide's motivation or capacity to ensure adequate environmental and industrial safety at its Bhopal plant, largely by diluting the degree of parent control and reducing the flow of relevant expertise into its affiliate. Union Carbide was reportedly required by Indian foreign investment laws to design, engineer, build, operate, and maintain its Bhopal plant with local labor, materials, equipment, and staff, unless it could prove to the authorities that needed resources were unavailable locally.

Union Carbide has asserted in court that Indian companies and officials had changed its design for the ill-fated pesticide plant "in innumerable ways" and that Indian government policies had barred the plant from using electronic safety equipment in favor of less sophisticated manual controls.[65] Others have noted that the very decision to manufacture MIC at Bhopal, rather than to continue importing and mixing it there, was forced by the government's self-sufficiency and technology transfer laws. Analyzing this and other decisions made about the Bhopal operation over the years led one observer to conclude, "at every phase of the Bhopal development, in every conceivable manner, national, state and local governments had given a green light to folly, irresponsibility and corruption. Incentives for safety, which ordinarily govern businesses in a free market, had been supplanted with the seductive carrots and the ominous sticks of industrial policy."[66]

At the time of the accident, the plant was totally managed by Indian nationals; the last U.S. technician had departed from the scene in 1982. When control over an affiliate is diluted (due to forced local participation requirements), and rewards from the activities of that affiliate are depressed, fewer resources are typically committed by the parent company. As recently noted in the *Wall Street Journal*, "intangible assets, such as proprietary technology, are less likely to be shared with a local partner, given the reduced flexibility of the venture and its limited responsiveness to the needs of the larger corporate structure. The multinational is less likely to fully include such a venture in its global information/expertise network in the presence of the 'free-riding' local partners. It is more likely to be held at arm's length."[67] It should be noted that the Indian government, via nationalized banks and insurance firms that were Union Carbide shareholders, owned approximately 23 percent of the Indian affiliate.[68]

Compliance. Before the accident the expected penalties associated with noncompliance perceived by Union Carbide managers may have been rather small. As one chief inspector of factories and boilers in India told the press, "the fines are so low that managements smilingly pay them and go back and commit the same offence."[69] Along with weak civil/criminal sanctions, it is not likely that local Union Carbide managers were very worried about negligence suits and liability laws in the preaccident Indian setting. The existing Indian legal system—involving long delays before trial, initial filing fees (where a claimant is often required to pay 10 percent of the sum requested in the suit), a paucity of tort precedent, no system of punitive damages, no arrangements for contingency fees to compensate lawyers out of money recovered, decisions coming an average 17.5 years after the events that led to litigation, and the susceptibility of district court officials to bribery—was surely seen as being strongly biased against effective adjudication of liability cases (the Indian government, in suing in America on behalf of Bhopal victims, admitted that a "just, speedy and equitable" resolution of claims was not possible in India).[70]

Even if plaintiffs did choose to traverse this long and difficult legal maze described above and they proved successful, damage awards would likely be tolerable for the defendant company in that they are based on expected lifetime earnings, and the frequently cited average annual income of residents near the Bhopal plant was below $200. Furthermore, given Union Carbide's estimated $200 million insurance policy covering pollution liability, these awards would be coming out of the coffers of about sixty insurance brokers led by Marsh & McLennon, Inc., the primary carrier, rather than the firm itself.[71] We should note that the Bhopal tragedy (along with record operating losses in the industry, mammoth jury awards and increasingly liberal U.S. court interpretations of liability) helped to induce an insurance crisis confronting hazard-intensive industries.[72] Following the accident, the supply of insurance for "sudden and accidental" pollution and "excess coverage" (that is, protection for companies in the event of major disasters) shrank dramatically. Given the emergence of a paranoid market regarding pollution liability, the short-term result was that an increasing number of firms in the chemical industry were forced to "go bare," that is, carry more and more of the risk themselves. Some firms, including Union Carbide, sought in 1985 to band together to form captive or mutual insurance companies to service their needs for excess liability policies, that is, coverage for claims exceeding $100 million.[73] As for the future, the prediction in 1986 was that markets would naturally adjust, with the supply of pollution-liability insurance increasing as companies gradually agreed to pay substantially higher premiums. The wrenching adjustments, of course, would force companies to either raise their returns (higher prices) and/or to reduce their risks (change their operations or product lines). The consensus was that hazard-prone chemical firms were likely to increasingly shy away from businesses with high risk (and thus high cost) exposures, both in terms of processes and locations. Such shifts were likely to be especially dramatic if the Bhopal suits ended up being adjudicated in the U.S. with notions of "multinational enterprise liability" being accepted into law.[74]

It must also be recalled that global "ambulance-chasing" on the part of plaintiffs' lawyers (typically pictured in editorial cartoons as a flock of legal vultures descending on Bhopal) had never been witnessed on such a scale before. As one of these American lawyers told the press, "If you hit them in the pocketbook, they will change . . . if you don't, they won't change."[75] Given limits on parent-company liability, barriers to piercing the "corporate veil," and other impediments to cross-border adjudication, it is unlikely that Union Carbide ever expected to be confronting the distinct possibility of having to litigate in U.S. courts damages for Indian deaths and injuries caused by its Bhopal operation.

"Out-of-sight, out-of-mind" is how the old saying goes. Along with traditionally being out-of-sight of home-nation lawyers, juries, and courts, it is important to also note that the hazardous operations of multinationals in developing nations, including Union Carbide's at Bhopal, have rarely attracted any significant international attention from the world's media, from environmental groups, from insurance underwriters, from home governments, or from international governmental organizations. No one else was carefully looking or meaningfully assisting; India and Union Carbide were very much alone in this tragic affair. This was recognized a half-year later at a Western summit meeting when the leaders of seven members of the Organization for Economic Cooperation and Development pledged that their countries "shall work with developing countries for the avoidance of environmental damage and disasters worldwide."[76]

# CHAPTER ELEVEN   The Disaster at Bhopal—Chemical Safety in the Third World

Wil Lepkowski

The disaster that befell the people of Bhopal the night of December 2–3, 1984, shows all signs of becoming a watershed event in the annals of Third World technology. That the event was bizarre and a profound shock to the developing countries is without question. That it generated agonizing self-examination by the global chemical industry is a matter of record. That the technocratic and legal wrangling over liability pushed into the background concern over the human impact of the tragedy is also, unfortunately, true.

Confusion, outrage, fear, and disbelief swept the world as news wires began carrying the details the next day. Well beyond the unofficial figure of 2,500 may have died; at least 150,000 were seriously injured, perhaps 40,000 permanently. There is no exact count. The medical effects, physicians widely believed, would linger for twenty to thirty years.

A further likelihood was development of birth defects among children born to pregnant women, and the possibility of genetic damage to the reproductive systems of everyone exposed. Long-term studies are needed to determine the latter, and these will be complicated. For a chemical so poisonous, surprisingly little was known about the detailed biochemical toxicology of methyl isocyanate (MIC)—its breakdown products in the body; the chemical paths by which the liver detoxifies it; its long-term effects on eyes, lungs, the reproductive system, and other organs. Moreover, few scientists could even conjecture what other chemical products were formed under the heat and pressures of the leak. These, including cyanide, are suspected by Indian scientists to have worsened the impact of the disaster.

The multinational corporations (MNC's) of the world will long remember Bhopal as they contemplate future investments in the developing countries. Liability risks for present and future investments are now a major concern in boardroom strategies.[1] Disaster insurance, long difficult to obtain for Third World operations, tightened even more after Bhopal.[2] Governments will insist on more guarantees of safety before granting licenses.

Major American chemical companies with plants in the Third World all displayed shock at the reported management failures and equipment flaws that prevailed at Bhopal before the accident occurred. The Monsantos, Dows, DuPonts all said that it was strict policy for their management to retain complete operating control of such plants and that they used technology at least the technological equal to counterpart factories at home.

In the view of multinationals, Union Carbide was an unfortunate exception to the way MNC's oversee their subsidiaries in the Third World. Union Carbide U.S.A. (UC-USA) regarded its affiliate, Union Carbide India, Ltd. (UCIL), almost as an autonomous, independent operation. Accordingly, UC-USA, in its report on the accident,[3] implied that the fault lay with UCIL by attributing the failures to management neglect. Complicating the issue was Carbide's suggestion that the immediate cause was likely "a deliberate act," further advancing the argument that the disaster was an Indian affair. Also at issue, and unresolved, is whether Indian restrictions or requirements concerning technology or technology transfer contributed to the disaster. The origin of process design and technology bears on the question of parent control, and thus the question of whether U.S. or Indian courts should settle claims for compensation.

Meanwhile, UCIL was itself accepting moral but denying legal guilt over the accident.[4] It maintained from the first that its plant was properly maintained and controlled. Its management considered itself by training and on its record as the equal to the best chemical operations anywhere in the world. Knitted within these assertions was the legal attempt, on the part of both Carbides, to convince judges that any trial should be held not in the United States but in India, where legal procedures are so slow that a sought for out-of-court settlement would be likely. A plea of innocence by UCIL, combined with evidence, if any, of sabotage, the reasoning went, would help assure such a venue.

The larger question Third World industry and governments face in the post-Bhopal years is whether the more profound issue—human, environmental, and economic development that does no harm—will be engaged. Labor critics and environmental and occupational health experts insist that multinational corporations exercise a less than ideal sense of patrimony toward workers and of parsimony toward the environment. They continue to assert that a double standard exists between safety and health practices in their home environments and their operations in the Third World.[5]

### Anatomy of an Industrial Calamity

The circumstances that contributed to the disaster deserve some review as a primer on the anatomy of a Third World industrial calamity.[6] The scene could just as well have been chemical operations around Jakarta, São Paulo, Cairo, Riyadh, or Lagos, where poor populations jam up against clusters of chemical operations.

Chemical plants in the ideal are technological orchestrations directed at converting molecules into other molecules under heat, cold, pressures, and vacuums, often by the ton. Valves, pipes, pumps, liquids, gases, and sensors all are automatically regulated and integrated so that reactions go as planned or, when they do not, are quickly detected and cut off immediately. In short, chemical plants are by all intellectual standards impressive contrivances.

All of them leak to some degree or other, but few ever run out of control as Bhopal's carbaryl pesticide plant did. And even that episode was unusual. For the accident did not involve part of the processing system. The plant wasn't making methyl isocyanate that night; it hadn't been for weeks. The accident involved a runaway, heat-building reaction of MIC in a storage tank.

No less than five failures of management and technology contributed to the disaster. The vent gas scrubber connected to the tank was apparently so overwhelmed by the force and volume of the discharge that it failed to work. Rusting had inactivated key components of the flare tower. The tank's refrigeration unit was long since shut down to conserve energy. A water curtain that was supposed to drench and dissolve the gas after such a leak failed to generate the pressure needed. The third tank, a spare, which was to have received any excess flow from the crucial tank, number 610, was already itself filled with methyl isocyanate. So the MIC, much of which was by then a hot gas, had no place to go but up through the unmaintained emergency system.

What added to the shock of Bhopal was that the entire community —from the shantytown dwellers living in proximity to the plant to officials in the city and the government of Madhya Pradesh state—was totally ignorant of key details of what the plant was producing and what to do in case of an acute emergency. Because the night was windless and the gas (or mixtures of several gases) merely crept through the city, the authorities had ample time to warn residents of impending danger. But curiously, plant officials had little information to give about the toxicity of MIC as a gas (under normal conditions it is a much less dangerous liquid), and the town itself had no evacuation plan in the event of such an emergency. So every reported response, from that of plant supervisors to the residents of Bhopal itself, was driven by panic. Ignorance and misinformation were not confined to the residents and officials of Bhopal and Madhya Pradesh. The plant's physician was, unbelievably, insisting for hours after the leak that MIC would have no long-term effects.

In accepting no legal blame for the disaster, UCIL officials insist that the Bhopal plant's technology was adequate to handle any emergency.[7] But they never really addressed the question of whether it was optimal. The distinction is important. Adequate means: (1) a technology that measures temperatures and pressures by gauges easily read by plant personnel; (2) a system that automatically cuts off a reaction when conditions run to an extreme; and (3) disaster prevention technology that keeps a unit from blowing up and gases from spreading outside the plant gates. Optimal is something more, something especially important in Third World industrial operations, with their reported high turnover of personnel who are only minimally trained in maintenance and operations. It implies the maximum use of automation processes so that safety does not depend on workers checking gauges and reporting abnormal readings to the control room by phone or on foot. It implies, in fact, control systems that are superior to those in countries already fully industrialized. In Bhopal the pressure in tank 610 was rising slowly, over many hours. But workers had no sense of any continuous pressure and temperature increase because these were not continuously recorded.

The MIC unit in Institute, West Virginia, had by contrast an automated monitoring and alarm system that has been upgraded since Bhopal. In these high-tech days, such a system is routine among chemical companies. But it is expensive. Union Carbide India engineers knew about it. UCIL management, working under India's mandate that technology be more labor- than capital-intensive, did not buy it.

So the controls in the Bhopal plant were considered "adequate." Except for the computerized monitoring of pressures, temperatures, and chemical concentrations, the safety systems were state-of-the-art, for India. The problem is that they were not maintained. And state inspectors, trained only as mechanical engineers, were not professionally qualified to detect chemical problems anyway.[8] Union Carbide U.S.A. would not force the subsidiary to be more vigilant. The answer as to why is not a technical issue; it is more a psychological and legal one. Why didn't Carbide U.S.A. insist on proper maintenance? Why didn't UCIL headquarters in Bombay keep a closer eye on safety problems in Bhopal? What barriers existed between the two companies that prevented better vigilance? Was Indian policy, which mandated the employment of indigenous labor-intensive technology in multinational enterprises, the real barrier?

What we have in Bhopal, then, is a precise case history of a Third World chemical disaster. What makes it an ideal object lesson is the fact that it occurred in a country that, while poor by conventional economic measurements, is nevertheless technologically sophisticated and on the brink, it believes, of technological takeoff under its young, technically educated Prime Minister, Rajiv Gandhi.[9] Other Third World countries, especially in Asia and Africa, can be expected to follow that model over time.

### Chemical Industrialization in Developing Countries

The process of "chemicalization" is proceeding quickly in the Third World. Latin America has a mature chemical industry. The Middle East has state-of-the-art petrochemical plants. The Republic of Korea, Singapore, and Taiwan already boast of plants technologically on a par with any in the West. All this implies, of course, a capably trained work force of engineers, managers, pipe fitters, electricians, and maintenance crews.

So the facts would suggest that the Third World is ready for the next step in industrialization: integration of the new electronic technology (commonly called "high tech") with traditional industries. The problem is that countries must start internalizing the value base needed for effective occupational safety policies: in short, values that assert lives are precious and that there are responsibilities and costs associated with producing toxic chemicals.[10] But not even in Latin America, with its Western cultural, religious, and technological tradition, has such a value base taken root. Clearly, the challenges are formidable.

No thought is being given to curtailing foreign investment. Because Third World countries know that growth comes from acquiring modern technology and adapting it to their needs, Bhopal, except for the disaster prevention factor, has had no discernible effect on their industrial development plans. More than ever, developing countries are welcoming investment by the multinational corporations.[11] Weeks after Bhopal, the chemical trade group of Tamil Nadu state in India issued a report cautioning officials not to react to the disaster by discouraging multinational investment in India.[12]

"This is a myopic view born out of ignorance of the history and growth of the chemical industry in the world," the group said in a post-Bhopal paper. "It must be remembered that it is the developing countries that invite the multinationals. Unlike East India Company days, they just cannot enter a country and carry on business as they like." The report did chastise the Indian government for looking the other way when facilities were built to produce under unsafe conditions chemicals deemed dangerous in the West: asbestos products, benzidine, DDT, polychlorinated biphenyls. And it deplored the licensing of mercury amalgam caustic soda plants when "safer and better technology has been available for some time."

Unfortunately there is no global inventory of occupational safety and health conditions around the developing world. But after Bhopal interest in doing one has naturally risen. The International Labour Organisation (ILO) reports that the rate of fatal industrial accidents is several times higher in developing countries than in the industrial world.[13] In half the twenty-four developing countries listed, the accident rate in 1983 was actually rising, because investment in occupational safety and health was inadequate. And while machinery in the North becomes safer to use, the ILO reported, the problems of technology transfer, poor maintenance, and inadequate safeguards have increased the hazards in the Third World.

The well-documented spectacle of Ciba-Geigy stationing children under an aerial pesticide spray operation in Egypt to test exposure levels is the insensitive image multinational industry labors under in the Third World.[14] This is one example of the double standard that industrial critics claimed MNC's practiced in their Third World operations. Simply and cynically put, if local laws put a low premium on human life, why should corporations not take the opportunity to maximize their profits by exploiting to save costs?

Episodes in Latin America further underscore the ethical dimension to the problem. The region began chemical industrialization as an appendage to American companies. Safety procedures today are advanced enough in Latin America so that there has not been anything like a Bhopal there. But needless slow-motion Bhopals keep occurring. In the cities around Rio de Janeiro's Guanabara Bay, according to a World Bank report, the regional environmental agency has found direct links between pollution in the bay and the area's extremely high infant mortality of 200 deaths per 1,000 live births.[15] Although some improvement has been reported around São Paulo, environmental conditions there are still dire. In Cubatão Valley, the air pollution is so severe that 40 of every 1,000 infants are stillborn and 40 die within a week of birth.

A 1982 study by the U.S. Embassy in Mexico said Mexico City residents, by inhaling city air, absorb the equivalent of forty cigarettes a day.[16] It said further that "United States air quality standards for sulfur dioxide, cadmium, zinc, copper, lead, iron, and particulate matter are repeatedly exceeded in Mexico City." But Bhopal did seem finally to persuade these countries that industry cannot be left to operate at the expense of public health and well-being. There are demands in Latin America that a clean environment be made a constitutionally based human right.

The overall goal after Bhopal is to bring the level of industrial safety in the Third World up to the standards set by society in the industrial world — a task that hardly stops at plant design. It involves worker training, the education of management, constant safety upgrading, emergency procedures, equipment standards, faithful inspection protocols, and community-wide warning and evacuation systems. And it is no surprise to any environmentalist or occupational health advocate that the industrial nations fall short of this ideal. One need think only of Seveso in Italy, site of a serious dioxin leak in 1976, or of Flixborough in England, where a chemical explosion took place in 1974, or indeed of the aldicarb oxime leak at Union Carbide in Institute, West Virginia, nine months after Bhopal.

Multinational manufacturing makes up only a small portion of Third World industrialization, however. No immediate figures are available but one suspects that the worst safety and environmental practices occur, all over the world, in government-run large factories or small, locally owned operations, such as fertilizer and pesticide mixing plants, foundries, ceramic kilns, cotton mills, scrap processing plants, and mines. Few of these are managed even indirectly by multinational companies.

Logic therefore dictates that industrialization in the Third World, in the wake of Bhopal, will demand a new and fuller perspective—that of safety, its ethical basis, and the industrial sociology that evolves out of it all. How Third World countries are going to import such a tradition is still problematical. But environmental and occupational safety and health issues are pressing that development. The solution obviously lies in training and education.

Two facts work in favor of Third World countries. One is that despite their vast cultural differences and immense swatches of poverty, their industrial layer is part of the single global "monoculture" of science, technology, and industry. Investment capital that drives the growth of technology flows through a uniform layer of professionals, whatever the nationality. Moreover, top engineering talent and management, often educated in the North, speak a single language. Efficiency is the byword. If efficiency has driven its roots so deeply there, so can safety, just as it has in industrial countries.

Second, enough technically trained people appear to exist in developing countries to form a strong work pool for a safe and healthy industrial environment. "In parts of West Asia and Africa, where there are indeed shortages [of technical people]," reports Indian journalist Dilip Mukerjee, "countries have faced no difficulty in harnessing skills from elsewhere in the Third World. This is strikingly evident in the Gulf States where thousands of well qualified and experienced personnel from India, Egypt, Pakistan, and the Philippines are currently employed."[17]

Thus many developing countries believe they have the technical wherewithal to care for themselves. But efficiency all too often is partly defined by the expendability of the individual worker in a region of labor surplus. What does not yet exist is a bridge between industrialist and environmentalist of the kind slowly materializing in the industrial countries, plus a sense that the quality of life of workers and the poor is a basic human right.

### A Reassessment of Industrial Risks in the Third World

Information on industrial safety reform is sparse during the first year after Bhopal. But from embassy commentary and press reports, indications are that countries are already tightening their occupational and environmental control laws and regulations to help prevent other Bhopals. For its part India is in the process of amending its Factories Act of 1948 to upgrade hazard prevention enforcement in its chemical industry. It is developing new regulations that would site new plants in zones permanently removed from populated areas. And its parliament has begun a lengthy assessment of the country's industrial safety and health problems. Politicians and governments know they are being held responsible for preventing industrial disasters in their countries. Third World countries can no longer claim helplessness before the policies and practices of multinational corporations. They have enough educated leaders, economists, and technical people to extract beneficial social and economic results from foreign investment. Moreover, given the examples of a $220 million World Bank loan to Brazil to reduce pollution in the Cubatão Valley near São Paulo, and International Finance Corporation industrial modernization projects, they have the international lending institutions to help them.

But until the necessary reforms take root, Third World countries will continue being seen as risks for corporations who establish operations there. After Bhopal it has become more obvious that developing countries are also risks to themselves as they industrialize. As B. Bowonder, Jeanne X. Kasperson, and Roger E. Kasperson point out:

> Host countries will need to institute licensing and regulatory structures that are sensitive to their own "risk-carrying capacities." They will need to stipulate more stringent requirements for highly toxic substances or for industries possessing potential for other catastrophic accidents. Such controls should emphasize the development of hazard data bases, which will need to be linked for easy communication and exchange of information. The Bhopal accident also highlights the need for more openness by both the host government and corporations in siting decisions, environmental impact assessments, accident injury reports, and basic information on hazards. India has no provision for public participation or public hearings, and most governmental and official documents are confidential. The "right to know" principle, if applied to India and other developing countries, would afford additional protection to workers and the public.[18]

Prescribing a post-Bhopal plan for developing countries from the comfortable vantage point of the North should be done cautiously. Their needs are complex, capital is in short supply, and industrial and environmental safety as a priority falls far behind basic economic requirements. Nigeria, to take one example of the difficult barriers in the way of viable development, has ambitious industrial plans. At present manufacturing makes up only 7 percent of the country's national income. Nigeria basically lacks not only a stable government but also the sort of infrastructure on which to base an economy as complex as one based on chemicals. Water supply is poor, power generation is unreliable, and rail and road transportation are still largely primitive. In short, though many factories produce there, Nigeria is not an industrial society, even though it is the most advanced black nation in Africa.

None of this is to say that countries such as Nigeria operate in an occupational safety and health vacuum. But it appears to be a climate that is unadapted to chemical safety. An ILO report on safety and health practices in multinational enterprises cites a Nigerian labor official remarking that Nigerian worker information on safety and health matters was limited usually to the need to wear protective clothing such as boots and gloves.[19] He believed that serious deficiencies exist in the workers' knowledge of the health effects resulting from exposure to hazardous substances. In general he considered that the multinational enterprises in Nigeria provided a much higher level of worker information regarding safety and health matters than the national firms. The multinationals were in fact depended on to set the standard for occupational safety and health in the country.

Nevertheless, visits by safety inspectors to multinational plants, according to the report, were "somewhat rare," indicating that the government regarded their safety and health performance as being "superior to those of most of the domestically owned enterprises." The ILO added: "There is thus a tendency for the inspectorate to direct their attention to the latter enterprises. The multinational enterprises were viewed as an important source of information for measures to protect the safety and health of workers." A continuing problem in Nigeria was in the training and retention of national inspectors: "Those achieving the highest levels of competence are typically recruited by industry with the offer of significantly better pay."[20]

The reassessment of industrial risks is not limited to authorities in the Third World. As mentioned earlier, liability insurance for major industrial disasters has become extremely expensive and difficult to obtain. The implication is that investment will be more expensive and less profitable, and on the margin some new investment may be discouraged. At the same time higher insurance premiums will help spur improvements in hazard protection technology and industrial safety management. MNC's may also seek some liability-limiting guarantees from host governments. On balance, though, the chemical industry will continue to expand, and MNC's will continue to invest as their resources remain attractive to host countries.

### Signs of Progress

The march toward reform received a boost in 1985 when the World Bank, largely in response to Bhopal, developed a set of hazard prevention guidelines that the bank's industrial loan officers must in the future apply as part of their system of planning funded projects. The guidelines were based on the "Seveso Guidelines" that the European Economic Community adopted soon after the accidental dioxin release in Italy.

The guidelines are essentially a step-by-step set of engineering and management procedures and processes that in the ideal would all but guarantee the safety of a plant and its surrounding area. Any recipient of World Bank industrial loans would be required to institute the safety procedures and design incorporated in the code. But again, its impact cannot be determined for several years. The key is whether the countries themselves can mount the enforcement laws and procedures required and whether the financial officers in the bank, in private banks, and in the countries themselves can agree that the safety and environmental aspects are worth the extra capital needed to follow the guidelines.

Steps were already being taken before Bhopal to establish voluntary codes for corporations. The United Nations has sets of such ethical principles relating to general social practices by multinational corporations. The philosophy would be extended to occupational safety matters as well. The United Nations Environment Programme had issued several studies on accident prevention in the Third World chemical industry. In a review of such studies UNEP's *Industry and Environment* summed up the issue in words that retain their timeliness even after Bhopal:

> Any accident prevention policy must have the full commitment of the management so that an effective accident prevention strategy is assured, and the work force must be fully involved through education and training. The role of governments and any regulatory agencies should be to provide an institutional framework including guidelines and incentives. International organizations also have a role to play in promoting the exchange of information and experience so that the lessons learned in one country are readily transferred to another, thus eliminat-

ing the situation in which individual enterprises can only learn from their own mistakes.[21]

Codes are important, but the key to improvements remains enforcement and the personnel, education, and facilities needed to begin that long trek toward a unified global occupational safety system. The training is available, mostly in the United States and Europe. But the engineering schools in those countries report—as safety officials have in Nigeria—that the most talented people seldom return to apply their expertise to their home countries. The professional environment is simply much better in the countries already industrialized. One question, then, is whether the financial aid and lending institutions are going to fund enough programs for the training of people in the field of industrial safety and whether the governments themselves will offer the inducements for students to return after their training.

There are signs also that universities are taking an interest in improving chemical process safety practices around the world. The University of Wisconsin has established a disaster management program with a focus especially on Third World countries and emphasis on worker training. Clark University and Carnegie-Mellon likewise are planning to adapt their programs in risk assessment and management to industrial plants in developing countries.

Public interest groups are also helping. In India the Delhi Science Forum in New Delhi and an educational group called Eklavya in Madhya Pradesh state have seized on the Bhopal disaster to educate the Indian public on the social and personal ramifications of chemical development. It was also hoped that Bhopal would spark the beginnings of a global labor/environmental coalition that would insist on high safety and environmental standards. Soon after Bhopal an information center was established at the Highlander Research and Education Center in New Market, Tennessee, to focus on the failure of Union Carbide and government groups in India to offer social and health benefits to the thousands of victims in Bhopal.

Among environmental groups the Natural Resources Defense Council launched a study of potentially dangerous plants around the world with hopes of developing policies that would protect workers and the public from industrial accidents. The project is being done with the International Organization of Consumers Unions. The study would determine how industrial procedures and equipment differ in the developing countries from those in the United States.

In safety technology the U.S. Agency for International Development (AID) had begun even before Bhopal a limited but systematic investigation of the level of safety technology and management at pesticide plants, beginning with a project in Egypt. The study included an assessment of the quality of worker and management training and the level of safety awareness among the workers. AID had also been supporting a project with the World Environmental Council, an industry-supported group in New York. This involves twenty American companies who contribute safety experts to countries planning to upgrade their environmental safety efforts. Two pilot projects, one a steel plant in Jordan and the other a cement plant in Tunisia, kicked off the project.

Whether or not the Bhopal tragedy goes to trial, the event is bound to have significant legal ramifications around the world. Legal scholar David Ott argues for a treaty that would bind all multinational corporations to adopt a set of principles for operating safely in Third World countries, involving control of operations and access to relevant information.[22] He believes that notions of national sovereignty and autonomy are no longer applicable in an era when economic borders virtually no longer exist.

The treaty would "establish an agreed international standard for determining what links with a court's jurisdiction would require that court to accept a suit. The treaty alternatively might emphasize the plaintiff's choice of jurisdiction by mandating acceptance of the suit unless the plaintiff's choice places an unreasonable burden on the defendant."

> All of these procedures would need in turn to be subject to government inspection, with mechanisms for compulsory improvement or sanctions for failure to meet the requirements. At the international level the treaty would make the state liable for harm resulting from inadequate enforcement, the state being obliged to provide detailed reports on its implementation of the treaty in the event of any incident giving rise to international claims.[23]

The ultimate guarantee that superior safety standards will be applied in chemical plants run by multinational corporations could well be through fear of liability costs. Third World industrial operations since Bhopal have virtually become uninsurable.[24] Until Bhopal corporations had scant interest in considering environmental and occupational liability around their operations. Now they must, or else future disaster could bankrupt them, as in the thousands of asbestos cases that threatened the viability of the Manville Corporation. The willingness of the public—and the legal profession—to take legal action against companies that misuse, misapply, or even misjudge their technologies is obviously rising.

### The Outlook for Safe Chemical Development

With these specifics of the Bhopal tragedy and the context in which it occurred in mind, it is possible to review some frequently asked questions concerning the implications and outlook for chemical development in the Third World.

*Are developing countries especially vulnerable to industrial accidents on the scale of Bhopal?* The impulse is to answer yes. Industrial safety and health practices in the developing countries are lax, in some countries technically trained workers are in short supply, and enforcement is inadequate. Still, an accident of the magnitude of Bhopal was unique: nothing like it had happened anywhere. If the potential for hazard has been so extreme in the developing countries, one has to ask why earlier Bhopals had not occurred. The question perhaps should be whether work around chemicals is more dangerous in the Third World. Unquestionably the answer is yes. These countries have a huge agenda before them if the slow deaths and injuries from exposure to toxic chemicals are to be reduced.

*Are standards of industrial safety lower in Third World countries?* Standards, which is to say ideals set down as declarations, are often on a par with those in the industrial countries. The practice is inferior for the reasons just mentioned. The safety infrastructure does not exist. The tradition of safety is not yet in place. And that can be seen as the failure of multinationals to set earlier examples of care for the human being in the workplace.

*What is the safety situation in Third World chemical plants run by multinational concerns?* From most accounts, good. But hazard prevention of the type laid down by the Seveso directive and the new World Bank guidelines is new even to the industrial countries. Improvement could come very quickly if the momentum after Bhopal persists.

*Who bears the major responsibility for plant safety—the corporation or the various government industrial safety bodies?* Both bear an equal responsibility —as they do in the industrial countries. But much more care and nurturing is needed to bring a sense of shared responsibility to Third World regulatory bodies and their industries.

*Are the management relationships between UC-USA and UCIL representative of the general pattern of joint venture arrangements between multinational corporations and local affiliates?* Apparently, no. UC-USA gave its affiliate much more autonomy than most multinationals do. Carbide has all but admitted its mistake and has put new monitoring and management procedures in place.

*Do environmental protection standards raise different issues from those of industrial safety?* They always have. The question is whether they should. Bhopal was a dramatic example of how the two areas ultimately intertwined. In the United States the Environmental Protection Agency is responsible for emissions that cause air and water pollution problems. The Occupational Safety and Health Administration regulates emissions within the plant gate. The plant gate is an artificial border between worker and community. Legally allowing corporations to expose their workers to higher levels of toxins than citizens can legally be exposed to under environmental laws is an archaic absurdity that the example of Bhopal could eventually eliminate.

*Will the experience of Bhopal change in any marked way the pattern of chemical development in the Third World?* It has, and it will. But the rapidity of needed changes is a huge unknown and each country will have to deal with the problem in its own way. Chemical development is a necessity for economic growth. One can question, as proponents of appropriate technology do, the social utility of intensive chemically based development, especially in agriculture. But the express train has long since begun its journey. It won't be stopped as long as the technology of health and safety can keep pace with the technology of what is known as progress.

# Guidelines for Growth

**Conference Statement***

The Challenges. Developing countries face serious environmental and resource management challenges. The problems arise from rapid economic growth and industrialization and, in some instances, from a vicious cycle of poverty, population pressures, and food demand that result in environmental degradation. These problems are serious, and developing countries have shown a willingness to find solutions to them.

The conflict between economic development and environmental quality has been exaggerated in the past. Many resources under stress are critical for long-term economic growth, and sound economic practice dictates that they be rationally managed. In some cases, such as in recycling and materials recovery, the same measure serves environmental and economic objectives. The concept that unites environmental and natural resource conservation and economic growth is "sustainable development." To realize this goal, many developing countries are establishing new environmental and natural resource management policies, and they are devoting considerable financial and human resources to the effort.

Multinational corporations (MNC's) play a critical role in many developing countries, supplying capital, technology, management skills, and markets. Directly and indirectly, they have considerable impact on the quality of the environment, on natural resource management and on health and safety in the workplace. They are well equipped to contribute positively and constructively to the wise use of these resources and to worker health and safety. As major

*The Conference Statement and Guidelines for Multinational Corporations and Host Countries emerged from an international conference on MNC's, environment, and development held in June 1984 and sponsored by the World Resources Institute. The Conference Statement reports areas of general agreement reached at the conference, but does not imply that each participant endorses every point. The views expressed are those of participants in their personal capacity and not necessarily those of the governments or the organizations with which they are associated.

repositories of data, expertise, and technology, MNC's can contribute to improved resource management and enhance their long-term cooperative relationships with host countries. Because of their position and resources, they can take a leadership role in many areas of environmental protection and management. The tasks are to find ways to avoid and minimize environmental conflicts and to encourage business to help make sustainable development a reality. A prime requirement is better communication on technical *and* policy issues between MNC's and host-country governments and non-government groups.

An anticipatory rather than a reactive strategy by governments reduces the need to rely on regulations, and it increases opportunities to use incentives and other economic instruments. Land-use planning is a good example of a means to anticipate environmental consequences. Anticipatory strategies, however, require government assessments of existing situations, including natural and environmental resource supply-and-demand projections. These assessments should be done by host governments, but with outside help where needed and invited. MNC's could play a positive role in this regard. A strengthening of a host country's capability to carry out assessments and resource surveys is in the interest of MNC's because it helps establish a rational base for durable policy, which, especially if it enjoys broad public support, strengthens the confidence of investors. It would also improve the image of MNC's in host countries.

Multinational corporations are sensitive to changes in the investment climate in developing countries, and many are responding to the increased concern for environmental and resource protection and management. Some multinational corporations, especially the larger firms, have internalized environmental concerns, established corporate environmental protection and management procedures and education programs, and have acted responsibly in their foreign activities whether or not required to do so by local authorities.

Steps for MNC's. MNC's that have taken these constructive steps should be encouraged, and their experiences studied and shared. Corporations that have not established effective environmental policies and procedures should do so, and should assign clear responsibility within the corporation to oversee execution. The emphasis should be on preventing environmental degradation and not on remedial action. MNC environmental responsibilities also extend to joint venture partners and subcontractors. Effective environmental procedures and education programs within the corporation are essential, as is full compliance with host-country regulations, including workplace health and safety standards. In countries with inadequate workplace protection regulations, MNC's have a special responsibility to protect their workers' health and safety.

Corporate environmental assessments for major projects should be prepared. They are useful to prevent environmental damage and to convey information to environmental officials in host countries, and they should be timely, comprehensive, and easily available to the public. Involving community groups in the planning for major investments also improves the investment climate and, thus, business conditions in the long term.

Voluntary guidelines or codes of conduct established at the industry level in specific sectors can influence less responsible firms to adhere to the industry's norm and can help improve relations with host countries. The International Chamber of Commerce has already published general environmental guidelines for private business. Industry-level associations can also play a valuable role in collecting and transmitting information on pollution abatement and resource management, and can influence counterpart business groups in developing countries. A more active role by industry associations, including self-regulation of hazardous exports and establishing industry standards for "good practices" in resource management, can reduce the need for governmental and intergovernmental regulations.

Strengthening the capacities of host countries for sound environmental management is of great importance. In this regard, multinational corporations should respond willingly to requests for technical information, data, and resource management expertise by host countries. Additional steps include supporting formal and informal training programs in pollution control and resource-management techniques, providing monitoring and testing equipment, conducting on-site corporate research directed toward solving local environmental problems, maintaining technical staffs in major foreign operations, and maintaining close contact with environmental, resource, and health officials, and with non-governmental organizations, in host countries.

*Steps for Developing Countries.* Developing-country governments that have not already done so should develop environmental protection and management policies, and infrastructure and incentive systems appropriate to their physical, economic, and social situation. Strong regulations, if fair and certain in their effect, are generally unlikely to discourage foreign investment that is in the long-run interest of the country. But delays, uncertainty, and unpredictable changes in environmental regulations do discourage investors, and should be avoided. Moreover, domestic firms (public and private) are often major polluters in many countries. Environmental regulations should be applied even-handedly to foreign and local firms alike.

Developing countries also need to improve their capabilities for environmental assessment and management so as to meet MNC's on a more equal footing and, more important, to establish policies that are consistent and stable because they are rational and enjoy popular support. Host countries should invite MNC's and other sources of expertise to assist in building local capabilities. The position of governmental environmental protection units relative to development, finance, and industry ministries should be strengthened, and they should be given additional financial and technical resources. Additionally, in some cases, inappropriate government economic policies inadvertently harm environmental objectives—as, for example, by underpricing water and energy. Such policies should be reviewed and changed. The use of "clean" technology, whether imported or domestic, should be encouraged. Enforcement of regulations and provision of consistent incentives are major challenges, and more attention and resources are needed.

Although MNC's are in a position to exercise leadership in many areas, they are also constrained, not least because they are more accustomed to responding to host-government requests. Therefore, developing-country governments should in many instances take the initiative to involve MNC's, and request the technical assistance the host countries deem most useful.

*Additional Steps for Home-Country Governments, International Organizations, and NGO's.* Both industrial-country governments and international organizations have resource management responsibilities, and both groups can play constructive roles. The program supported by the U.S. Agency for International Development and administered by the World Environment Center to involve U.S.-based MNC's in short-term technical assistance in pollution control in developing countries is a good example. The U.S. Export-Import Bank and the Overseas Private Investment Corporation, which help U.S. exporters and foreign direct investors, often in environmentally sensitive sectors, should be used as vehicles for improving environmental management, but should not require extension of U.S. standards to the foreign activities of U.S.-based MNC's. Counterpart trade and investment promotion agencies that deal with MNC's in other industrial countries should also have procedures for assessing the environmental effects of the projects they finance and insure.

The Organization for Economic Cooperation and Development, the United Nations Environment Programme, and the International Union for the Conservation of Nature's Development Center, and the U.N. Center on Transnational Corporations have capabilities with which to respond to governments needing assistance in strengthening natural resource assessment and management capacity. Guidelines or codes for the environmental activities of MNC's established at the international level by, for example, the OECD or the UN, can be useful if MNC's are adequately involved.

Conservation, environmental, and other citizen groups are a growing force for sound environmental and resource management in many developing countries, and deserve support and encouragement. Counterpart private organizations in industrial countries can assist them, as well as work directly with governments and MNC's on resolving critical environmental issues.

The responsibilities for achieving wise resource management must be shared. Working together, international business, governments and private organizations in developing countries, home-country governments, and international and conservation organizations can meet the Third World's environmental challenges, and a durable partnership can help turn sustainable development from a goal into the norm.

### Guidelines for Multinational Corporations and Host Countries*

Improving environmental management in developing countries takes the active commitment of both multinational companies and host governments. Progress can be accelerated if there is a parallel commitment by both parties.

What Multinational Companies Can Do to Improve Environmental Management in Developing Countries.

Multinational companies should:

– adhere to all host-government environmental and health laws and regulations;
– have an environmental policy statement or code of conduct, which should be firmly supported by corporate leadership, widely circulated inside the company, and publicized outside the company in the host country; and
– establish clearly defined responsibility for implementation of this policy or code of conduct.

Company policy in the host country should follow environmental principles that the corporation has established and follows in the home country. Any exceptions by subsidiaries should be agreed to by home-country management.

Every major project should have an environmental assessment, which should be made available to the public and to host-country governments in a timely manner. Guidelines and

*A synthesis of recommendations emerging from three working groups of the Conference.

standards should conform to host-country laws and company policy. Environmental and health effects audits should be conducted periodically during the life of the project.

Companies have a responsibility to inform host governments of any adverse environmental and health consequences of their operations when such information becomes available to the company. Without violating proprietary information, companies should also communicate, as appropriate, to customers, contractors, local communities, and the public such potential hazard information. Companies should be more active in assuring that critical information reaches those who need it in a timely manner.

Companies should respond in a positive manner to host-country requests for environmental and health information, technical data and training. This extends to a general strengthening of the host-country's capacity for sound environmental management, e.g., public education, collection of data, support of local academic and research activities, etc. The aim is to develop local capabilities to deal with environmental problems.

Every exporter of potentially hazardous materials has a responsibility to fully inform the importing country of appropriate information concerning the nature of the hazard, and to indicate whether the materials are banned or severely restricted in their country of origin. There should be timely and adequate notice given with appropriate labeling and requirements for safe use.

Companies that are engaged in joint ventures or that employ contractors and/or distributors should make a diligent good faith effort to assure that these parties conform to sound environmental and health practices.

The greatest opportunity for exercising creative leadership probably lies with sectoral level and general business organizations such as the International Chamber of Commerce, the Business Roundtable, the International Group of National Associations of Agrochemical Manufacturers, and others. Initiatives that can be undertaken by such groups include creation of sectoral codes of conduct, environmental assessment guidelines, and other means to transfer environmental management information to host governments.

What Developing Countries Can Do to Improve Environmental Management and Cooperation With Multinational Companies.

Host governments should:

–provide a stable and predictable business climate;
–establish a regulatory process that is fair, efficient, predictable and allows participation by all concerned parties; and
–enforce their environment and health regulations evenhandedly among multinationals, state enterprises, and domestic companies.

Host governments should strengthen their technical capabilities in order to determine appropriate health and environmental standards and to improve monitoring ability.

There should be clearly defined environmental and health responsibilities within the host-country government structure. This will allow companies to know which agencies to deal with and will assure that appropriate environmental and health agencies are fully involved in decisions.

Governments should request assistance from multinationals and international development assistance organizations to upgrade the level of environmental expertise.

All appropriate government agencies should actively participate along with companies in the development of environmental assessments. Governments should assure adequate and timely representation by other interested parties—local governments, non-governmental organizations, and the affected public.

Government agencies should upgrade their capability to adequately assess information concerning imported hazardous materials.

Governments should strengthen the position of environmental agencies in investment and development decisions and incorporate environmental considerations in development planning.

# Notes

### Chapter One

1. For a discussion of the relations between environmental quality and economic development, see Charles S. Pearson, *Down to Business: Multinational Corporations, The Environment and Development* (Washington, D.C.: World Resources Institute, 1985), chap. 2.

2. Robert D. Munro, "Twenty Years After Stockholm: Past Achievements and Future Issues," *Mazingira* 6, no. 1 (1982): 47.

3. "Turn to Pollute," *New York Times*, February 23, 1972.

4. See "Environment and Development: The Founex Report on Development and Environment," *International Conciliation*, January 1972.

5. See "Draft Report on the UNEP/UNCTAD Symposium on Patterns of Resource Use, Environment and Development Strategies: Cocoyoc, Mexico, October 1974" (UNEP Document GC (III)/Inf. 4, April 16, 1975) and "The Cocoyoc Declaration," *Bulletin of the Atomic Scientists*, March 1975, 8.

6. United Nations Environment Programme, "Ecodevelopment," UNEP Document/GC/80, Nairobi, January 15, 1976, 1.

7. See Mostafa K. Tolba, *Development Without Destruction* (Dublin: Tycooly International Publishing, 1982).

8. A. W. Clausen, "Sustainable Development: The Global Imperative," *Mazingira* 5, no. 4 (1981): 2–13.

9. Asit Biswas, "Sustainable Development," *Mazingira* 4, no. 1 (1980): 11.

10. Mostafa K. Tolba, "Profiting from the Environment," *Mazingira* 8, no. 1 (1984): 3; see also World Resources Institute, *The Global Possible*, The Statement and Action Agenda of an International Conference on Resources, Development and the New Century (Washington, D.C., 1984).

11. John H. Dunning, *International Production and the Multinational Enterprises* (London: George Allen and Unwin, 1981), 397.

12. H. Jeffrey Leonard and Christopher J. Duerksen, "Environmental Regulations and the Location of Industry: An International Perspective," paper presented at the Conservation Foundation Conference on the Role of Environmental and Land-Use Regulation in Industrial Siting, Washington, D.C., June 21, 1979, 23.

13. S. Lall, "Transnationals, Domestic Enterprises, and Industrial Structure in Host LDCs: A Survey," *Oxford Economic Papers*, July 30, 1978, 217–48.

14. Michael G. Royston, "Control by Multinational Corporations: The Environmental Case for Scenario 4," *Ambio* 8, no. 2/3 (1979): 84–89.

15. Thomas N. Gladwin and Ingo Walter, *Multinationals Under Fire: Lessons in the Management of Conflict* (New York: John Wiley, 1980).

16. Ingo Walter, *International Economics of Pollution* (London: Macmillan, 1975).

17. Ingo Walter, "Implications of Environmental Policies for the Trade Prospects of Developing Countries: Analysis Based on an UNCTAD Questionnaire," UN Conference on Trade and Development, Geneva, mimeograph, 1976, and U.S. Agency for International Development (AID), *Environmental and Natural Resource Management in Developing Countries: A Report to Congress*, vol. 1: Report (Washington, D.C., 1979).

18. World Environment Center, *World Environment Handbook* (New York: 1983).

19. Mostafa K. Tolba, "The Global Environment: Retrospect and Prospect," *Mazingira* 6, no. 2 (1982): 28.

20. G. K. Sammy, "Environmental Assessment in Developing Countries," Ph.D. Thesis, University of Oklahoma, 1982.

21. OECD Environment Committee, "Environmental Assessment and Development Assistance," ENV (84) 17, Paris, November 1984, Annex 4.

22. Pearson, *Down to Business*, chap. 3; Jeffrey Leonard and David Morell, "Emergence of Environmental Concern in Developing Countries: A Political Perspective," *Stanford Journal of International Law* 17 (1981): 281–313; OECD Environment Committee, "Environmental Assessment"; and International Institute for Environment and Development, for U.S. AID, *Legal, Regulatory, and Institutional Aspects of Environmental and Natural Resources Management in Developing Countries* (Washington, D.C.: National Park Service, 1981).

23. Maynard M. Hufschmidt et al., *Environment, Natural Systems, and Development: An Economic Valuation Guide* (Baltimore: The Johns Hopkins University Press, 1983), 6–7.

24. Pearson, *Down to Business*, chap. 3.

25. This section draws heavily on UN Centre on Transnational Corporations, *Environmental Aspects of the Activities of Transnational Corporations: A Survey* (New York: United Nations, 1985), 38–42.

26. Karl P. Sauvant, "Controlling Transnational Enterprises: A Review and Some Further Thoughts," in Karl P. Sauvant and Hajo Hasenpflug, eds., *The New International Economic Order* (Boulder, Colo.: Westview Press, 1977), 359.

27. C. Fred Bergsten, Thomas Horst, and Theodore H. Moran, *American Multinationals and American Interests* (Washington, D.C.: The Brookings Institution, 1978), 369–70.

28. Michael Z. Brooke and H. Lee Remmers, *The Strategy of Multinational Enterprise: Organization and Finance* (New York: American Elsevier, 1970), chap. 3.

29. See H. de Bodinat, "Influence in the Multinational Corporation: The Case of Manufacturing," D.B.A. Thesis, Graduate School of Business Administration, Harvard University, 1975.

30. Richard E. Caves, *Multinational Enterprise and Economic Analysis* (Cambridge: Cambridge University Press, 1982), 78.

31. This is the central conclusion of OECD, *Responsibility of Parent Companies for Their Subsidiaries* (Paris: 1980).

32. See Rice Odell, "Pollution Victims Rarely Get Compensated," *Business and Society Review*, Fall 1981: 23–28; OECD, *The Costs of Oil Spills* (Paris: 1982); and OECD, *Compensation for Pollution Damages* (Paris: 1981).

33. Thomas N. Gladwin and John G. Wells, "Environmental Policy and Multinational Corporate Strategy," in Ingo Walter, ed., *Studies in International Environmental Economics* (New York: John Wiley, 1976), 177–224.

34. Thomas N. Gladwin and Ingo Walter, "Multinational Enterprise, Social Responsiveness, and Pollution Control," *Journal of International Business Studies*, Fall-Winter 1976: 64.

35. See Thomas N. Gladwin and John G. Wells, "Multinational Corporations and Environmental Protection: Patterns of Organizational Adaptation," *International Studies of Management and Organization*, Spring-Summer 1976: 160–84.

36. This section is based on Gladwin and Walter, Multinational Enterprise, Social Responsiveness, and Pollution Control," 65–66.

37. "Managing Environment," *Chemical Week*, March 5, 1980: 32.

38. See John B. Elkington, *The Ecology of Tomorrow's World: Industry's Environment* (London: Associated Business Press, 1980).

39. See "Decentralizing Environmental Burdens," *Chemical Week*, March 3, 1982: 37–38.

40. Gladwin and Wells, "Multinational Corporations and Environmental Protection," 168 n. 5.

41. Thomas N. Gladwin, *Environment, Planning and the Multinational Corporation* (Greenwich, Conn.: JAI Press, 1977).

42. For a description of what an environmentally-oriented mode of planning entails, see Thomas N. Gladwin and Michael G. Royston, "An Environmentally-Oriented Mode of Industrial Project Planning," *Environmental Conservation*, Autumn, 1975: 189–98.

43. Gladwin, *Environment, Planning and the Multinational Corporation*, chaps. 10 and 11.

44. "Dow's Big Push for Product Safety," *Business Week*, April 12, 1973: 82–85, and "Product Stewardship: Responsibility Never Ends," *Chemical Week*, October 3, 1973: 45–46.

45. For general surveys of the hazardous-export issue, see Gladwin and Walter, *Multinationals Under Fire*, chap. 10; Committee on Government Operations, *Report on Export of Products Banned by US Regulatory Agencies* (Washington, D.C.: U.S. Government Printing Office, 1978); Robert J. Ledogar, *Hungry for Profits: US Food and Drug Multinationals in Latin America* (New York: IDOC/North America, 1975); Patrick B. Seferovich, "United States Export of Banned Products: Legal and Moral Implications," *Denver Journal of International Law and Policy* 10 (1981): 537–60; and Annie Street and James E. Zorn, "Toward Controlling the International Movement of Hazardous Products," *The Corporate Examiner*, July 1983: 3A–3D.

46. James Brady, "An Export Trade in Death," *Advertising Age*, May 15, 1978: 99; Mark Dowie, "The Corporate Crime of the Century," *Mother Jones*, November 1979: 23–49.

47. See David Weir and Mark Schapiro, *Circle of Poison: Pesticides and People in a Hungry World* (San Francisco: Institute for Food and Development Policy, 1981); "U.K. Agrochemical Firms Under Fire Over Hazardous Exports," *European Chemical News*, July 26, 1982: 17; David Weir and Mark Schapiro, "Pesticide Pollution Goes Multinational," *Business and Society Review*, Spring, 1980–81: 47–53; and David Bull, *A Growing Problem: Pesticides and the Third World Poor* (Oxford: Oxfam, 1982).

48. These concerns are spelled out and documented in Francine Schulberg, "Comment: United States Export of Products Banned for Domestic Use," *Harvard International Law Journal*, Spring 1979: 331–83; OECD Environment Directorate, "Information Exchange Related to Export of Hazardous Chemicals/Report on Current International Exchange Schemes," ENV/CHEM/CM/83.7, Paris, April 20, 1983; and A. Karim Ahmed and S. Jacob Scherr, "Poisons for Export," *Business and Society Review*, Winter 1981–82: 4–8.

49. For a general survey of the global hazardous-waste problem, see UNEP, *The State of the Environment 1983: Selected Topics* (Nairobi: 1983), chap. 2; see also "Europe's Plan for Coping with Toxic Waste," *Chemical Week*, March 21, 1983: 76–77. For some case examples, see "Hazardous Waste Dump?" *World Press Review*, May 1980: 16; "Dumping Ground Third World," *Environmental Policy and Law*, 1980: 96–97; Philip Shabecoff, "US Aroused by Industry Plans to Ship Toxic Wastes Overseas," *New York Times*, January 25, 1980; and K. Karim Ahmed and S. Jacob Scherr, "Do Unto Others," *The Amicus Journal*, Summer 1981: 39.

50. Gladwin and Wells, "Multinational Corporations and Environmental Protection," 168.

51. For example, Barry Castleman, "How We Export Dangerous Industries," *Business and Society Review*, Fall 1978: 7–14.

52. Royston, "Control by Multinational Corporations," 86.

53. Ibid., 89.

54. Michael G. Royston, "Making Pollution Prevention Pay," *The Harvard Business Review*, November-December 1980: 6–27; also Cynthia J. Duncan, ed., *Business and Environment: Some Case Studies* (New York: U.S. Council for International Business, 1982), 15.

55. Royston, "Making Pollution Prevention Pay," 12, and UN Centre on Transnational Corporations, *Transnational Corporations in World Development: Third Survey* (New York: United Nations, 1983), 224.

56. See Jeffrey Leonard, "Environmental Regulations, Multinational Corporations and Industrial Development in the 1980s," *Habitat International* 6, no. 3 (1982): 9.

57. Barry I. Castleman, "The Double Standard in Industrial Hazards," *International Journal of Health Services* 13, no. 1 (1983): 5–14.

58. International Labour Office, *Safety and Health Practices of Multinational Enterprises* (Geneva: 1984).

59. Ibid., 71.

60. Ibid., 58–59.

61. Ibid., 72.

62. Ibid., 33.

63. This framework is presented in full in Gladwin and Walter, *Multinationals Under Fire*, 565–72.

64. Ibid., 568.

65. See Thomas N. Gladwin, "Environmental Policy Trends Facing Multinationals," *California Management Review*, Winter 1977: 81–93.
66. See, for example, Eugene V. Coan, Julia N. Hillis, and Michael McCloskey, "Strategies for International Environmental Action: The Case for an Environmentally-Oriented Foreign Policy," *Natural Resources Journal*, January 1974: 87–102.
67. Discussion of these various measures can be found in David A. Kay and Eugene B. Skolnikoff, eds., *World Eco-Crisis: International Organizations in Response* (Madison: University of Wisconsin Press, 1972); David A. Kay and Harold K. Jacobsen, eds., *Environmental Protection: The International Dimension* (Totowa, N.J.: Allanheld, Osmun, 1983); James J. Barrow and D. M. Johnston, *The International Law of Pollution* (New York: Free Press, 1974); Oran R. Young, *Resource Management at the International Level* (New York: Nichols, 1977); OECD, *Instruments for Solving Transfrontier Pollution Problems* (Paris: OECD, 1973); Hans W. Baade, "Code of Conduct for Multinational Enterprises: An Introductory Survey," in Norbert Horn and E. R. Lanier, eds., *Legal Problems of Codes of Conduct for Multinational Enterprises*, vol. 1 (Frankfurt: Kluwer, 1980); Bo Johnson, "International Environmental Conventions," *Ambio* 5, no. 2 (1976): 55–65; OECD Environmental Directorate, "Information Exchange"; and Henri Smets, "Legal Principles Adopted by the OECD Council," *Environmental Policy and Law*, 1982: 110–16.
68. See "Environmental Aspects of Multinational Investment," in OECD, *Economic and Ecological Interdependence* (Paris: OECD, 1982).
69. Environment Committee—Group of Economic Experts, "Proposal for a Possible Chapter on Environment to be Included in the OECD Guidelines on Multinational Enterprises," ENV/ECO/85.1, Paris, OECD, January 28, 1985. The original 1976 guidelines can be found in OECD, *International Investment and Multinational Enterprises: Revised Edition* (Paris: 1979).
70. "British Appear Alone in Opposition to Draft Guidelines for Multinationals," *International Environment Reporter*, April 10, 1985: 124.
71. UN Commission on Transnational Corporations, *Report of the Special Session, 7–18 March and 9–21 May 1983*, Economic and Social Council, Official Records, 1983 (Supplement no. 7) (New York: United Nations, 1983), 19–20.
72. This research agenda draws on Thomas N. Gladwin, "Draft Workplan: Industry and Sustainable Development," prepared for the World Commission on Environment and Development, Geneva, March 4, 1985, and on UN Centre on Transnational Corporations, *Environmental Aspects of the Activities of Transnational Corporations*, chap. 6.

## Chapter Two

1. The participants in KE were the German metal processor, Metallgesellschaft AG (MG); the precious metal and chemical producer, DeGussa; the metal fabricator, Kabel Und Gutegoffnungschutte AG; and the industrial firm, Siemens AG.
2. Following Kennecott's withdrawal, the government assumed control of the exploration project and proposed several innovative technical ideas and geological interpretations.
3. Design criteria for Ok Tedi were based on a Mercalli 8 event, which is the equivalent of a Richter 6 rating and would be "very destructive to weak structures."
4. Although the social consequences of the mine were always a high priority, major social studies were not available during this immediate postfeasibility period.

5. Over the author's four years in PNG he briefed the cabinet fourteen times on Ok Tedi. At each briefing the questions of environmental damage and cultural impact were raised by various ministers.

6. The hydraulic equations were developed to study deposition in Bougainville's Jaba River.

7. "AMOCO Environmental Impact Assessment of Cyanide Effluents from Ok Tedi Project," paper presented to Ok Tedi Operating Committee, PNG, August 1980.

8. This conclusion follows from (a) the principles of financial discounting, in which future expenditures are less costly than present expenditures, and (b) the fact that using the total tax deductibility of costs as an operating expense would be more advantageous than a multiyear depreciation of a capital investment.

9. Behre Dolbear and Co., letter, November 27, 1979, 2.

10. The location of Ok Tedi in a sparsely settled, inhospitable area implies that even under the worst imaginable environmental catastrophe, compensation would be well within the capacity of the mining company without jeopardizing debt service or amortization. Nevertheless, the particular circumstance should not confuse the general point that unlimited environmental liability can affect the risk assessment of lenders. An example of this circumstance in an industrial nation is the limits and provisions for nuclear accidents liability in the United States, without which nuclear reactors could not be financed.

11. Everett and Associates, *Estimate of Geochemical Processes and Chemical Concentrations in the Fly River Drainage that May Result from Development of the Ok Tedi Project*, Consultant Report to PNG Department of Minerals and Energy, vol. 2, chap. 7, p. 2.

12. Historical records of $850 per troy ounce were reached in late January 1980 against a feasibility assumption of $350 per troy ounce.

13. Clause 3.3 Mining (Ok Tedi Agreement) Act of 1976, Approval of Proposals document.

14. Such a reopening clause was, in fact, incorporated in the agreement of the Bougainville mine, and the PNG government would have found it difficult to repudiate this precedent.

15. Mining (Ok Tedi Supplemental Agreement) Act 1980, clause 9.1.

16. Maunsell and Partners, *Ok Tedi Environmental Study*, Consultant Report to Ok Tedi Mining Ltd., vol. 2 (June 1982), 281–82.

17. Ibid., vol. 4, 140–41.

18. R. T. Jackson, C. A. Emerson, and R. Welsch, *The Impact of the Ok Tedi Project*, Consultant Report to PNG Government (July 1980).

19. *Post Courier*, January 16, 1984.

20. *The Times* (Papua New Guinea), February 9, 1984.

**Chapter Three**

1. Malcolm Gillis, "Episodes of Economic Growth in Indonesia," in A. C. Harberger, ed., *Problems in World Economic Growth* (San Francisco: Institute of Contemporary Studies, 1984).

2. World Bank, *World Development Report 1983* (Washington, D.C.: 1983), table 1 (appendix).

3. Gillis, "Episodes of Economic Growth in Indonesia."

4. Malcolm Gillis, "Foreign Investment in the Forest-Based Sector of the Asia-Pacific Region," prepared for the UN Food and Agriculture Organization, Rome, July 1981, 104–106.

5. Total taxes have been a smaller share of timber export values in Indonesia than in some other countries: between 1974 and 1979, taxes paid by the forest sector as a percent of reported export values were about half those for neighboring Sabah. Malcolm Gillis et al., "Foreign Investment in the Forest-Based Sector in Africa," prepared for the UN Food and Agriculture Organization, Rome, April 1983, chap. 4. Nevertheless, taxes as a percent of export value were higher in Indonesia than in any African country in the late 1970s. Gillis, "Foreign Investment in the Asia-Pacific Region," 107.

6. Gillis et al., "Foreign Investment in the Forest-Based Sector in Africa," 3–39.

7. Gillis, "Foreign Investment in the Asia-Pacific Region," 86.

8. J. S. Bechtel et al., "The Role of U.S. Multinational Corporations in Commercial Forestry Operations in the Tropics," submitted to the U.S. Department of State, Washington, D.C., March 1982, 261.

9. Gillis, "Foreign Investment in the Asia-Pacific Region," 44–47.

10. Team Kaju, *LAPORAN* (Jakarta: August 1980), 1–14.

11. Technical versions may be found in Peter Ashton, "The Biological Significance of Complexity in Lowland Tropical Rain Forest," *Journal of Indian Botanical Society* 50A (1972): 530–37; and in Office of Technology Assessment, *Technologies to Sustain Tropical Forest Resources* (Washington, D.C.: U.S. Government Printing Office, 1984).

12. Bayard Webster, "Devastated Forest Offers a Rare View of Rebirth," *New York Times*, April 24, 1984.

13. Confidential assessments by a German team of forest experts, December 12, 1983.

14. Mark Leighton and Nengah Wirawan, "Catastrophic Drought and Fire in Bornean Tropical Rain Forest Associated with the 1982–83 ENSO Event" (Cambridge, Mass., Harvard University, unpublished MS, January 6, 1985).

15. Quoted in Office of Technology Assessment, *Tropical Forest Resources*, 267.

16. Ashton (1980) avers that the East Kalimantan forest may also contain 3,500 tree species, versus a total of 700 in North America.

17. Kartawinata Kuswata, "East Kalimantan: A Comment," *Bulletin of Indonesian Economic Studies* (November 1980): 120–21.

18. The figures in table 3.6 understate the relative role of foreign firms in the Indonesian timber sector. A large but unknowable share of what is recorded as domestic investment in forestry in reality has its origins in other Asian countries, particularly Singapore and Hong Kong. Also, many domestic firms with forest concession rights have contracted with foreign enterprises for logging operations without the knowledge or prior approval of the Forestry Department. One recent study concludes that fully 100 domestic firms with forestry concession rights (one-fourth of the total of domestic firms in timber) have placed foreign contractors in complete charge of their operations. Office of Technology Assessment, *Tropical Forest Resources*, 267.

19. Biro Pusat Statistik, *Statistik Indonesia 1982* (Jakarta: 1983), 248.

20. Timber royalties vary according to species and grade, but in recent years have averaged about 7.5 percent of the f.o.b. export value of "meranti" logs, which account for about 60 percent of the annual harvest. License fees or area taxes on concessions are $1.60 per hectare.

21. P. T. Data-Consult, *A Comprehensive Report on the Indonesian Plywood Industry* (Jakarta: April 1983), 10–23.

22. "Indonesian Timber Companies Cry Foul," *Wall Street Journal*, April 11, 1984. This article places job loss in the forest-based sector at 50,000, but this is clearly overstated.

23. Robert Conrad and Malcolm Gillis, "The Indonesian Tax Reform of 1983," Harvard Institute for International Development, Cambridge, Massachusetts, January 1984, 3–7.

24. Gillis, "Foreign Investment in the Asia-Pacific Region," chap. 4.

25. See Kuswata, "East Kalimantan"; Office of Technology Assessment, *Tropical Forest Resources*; Malcolm Gillis, "Fiscal and Financial Issues in Tropical Hardwood Concessions," Harvard Institute for International Development, Cambridge, Massachusetts, December 1980; Gillis, "Foreign Investment in the Asia-Pacific Region."

26. Bechtel et al., "Role of U.S. Multinational Corporations," 61.

27. Kenneth Davey, *Central Local Financial Relations* (Jakarta: Ministry of Finance, 1980); Gillis, "Foreign Investment in the Asia-Pacific Region."

28. Gillis, "Foreign Investment in the Asia-Pacific Region," 120–25.

29. Ibid., chaps. 2–3.

30. U.S. Interagency Task Force, *The World's Tropical Forests: A Policy, Strategy and Program for the United States* (Washington, D.C.: U.S. Department of State, 1980), 24.

31. Bechtel et al., "Role of U.S. Multinational Corporations," 259.

32. U.S. Interagency Task Force, *The World's Tropical Forests*, 18.

33. Bechtel et al., "Role of U.S. Multinational Corporations," 263.

34. BKPM, *Almanac of Investment*, 38.

35. U.S. Interagency Task Force, *The World's Tropical Forests*, 24.

## Chapter Four

1. See Victor M. Goneaga B., "La industria de plaguicidas en el panorama nacional," 22nd Annual Assembly of the Asociacion Mexicana de la Industria de Plaguicidas y Fertilizantes, Ixtapa, Zihuatanejo, November 23, 1984.

2. For a statement of the critical viewpoints see Lilia Albert et al., "Informe preliminar sobre el uso de plaguicidas sinteticas en Mexico y sus efectos en la salud y en el ambient," Mexico City, February 23, 1984.

3. For a comprehensive discussion of integrated pest management, see Dale G. Bottrell, *Integrated Pest Management* (Washington, D.C.: U.S. Government Printing Office, 1979).

4. Goneaga, op. cit.

5. See Louis W. Goodman, et al., "Mexican Agriculture: Rural Crisis and Policy Response," Working Paper No. 168, Woodrow Wilson International Center for Scholars, Washington, D.C., July 1985.

6. Laurie Becklund and Ronald Taylor, "Pesticide Use in Mexico—A Grim Harvest," *Los Angeles Times*, April 27, 1980.

7. A recent summary of her research appears in J. Miyamoto et al., IUPAC *Pesticide Chemistry: Human Welfare and the Environment* (New York: Pergamon Press, 1983), 153–58.

8. Ibid., 158.

9. Lilia Albert et al., *Biotica* (in press), cited in Lilia A. Albert, "Pesticide Residues in Food in Mexico," in Miyamoto et al., IUPAC *Pesticide Chemistry*.

10. Lilia Albert, P. Vega, and A. Portales, "OP Residues in Human Milk Samples from

Comarca Lagunera, Mexico, 1976," *Pesticides Monthly Journal*, December 1981.

11.  Lilia Albert, Mirtha Martinez, and Maria Eugenia Gonzales, "Residuos de insecticidas OP en algunos alimentos mexicanos," *Revista Quimica Mexicana* 23 (1979): 189–97.

12.  Lilia Albert and Felipe Mendez, "OC Pesticide Residues in Human Adipose Tissue in Mexico: Results of a Preliminary Study in Three Mexican Cities," *Archives of Environmental Health*, September 1980, 262–69.

13.  *Excelsior*, February 28, 1983.

14.  Reported in Asesores del C. Presidente, "Sistema Alimentario Mexicano: medidias operativas agropecuarios y pesqueras, estrategia de comercializacion, transformacion, distribucion y consumo de los productos de la canasta basica recomendable," Mexico, unpublished, 1980.

15.  Georgeanne Chapin and Robert Wasserstrom, "Agricultural Production and Malaria Resurgence in Central America and India," *Nature*, September 17, 1981, 181–85.

16.  For a summary discussion of literature on the evolution of pesticide resistance, see Bottrell, *Integrated Pest Management*, 9–12.

17.  Data for 1979 provided by the United Nations Centre on Transnational Corporations.

18.  Data in this section have been provided by the Office of Planning of FERTIMEX and the Asociacion Mexicana de la Industria de Plaguicidas y Fertilizantes.

19.  *Dallas Morning News*, February 15, 1981, 18, as reported by Howard G. Applegate and C. Richard Bath in "Hazardous and Toxic Substances in U.S.-Mexico Relations," *Texas Business Review*, Sept.–Oct. 1983, 233.

20.  Applegate and Bath, "Hazardous and Toxic Substances," 232, reporting on Senate Subcommittee on Foreign Agricultural Forestry, *Inspection Standards of Vegetable Imports*, 95th Congress, 2nd Session, May 25, 1978, 69, 79–82.

21.  General Accounting Office, "Better Regulation of Pesticide Exports and Pesticide Residues in Imported Foods is Essential," CED-79-43, June 22, 1979.

22.  Applegate and Bath, "Hazardous and Toxic Substances," 232–33; Donald R. Clark, Jr., "DDT Hot Spots in New Mexico and Arizona," Patuxent Wildlife Research Center, Patuxent, Md., 1982, unpublished.

### Chapter Five

1.  For convenience, the discussion is in terms of pollution abatement standards, but the analysis can be extended to other environmental protection measures such as land reclamation of surface mines or reforestation.

2.  In economic terms this requires equal marginal abatement costs among different pollution sources. In theory this could be accomplished by a pollution tax. Such taxes have not been widely used in the United States.

3.  Goodman, in chapter 4 in this volume, notes allegations that enforcement of U.S. pesticide residue limits on imports of Mexican fruits and vegetables varies with different market conditions in the United States. A 1973 Canadian restriction on U.S. beef exports ostensibly was due to the growth hormone diethylstilbestrol, but allegedly aimed to limit a sharp surge of U.S. beef exports to Canada. *Washington Post*, April 10, 1974. For an analysis of environmentally related product standards, see Charles Pearson, *Environmental Policies and Their Trade Implications for Developing Countries, with Special Reference to Fish and Shellfish, Fruit and Vegetables* (New York: UN Conference on Trade

and Development, 1982).

4. See chapter 7 in this volume.

5. See Maynard Hufschmidt et al., *Environment, Natural Systems and Development: An Economic Valuation Guide* (Baltimore, Md.: The Johns Hopkins University Press, 1983).

6. Capital and labor markets can also be distorted, but the indicators of distortion such as unemployment and rationing are easier to spot.

7. Charles Pearson and Anthony Pryor, *Environment North and South* (New York: John Wiley, 1978), chap. 2.

8. For more comprehensive reviews, see Thomas Gladwin and John Wells, "Environmental Policy and Multinational Corporate Strategy," in Ingo Walter, ed., *Studies in International Environmental Economics* (New York: John Wiley, 1976); Pearson and Pryor, *Environment North and South*; Ingo Walter, "Environmentally Induced Industrial Relations to Developing Countries," in Seymour Rubin and Thomas Graham, eds., *Environment and Trade* (Totowa, N.J.: Allenheld, Osmon and Co., 1982); Christopher Duerksen, *Environmental Regulations of Plant Siting* (Washington, D.C.: The Conservation Foundation, 1983); H. Jeffrey Leonard, *Are Environmental Regulations Driving U.S. Industry Overseas?* (Washington, D.C.: The Conservation Foundation, 1984).

9. J. David Richardson and John Mutti, "Industrial Displacement Through Environmental Controls," in Ingo Walter, ed., *Studies in International Environmental Economics* (New York: John Wiley, 1976).

10. Charles Pearson, *Implications for the Trade and Investment of Developing Countries of United States Environmental Controls* (New York: UN Conference on Trade and Development, 1976).

11. Christopher Duerksen and H. Jeffrey Leonard, "Environmental Regulations and the Location of Industries: An International Perspective," *Columbia Journal of World Business*, Summer 1980, 52–58; Duerksen, *Environmental Regulations of Plant Siting*; Leonard, *Are Environmental Regulations Driving U.S. Industry Overseas?*

12. Howard Stafford et al., "The Effects of Environmental Regulations on Industrial Location: A Summary," University of Cincinnati, Cincinnati, Ohio, June 1983, mimeographed.

13. Gabriele Knödgen, "Environment and Industrial Siting: Results of an Empirical Survey of Investment by West German Industry in Developing Countries," *Zeitschrift für Umweltpolitik* 2 (1979).

14. Barry Castleman, "The Export of Hazardous Factories to Developing Countries," mimeographed, 1978.

15. See H. Jeffrey Leonard, *Pollution and Multinational Corporations in Rapidly Industrializing Nations* (Washington, D.C.: The Conservation Foundation, 1984).

**Chapter Six**

1. See S. Jacob Scherr and Ellen Spitalnik, "National Laws Relating to Exports of Chemicals, In Particular Pesticides: A Selected Review," a report prepared for the Environmental Liaison Centre, Nairobi, March 1984.

2. 42 *Federal Register* 18, 850–52 (1977).

3. 43 *Federal Register* 25, 711 (1978).

4. L. Kramer, "CPSC Probes Possible TRIS-Treated Exports," *Washington Post*, May 9, 1978.

5. Nor did the TRIS incident end in 1977. In 1981 TRIS-treated clothing processed in Ghana was being illegally marketed in the United States. "More U.S. Sales of TRIS-Treated Clothes Reported," *Washington Post*, February 21, 1981. TRIS was also found in the semen of Florida college students tested in 1981. R. Severo, "Chemical TRIS Found To Be in Seminal Fluid of Students in Florida," *New York Times*, February 22, 1981.

6. A similar example is the Dalkon Shield: the manufacturer withdrew it from the domestic market after seventeen women using it died in the United States but continued selling over half a million of the devices overseas. *New Internationalist*, November 1983, 7.

7. The Subcommittee on Commerce, Consumer, and Monetary Affairs of the House Committee on Government Operations held hearings in the summer of 1978 on the export of banned products. The subcommittee determined that over 300 pesticides, consumer products, food additives, medical devices, and other goods have been banned from domestic sale by the Environmental Protection Agency (EPA), the Food and Drug Administration, and the Consumer Product Safety Commission (CPSC). U.S. House of Representatives, Committee on Government Operations, *Report on Export of Products Banned by U.S. Regulatory Agencies*, H. R. Rep. No. 1686, 95th Cong., 2d Sess., 1978, 13. This number does not include other hazardous exports such as wastes. The subcommittee also concluded that, although it could not pinpoint the quantity of these products being exported, the volume was significant and the incidence of harm to foreign consumers was high enough to warrant a change in policy.

8. U.S. General Accounting Office, "Better Regulation of Pesticide Exports and Pesticide Residues in Imported Food Is Essential," Report to the Congress, CED-79-43, Washington, D.C., June 22, 1979, 50.

9. David Bull, *A Growing Problem: Pesticides and the Third World Poor* (Oxford: Oxfam, 1982), 6.

10. Ibid.

11. World Health Organization, *Safe Use of Pesticides*, 20th Report of the WHO Expert Committee on Insecticides, Technical Report Series No. 513 (Geneva, 1973). These are generally considered conservative estimates, since a large number of poisonings are either not diagnosed or not reported.

12. Bull, *A Growing Problem*, 37–38. Bull's investigation of pesticide poisonings in Sri Lanka indicates that poisonings in the Third World may be much higher than this (although a substantial number of deaths from pesticide poisoning are suicides): "From a population of only just over 14 million, two and a half times as many people are hospitalized for pesticide poisonings as in the U.S. and nearly five times as many die." Ibid., 43.

13. *Washington Post*, December 10, 1976.

14. E. Hughes, "How the Pink Death Came to Iraq," *Times of India*, September 9, 1973. See also Statement of Natural Resources Defense Council to the Subcommittee on International Economic Policy and Trade, House Foreign Affairs Committee, Concerning Exports of Hazardous Products, June 5, 1980.

15. See David Weir and Mark Schapiro, *Circle of Poison: Pesticides and People in a Hungry World* (San Francisco: Institute for Food and Development Policy, 1981). Bull, in chapters 4 and 5 of *A Growing Problem*, extensively documents a number of occupational and accidental poisonings in East Asian countries.

16. See Statement of Roque Sevilla of Fundacion Natura to the Subcommittee on Department Operations, Research, and Foreign Agriculture, House Committee on Agriculture, October 6, 1983.

17. David Kay, *The International Regulation of Pharmaceutical Drugs* (Washington, D.C.: American Society of International Law, 1975), 43.

18. J. Worrall, "Kenya Focusses on Drug Dumping in Third World," *Christian Science Monitor*, February 25, 1980. In 1981 Indian Prime Minister Indira Gandhi, in an address to the World Health Assembly, similarly expressed concern that "sometimes dangerous drugs [are] tried out on populations of weaker countries although their use [is] prohibited within the countries of manufacture." United Nations Office of Public Information, Press Section, "Prime Minister of India Addresses 34th World Health Assembly Currently Meeting in Geneva," Press Release H/2616, New York, May 6, 1981.

19. See Charles Medawar, *Insult or Injury?: An Inquiry Into the Marketing and Advertising of British Food and Drug Products in the Third World* (London: Social Audit, Ltd., 1979); "Statement of Dr. Milton Silverman," in *The Drug Regulation Reform Act of 1978: Hearings on H.R. 11611 Before the Subcommittee on Health and the Environment of the House Comm. on Interstate and Foreign Commerce*, 1978, 1322.

20. Morton Mintz, "The Dump That Killed Twenty Thousand," *Mother Jones*, November 1979, 43.

21. Alan Guttmacher Institute, "Special Report: The House Committee on Population," Washington, D.C., September 1, 1978, 2. The FDA bases its denial on the lack of a significant number of American patients requiring the drug.

22. H. Logan, "Third-World Demand for Contraceptive Raises Moral Issue," *Washington Post*, June 28, 1978.

23. See U.S. House of Representatives, Subcommittee on International Economic Policy and Trade of the Committee on Foreign Affairs, *Export of Hazardous Products*, Hearings, 96th Cong., 2nd Sess., 1980.

24. U.S. House of Representatives, *Report on Export of Products Banned*, 10.

25. Ibid.

26. "Inside: CPSC," *Washington Post*, May 3, 1984.

27. Organization for Economic Cooperation and Development, Letter to the Delegates to the Committee on Consumer Policy, DAF/CCP/943, EL/MM, January 2, 1980.

28. U.S. House of Representatives, *Report on Export of Products Banned*, 14.

29. For example, contaminated shrimp violating FDA regulations were exported to unnamed countries "less protective of citizens' health" in 1982. M. Hinds, "Tainted Shrimp," *New York Times*, April 30, 1982. PCB-contaminated eels from Lake Ontario that could not be sold in the United States were exported to Germany and the Netherlands. "A Slippery Deal: We Sell Eels We Can't Eat," *The Knickerbocker News* (Albany, N.Y.), July 28, 1981.

30. See, e.g., "Milestones: Ten Years of Struggle to Prevent 'Bottle Baby Disease'," Brief, Interfaith Center on Corporate Responsibility, New York, 1983. The infant formula campaign also led to adoption of a WHO code of conduct on infant formula marketing in May 1981.

31. "Baby Foods Row Renewed," *New Scientist*, May 17, 1984, 6; Consumers Union of Penang, "The Other Baby Killer," Penang, Malaysia, 1981.

32. Douglas M. Costle, Administrator, Environmental Protection Agency, remarks at National Governors Conference, Washington, D.C., February 27, 1979. Under Section 1004(5) of the Resources Conservation and Recovery Act of 1976 (42 U.S.C. 6903(4)), the term "hazardous wastes" is defined as "a solid waste, or combination of solid wastes which, because of its quantity, concentration, or physical, chemical, or infectious characteristics may:

(A) cause, or significantly contribute to an increase in mortality or an increase in serious irreversible, or incapacitating irreversible illness;

(B) pose a substantial present or potential hazard to human health or the environment when improperly treated, stored, transported, or disposed of, or otherwise managed."

33. Costle, remarks at National Governors Conference.

34. Philip Shabecoff, "U.S. Aroused by Industry Plans to Ship Toxic Wastes Abroad," *New York Times*, January 25, 1980; B. Richards, "U.S. Fights Export of Hazardous Wastes," *Washington Post*, January 26, 1980.

35. Richards, "U.S. Fights Exports." The State Department became concerned about possible adverse reactions to this proposal, warning that African nations might condemn the United States for "dumping its wastes in the black man's backyard." Despite the lack of any formal requirements on hazardous waste exports, in both this instance and several months later in regard to a proposal to ship wastes to Haiti, the State Department was concerned enough about the public health and foreign policy implications to undertake a number of diplomatic steps to discourage the proposals.

36. Richards, "U.S. Fights Exports."

37. D. Weissman, "Toxic Wastes May Find Way to Haitian Sites," *Sunday Star Ledger* (Newark, N.J.), February 10, 1980.

38. "Alabama and EPA to Examine Company's Waste Disposal Plan," *New York Times*, December 28, 1980.

39. "Deadly Exports," *Houston City Magazine*, March 1981.

40. David Dickson, "The Embarrassing Odyssey of Seveso's Dioxin," *Science*, June 24, 1983, 1362–63.

41. The relevant original statutes include the Federal Food, Drug, and Cosmetics Act; the Federal Insecticide, Fungicide, and Rodenticide Act (FIFRA); the Flammable Fabrics Act; the Toxic Substances Control Act; the Consumer Product Safety Act; and the Occupational Safety and Health Act. For a summary of the provisions' relation to exports of hazardous products, see the Carter administration's *Hazardous Substances Export Policy Draft Report*, attachment A, 45 *Federal Register* 53765-67 (1980).

42. U.S. House of Representatives, *Report on Export of Products Banned*, 3.

43. Consumer Product Safety Act, 15 U.S.C. 2051–81; the Flammable Fabrics Act, 15 U.S.C. 1191–1204; and the Federal Hazardous Substances Act, 15 U.S.C. 1261–74.

44. 7 U.S.C. 136 (1)(a). FIFRA also requires EPA to transmit to foreign nations and international agencies notification of the cancellation or suspension of domestic registration of pesticide products. 7 U.S.C. 136(1)(b).

45. 45 *Federal Register* 53754.

46. Joanne Omang, "Carter Limits U.S. Export of Banned Items," *Washington Post*, January 16, 1981.

47. Executive Order 12290, February 17, 1981.

48. Memorandum from President Reagan to the Secretary of Commerce and the Secretary of State, February 17, 1981.

49. Malcolm Baldridge, Secretary of Commerce, and Alexander M. Haig, Jr., Secretary of State, "Report to the President on the Review of U.S. Hazardous Substance Export Policy" (May 10, 1982), reprinted in *International Environment Reporter*, June 9, 1982, 267–71.

50. C. Mayer, "New Rules on Exports Supported," *Washington Post*, May 27, 1982.

51. Baldridge and Haig, "Report to the President," 269. Yet the Reagan Administration recognized that some controls on certain categories of hazardous exports should be retained. The Baldridge-Haig report did not recommend an end to export notices for defective consumer products and hazardous wastes.

52. Baldridge and Haig, "Report to the President," 268.

53. "Statement of Mary Rose Hughes," Deputy Assistant Secretary of State for Environment, Health, and Natural Resources, in U.S. House of Representatives, Subcommittee on Department Operations, Research and Foreign Agriculture, Committee on Agriculture, *Regulation of Pesticides*, 98th Cong., 1st Sess., 1983, 42.

54. Noncomplying items produced for export only can be shipped overseas with thirty days' notice to the CPSC under the 1978 amendments.

55. *Washington Post*, May 17, 1984.

56. Public Law 98–616, Title II, Sec. 245(a), November 8, 1984, 42 U.S.C. 6938.

57. *Congressional Record* H8163-4 (October 6, 1983).

58. 42 U.S.C. 6938(f).

59. *The Standard* (Nairobi, Kenya), May 11, 1977, 3.

60. United Nations Environment Programme, Compendium of Legislative Authority 244, "Human and Environmental Health," Decision 85(v), reprinted in U.S. House of Representatives, *Report on Export of Products Banned*, 76.

61. See UN General Assembly, resolutions 34/173, December 12, 1979; 35/186, December 15, 1980; and 36/166, December 16, 1981; and UN Document UNEP/GC.6/L8/Add.3, 1978.

62. See "OECD Council Adopts Recommendation on Export of Banned, Restricted Chemicals," *International Environment Reporter*, April 11, 1982, 100.

63. See "UNEP Group Agrees on Provisional Plan for Information Exchange on Chemicals," *International Environment Reporter*, April 11, 1984, 99.

64. Ibid.

65. UN Doc. a/37/679/Add.1, December 17, 1982.

66. "Consolidated List of Products Whose Consumption and/or Sale have been Banned, Withdrawn, Severely Restricted or Not Approved by Governments," First Issue, UN Secretariat, New York, December 30, 1983.

67. This language is from the fifth draft of the code; apparently there have not been significant changes in later drafts in the sections quoted here. Personal communication.

68. World Health Assembly, 37.33, May 17, 1982.

69. *Business International*, May 25, 1984.

70. "Statement of Mr. Robert Oldford," Vice Chairman, National Agricultural Chemicals Association, before the U.S. House of Representatives, Subcommittee on Department Operations, Research, and Foreign Agriculture, Committee on Agriculture, 98th Cong., 1st Sess., June 9, 1983, 175.

71. See, e.g., Jeane Kirkpatrick, "Global Paternalism: The U.N. and the New International Regulatory Order," *Regulation: The AEI Journal on Government and Society*, January/February 1983.

72. See Statement of Congressman Gibbons, U.S. House of Representatives, Subcommittee on International Economic Policy and Trade, Committee on Foreign Affairs, *Export of Hazardous Products*, Hearings, 96th Cong., 2nd Sess., 1980, 121.

73. See, e.g., letters from Patricia Sheehan, Johnson and Johnson, to Esther Peterson, October 28, 1980, and from Ira Frost, Norwich-Eaton Pharmaceuticals to Esther Peterson, September 10, 1980.

74. See letter from A. A. Abbass, Embassy of Nigeria, to Representative J. B. Bingham, July 22, 1980, reprinted in U.S. House of Representatives, *Export of Hazardous Products*, 405.

75. Mark Dowie, "The Corporate Crime of the Century," *Mother Jones*, November, 1979, 38.

76. U.S. General Accounting Office, "Better Regulation."

77. See Faith Halter, Attorney, EPA, "How to Improve International Notification Procedures and Toxic Substances under the United States Law," Washington, D.C., April 1984.

78. See Baldrige and Haig, "Report to the President"; letters from P. C. Carra, Upjohn Company, to Jack Blanchard, Department of State, July 1, 1983, and from George Ingle and Gabrielle Williamson, Chemical Manufacturers Association, to Jack Blanchard, July 6, 1983.

79. See statement of Susan B. King, Chairperson, CPSC, in U.S. House of Representatives, *Export of Hazardous Products*, 92.

80. Shabecoff, "U.S. Aroused by Industry Plans"; Richards, "U.S. Fights Export"; Wiessman, "Toxic Wastes May Find Way to Haitian Sites"; "Alabama and E.P.A. to Examine Plan," *New York Times*.

81. See, e.g., "Statement of Mr. Robert Oldford," before U.S. House of Representatives, Committee on Agriculture, 98th Cong., 1st Sess., June 9, 1983.

**Chapter Seven**

1. Rene Mendes, Pan American Health Organization, private communication, 1983.

2. A. C. Revkin, "Paraquat," *Science Digest*, June 1983, 36.

3. W. O. Phoon, "The Impact of Industrial Growth on Health in South-East Asia," in *Health and Industrial Growth* (Amsterdam: Elsevier Publishing Company, 1975), 107–26.

4. A. W. Hayes, ed., *Principles and Methods of Toxicology, Student Edition* (New York: Raven Press, 1984), 81–87.

5. Z. M. Khalfan, "Danger: Development at Work," *I.D.R.C. Reports*, October 1983, 12–15.

6. M. A. El Batawi, "Special Problems of Occupational Health in Developing Countries," in R. S. F. Schilling, ed., *Occupational Health Practice*, 2d ed. (London: Butterworths, 1981), 27–46.

7. Phoon, "Impact of Industrial Growth."

8. Christopher J. Duerksen, *Environmental Regulation of Industrial Plant Siting* (Washington,

D.C.: Conservation Foundation, 1983), 45–46; H. Jeffrey Leonard, *Are Environmental Regulations Driving U.S. Industry Overseas?* (Washington, D.C.: Conservation Foundation, 1984), 15–123.

9. R. R. Bonczek, Director of Safety, Health and Environmental Affairs, E. I. DuPont de Nemours Company, letter to B. Castleman, March 6, 1984.

10. Barry I. Castleman, "The Double Standard in Industrial Hazards," *International Journal of Health Services* 13, no. 1 (1983): 5–14; Barry I. Castleman and Manual J. Vera Vera, "Impending Proliferation of Asbestos," *International Journal of Health Services* 10 (1980): 389–403; Barry Castleman, "Double Standards: Asbestos in India," *New Scientist*, February 26, 1981, 522–23; Robert Wyrick, "Hazards for Export" (ten-part series), *Newsday*, December 1981; Mark Dowie, "The Corporate Crime of the Century," *Mother Jones*, November 1979, 23–49; Jerry S. Purswell et al., *Safety and Health Practices of Multinational Enterprises* (Geneva: International Labour Office, 1984), 70–72.

11. Castleman, "Asbestos in India"; Wyrick, "Hazards for Export."

12. Barry I. Castleman and Stephen L. Berger, *Asbestos: Medical and Legal Aspects* (New York: Law and Business, 1984), 295–353, 546; D. Berman, "Asbestos in Brazil: Bhopal in Slow Motion," *Exposure* (Environmental Action Foundation), January 1985, 1.

13. D. B. Hilder, "Insurance Industry Is Changing Policy for Basic Business Liability Coverage," *Wall Street Journal*, January 5, 1984.

14. Stuart Diamond, "Insurance Against Pollution is Cut," *New York Times*, March 11, 1985; D. Katzenberg, "Coping with the Insurance Shortage," *Chemical Week*, May 15, 1985, 21–22.

15. Castleman, "Double Standards in Industrial Hazards"; Castleman and Vera Vera, "Proliferation of Asbestos"; Castleman, "Asbestos in India"; Wyrick, "Hazards for Export"; Dowie, "Corporate Crime of the Century"; Castleman, *Asbestos*; Ruth Norris and A. Karim Ahmed, eds., *Pills, Pesticides, and Profits: The International Trade in Toxic Substances* (Croton-on-Hudson, N.Y.: North River Press, 1982); David Weir and Mark Schapiro, *Circle of Poison: Pesticides and People in a Hungry World* (San Francisco: Institute for Food and Development Policy, 1982); David Bull, *A Growing Problem: Pesticides and the Third World Poor* (Oxford: Oxfam, 1982); Milton Silverman and Philip R. Lee, *Prescriptions for Death: The Drugging of the Third World* (Berkeley, Calif.: University of California Press, 1982); T. Heller, *Poor Health, Rich Profits: Multinational Drug Companies and the Third World* (Nottingham, England: Spokesman Books, 1977).

16. Bonczek, letter to Castleman.

17. Castleman, "Asbestos in India"; Wyrick, "Hazards for Export."

18. *Domingo, Castro, Alfaro et al. v. Dow Chemical Co. et al.*, 113th Judicial District Court, Harris County, Texas, no. 84-17171.

19. "DBCP Victims Settle Suit," *Chemical Week*, January 4, 1984, 15.

20. Anil Agarwal, Juliet Merrifield, and Rajesh Tandon, *No Place to Run: Local Realities and Global Issues of the Bhopal Disaster* (New Market, Tenn.: Highlander Research and Education Center, 1985); Barry I. Castleman and Prabir Purkayastha, "The Bhopal Disaster as a Case Study in Double Standards," in *The Export of Hazard*, ed. Jane H. Ives, (Boston: Routledge & Kegan Paul, 1985).

21. Castleman, "Asbestos in India."

22.  R. K. Rangan, "Proof of Cancer Among Men in Asbestos Units," *Times of India*, March 27, 1981.

23.  Centre for Education and Documentation, "Asbestos: The Dust That Kills," Bombay, India, July 1983.

24.  Wyrick, "Hazards for Export."

25.  Yorkshire Television, "Alice: A Fight for Life," broadcast on July 14, 1982.

26.  Centre for Education and Documentation, "Asbestos."

27.  Ibid.

28.  Barry I. Castleman, "The Export of Hazardous Factories to Developing Countries," *International Journal of Health Services* 9 (1979): 569–606.

29.  M. A. Mendoza, "La Muerte Fra un Polvo Amarililo Sobre Lecheria," *Excelsior* (Mexico City), June 6, 1978.

30.  Wyrick, "Hazards for Export"; A. Hassan et al., "Mercury Poisoning in Nicaragua," *International Journal of Health Services* 11 (1981): 221–26.

31.  D. Kowalewski, "Pennwalt—Under Pressure—Cleans Up Mercury Contamination," *Multinational Monitor*, April 1983, 8.

32.  T. Kirayama, "Exporting Pollution," *Kogai—The Newsletter from Polluted Japan*, Winter 1974; "Action Committee to Stop Toyama Kagaku's Pollution Export: The Voices of the People of Japan and South Korea Encircle Nihon Kagaku," *AMPO: Japan-Asia Quarterly Review*, October–December 1975; *Kogai—The Newsletter from Polluted Japan*, Spring 1975.

33.  J. Rocamora, "Japanese Capital in the Philippines: Exploiting to Develop," *Southeast Asia Chronicle*, February 1983, 10–13.

34.  Yamaka Junko, "More Pollution Export by Japan," *AMPO: Japan-Asia Quarterly*, January–March 1985.

35.  Ibid.

36.  "Showdown for Drug Firms in Bangladesh," *New Scientist*, November 11, 1982, 344; M. Cross, "Kenya to Ban Dangerous Pesticides," *New Scientist*, March 27, 1983, 705.

37.  J. Martin, "Consumer and Corporate Codes Widen North-South Split," *Multinational Monitor*, February 1984, 5–6.

38.  Eileen Nic, Coordinating Committee on Toxics and Drugs, Natural Resources Defense Council, New York, personal communication, June 28, 1985.

39.  Marcos Arruda, ed., *Transnational Corporations, Technology, and Human Development* (Geneva: World Council of Churches, 1981), 13.

40.  Agricultural Chemicals Dialog Group, "Guidelines for Advertising Practices in the Promotion of Pesticide Products in the Developing Areas of the World," National Agricultural Chemicals Association, October 1983; "A Meeting of Minds on Pesticides Ads Overseas," *Chemical Week*, November 9, 1983, 29–30; "Coalition Adopts Pesticide Labeling Guidelines," *Chemical Week*, April 10, 1985, 44.

41.  "Hazard Export: A Case for International Concern" (editorial), *Nature*, June 8, 1978, 415; "Trouble for Export" (editorial), *Washington Post*, August 27, 1979.

42.  International Labour Office, *Occupational Safety, Health, and Working Conditions, and the Transfer of Technology* (Geneva: 1982).

43.  World Health Organization, "Global Medium-Term Programme/Programme 9.3/Workers' Health," Geneva, June 1983.

44.  Ibid.

45. UN Environment Programme, "Interagency Consultations on Follow-up to the *Ad Hoc* Meeting of Senior Government Officials Expert in the Environmental Law—Phase I, No. 83-5300," Geneva, February 14, 1983.

46. Ibid.

47. Sheldon Samuels, *National Stewardship: Unilateral International Regulation of Occupational and Environmental Hazards* (Washington, D.C.: Industrial Union Dept., AFL-CIO, 1980).

48. Barry Castleman, "Reply to Levenstein-Eller Critique," *International Journal of Health Services* 11 (1981): 311.

49. "Ban on Benzidine Import Proposed to Protect U.S. and Foreign Workers," *Occupational Safety and Health Reports*, February 28, 1985, 747–48.

50. "S. Africa Sanctions Okd," *Baltimore Sun*, May 5, 1983.

51. G. M. Kober and E. R. Hayhurst, *Industrial Health* (Philadelphia: P. Blackiston & Son, 1924), 24.

52. W. G. Simeral, "One View: The Chemical Industry and the Environment," paper presented at the General Policy Committee of the Council of Chemical Manufacturers' Federations, Brussels, December 6, 1983.

**Chapter Eight**

1. This section draws on Environmental Problems Foundation of Turkey, *Environmental Profile of Turkey* (Ankara: 1981), which should be consulted for a more complete description of Turkish environmental problems and for references to the studies cited here.

2. World Health Organization, *Air Quality Criteria and Guides for Urban Air Pollutants*, Technical Report 506 (Geneva: 1972).

3. The tables are based on data in Ridvan Karluk, *Türkiye'de Yabanci Sermaye Yatirimlari* (Foreign Private Investment in Turkey) (Istanbul, 1983); Kazim Oksay, *Guide to Foreign Capital Investment in Turkey* (Ankara: 1967); Türkiye Çevre Sorunlari Vakfi, Turkiye'nin Çevre Sorunlari (Ankara: Environmental Problems Foundation of Turkey, 1983); T. Gungor Uras, *Yabanci Sermaye Yatirimlari* (Foreign Private Investment) (Istanbul: Economic Publications Ltd., 1979); and Nuri Yildirim, *Uluslararasi Sirketler* (Multinational Corporations) (Istanbul: United Publications Ltd., 1979).

4. Fourth Five Year Development Plan, *Official Gazette*, December 12, 1978.

5. English translation of the Environment Law published by the Environmental Problems Foundation of Turkey, November 1983.

**Chapter Nine**

1. R. V. Costa, "Demographic Growth and Environmental Pollution," BNH Information Office, Rio de Janeiro, Brazil, undated.

**Chapter Ten**

1. See Russell Mokhiber, "Paying for Bhopal: Union Carbide's Campaign to Limit Its Liability," *Multinational Monitor*, July 31, 1985, 1–5; "Union Carbide Fights for Its

Life," *Business Week*, December 12, 1984, 52–61; Stuart Diamond, "Doing Business in the Third World: Chemical Leak Prompts Debate," *New York Times*, December 16, 1984; Robert Engler, "Many Bhopals: Technology Out of Control," *The Nation*, April 27, 1985, 488–500; Gus Speth, "No More Bhopals," *The Amicus Journal*, Winter 1985, 3–4; and Charles S. Pearson, "What Has to be Done to Prevent More Bhopals," *Washington Post*, December 9, 1984.

2. For general surveys of the tragedy, see "Bhopal: City of Death," *India Today*, December 31, 1984, 4–25; Richard I. Kirkland, Jr., "Union Carbide: Coping with Catastrophe," *Fortune*, January 7, 1985, 50–53; "Indian Tragedy Raises Big Questions," *Not Man Apart*, January 1985, 1; "It Was Like Breathing Fire," *Newsweek*, December 17, 1984, 26–44; "India's Bhopal Disaster: Chemical Mishap Raises Thorny Issues," *Chemical and Engineering News*, December 17, 1984, 22–24; "Gassed in Bhopal," *The Economist*, December 15, 1984, 12–14; "Home Truths About Bhopal," *New Scientist*, December 13, 1984, 2; "India's Bhopal Disaster Raises Important Issues for MNCs, Governments," *Business Asia*, December 14, 1984, 393–94; Robert D. McFadden, "India Disaster: Chronicle of a Disaster," *New York Times*, December 10, 1984; "Bhopal Report," *Chemical and Engineering News*, February 11, 1985, 16–65; Stuart Diamond, "The Disaster in Bhopal: Lessons for the Future," *New York Times*, February 3, 1985; and Stephen J. Adler, "Carbide Plays Hardball," *The American Lawyer*, November 1985, 27–62.

3. See Stuart Diamond, "Combined Bhopal Suit is Filed," *New York Times*, June 29, 1985; "Spurred by Bhopal, Florio Readies a Batch of Bills," *Chemical Week*, January 30, 1985, 82; "Bhopal: Legislative Fallout in the U.S.," *Chemical Week*, February 6, 1985, 26–28; "Bhopal: A Less Frenzied Legislative Pace Abroad," *Chemical Week*, February 6, 1985, 29–30; Patrick P. McCurdy, "Bridging the Bhopal Gap," *Chemical Week*, May 1, 1985, 3; Barry Meier, "Use of Right to Know Rules is Increasing Public's Scrutiny of Chemical Companies," *Wall Street Journal*, May 23, 1985; and Stuart Diamond, "Warren Anderson: A Public Crisis; a Personal Ordeal," *New York Times*, May 19, 1985.

4. "Union Carbide on Bhopal: Excerpts from Report and Comments on Company's Inquiry," *New York Times*, March 21, 1985; Barry Meier and Robert Friedman, "Union Carbide Corp. Suggests Sabotage Caused Disastrous Leak of Gas in India," *Wall Street Journal*, August 5, 1985.

5. Stuart Diamond, "Union Carbide's Inquiry Indicates Errors Led to India Plant Disaster," *New York Times*, March 21, 1985.

6. "A New Legal Claim: Multinational Enterprise Liability," *Multinational Monitor*, July 31, 1985, 5; Barry Meier, "Union Carbide's Report on Bhopal Criticized by India," *Wall Street Journal*, March 22, 1985.

7. Thomas J. Lueck, "Carbide a Year After Bhopal," *New York Times*, December 3, 1985.

8. For a survey of the issues regarding forum, see Adler, "Carbide Plays Hardball."

9. Adler, "Carbide Plays Hardball."

10. Tamar Lewin, "Carbide is Sued in U.S. by India in Gas Disaster," *New York Times*, April 9, 1985; "India Sues Carbide in New York," *Chemical Week*, April 17, 1985, 15; Barry Meier, "Union Carbide Chief Criticizes Indians for Rejecting Offer on Bhopal Claims," *Wall Street Journal*, April 25, 1985; "Carbide Talks Peace But Girds for War," *Business Week*, April 29, 1985, 28–29; "Gandhi Sees Slim Hope for Bhopal Settlement,"

*New York Times*, June 5, 1985; Stuart Diamond, "Meetings on Bhopal Resuming," *New York Times*, June 17, 1985; Barry Meier and James B. Stewart, "A Year After Bhopal, Union Carbide Faces a Slew of Problems," *Wall Street Journal*, November 26, 1985.

11. Stuart Diamond, "Carbide-India Talks On Bhopal Resume," *New York Times*, January 27, 1986; Barry Meier, "Carbide Stock Price Soars on Speculation That Assets Sale May Bring $2.5 Billion," *Wall Street Journal*, February 27, 1986.

12. Diamond, "Carbide-India Talks On Bhopal Resume."

13. This section draws upon Thomas N. Gladwin, "The Bhopal Tragedy: Lessons for Management," *NYU Business*, Spring/Summer 1985, 17–21.

14. See Thomas N. Gladwin and Ingo Walter, "Bhopal and the Multinational," *Wall Street Journal*, January 16, 1985.

15. "Union Carbide Starts Inspecting Two U.S. Plants," *Wall Street Journal*, December 5, 1984.

16. Barry Meier, "Union Carbide Wanted Large Amounts of Chemical at Bhopal, Ex-Aide Asserts," *Wall Street Journal*, February 4, 1985.

17. Ron Winslow, "Union Carbide Confirms That Problems With Tanks in India Were Found in 1982," *Wall Street Journal*, December 11, 1984; Thomas J. Lueck, "1982 Report Cited Safety Problems at Plant in India," *New York Times*, December 11, 1984.

18. Stuart Diamond, "The Disaster in Bhopal: Workers Recall Horror," *New York Times*, January 30, 1985.

19. Philip Shabecoff, "Union Carbide Had Been Told of Leak Danger," *New York Times*, January 26, 1985; Christopher Joyce, "Bhopal's Engineers Not Told of Safety Fears," *New Scientist*, January 31, 1985, 4.

20. Diamond, "The Disaster in Bhopal: Lessons For The Future"; see also Cathy Frost, "Danger Zone: Chemical Plant Safety is Still Just Developing in Developing Nations," *Wall Street Journal*, December 13, 1984.

21. "Belated Awakening," *India Today*, January 31, 1985, 62–63.

22. Stuart Diamond, "The Bhopal Disaster: How It Happened," *New York Times*, January 28, 1985.

23. Charles Perrow, *Normal Accidents: Living with High Risk Technology* (New York: Basic Books, 1984).

24. Diamond, "The Bhopal Disaster: How It Happened."

25. For summaries of these investigations, see "Questions Unfold Over Bhopal," *Chemical Week*, August 7, 1985, 8–9; Steven R. Weisman, "Bhopal Leak Not Sabotage, Report Says," *New York Times*, December 21, 1985.

26. Diamond, "The Bhopal Disaster: How It Happened"; see also Inderjit Badhwar, "Exporting Hazards," *India Today*, January 15, 1985, 54–57.

27. Diamond, "The Bhopal Disaster: How It Happened"; see also Barry Newman, "Death in Bhopal: Compensation Seems Not Quite the Point," *Wall Street Journal*, December 19, 1984, and Sanjoy Hazarika, "An Indian Union Leader Blames Both State and Managers for Leak," *New York Times*, December 17, 1984.

28. Stuart Diamond, "1982 Inspector Says Indian Plant Was Below U.S. Safety Standards," *New York Times*, December 12, 1983.

29. Mokhiber, "Paying for Bhopal: Union Carbide's Campaign to Limit Its Liability."

30. "Carbide's Report: How Bhopal Happened," *Chemical Week*, March 27, 1985, 8; Barry

Meier, "Union Carbide Says Bhopal Facility Should Have Been Shut Before Accident," *Wall Street Journal*, March 21, 1985.

31. "Bhopal: City of Death," *India Today*, 9–10.

32. "Publication Says Carbide Tried to Sell Bhopal Plant," *Wall Street Journal*, December 17, 1984; "India Frees 2 Carbide Officials," *New York Times*, December 15, 1984; "Carbide Did Not Know of Plant Details," *Financial Times* (London), December 12, 1984; Robert Reinhold, "Disaster in Bhopal: Where Does Blame Lie?" *New York Times*, January 31, 1985; "Pesticide Plant Started as a Showpiece but Ran into Troubles," *New York Times*, February 3, 1985; Stuart Diamond, "Discrepancies Are Seen in Bhopal Court Papers," *New York Times*, January 3, 1986.

33. Diamond, "The Bhopal Disaster: How It Happened."

34. Diamond, "The Disaster in Bhopal: Workers Recall Horror."

35. Wil Lepkowski, "People of India Struggle Toward Appropriate Response to Tragedy," *Chemical and Engineering News*, February 11, 1985, 19.

36. William K. Stevens, "Workers At Site of Leak Described as Unskilled," *New York Times*, December 6, 1984.

37. "Indian Tragedy Raises Big Questions," *Not Man Apart*.

38. "Bhopal: City of Death," *India Today*, 10.

39. Diamond, "The Bhopal Disaster: How It Happened."

40. Diamond, "Warren Anderson"; "Carbide Did Not Know of Plant Details," *Financial Times*; "Union Carbide: The Safety Factor," *The Economist*, December 22, 1984, 72; "Carbide's Search For Answers," *Chemical Week*, December 19, 1984; "Questions Unfold Over Bhopal," *Chemical Week*, August 7, 1985.

41. See Gladwin and Walter, "Bhopal and the Multinationals." "Local adaptation" is a rather common pattern for MNC's in the environmental area. See Thomas N. Gladwin and Ingo Walter, *Multinationals Under Fire: Lessons in the Management of Conflict* (New York: John Wiley, 1980), chap. 12.

42. "Union Carbide on Bhopal," *New York Times*.

43. Diamond, "The Bhopal Disaster: How It Happened."

44. Diamond, "Union Carbide's Inquiry Indicates Errors."

45. Ron Winslow, "Union Carbide Move to Ban Accident at U.S. Plant Before Bhopal Tragedy," *Wall Street Journal*, January 28, 1985; Barry Meier and Ron Winslow, "Union Carbide Faces a Difficult Challenge Even Without Bhopal," *Wall Street Journal*, December 27, 1984.

46. "Carbide's Report," *Chemical Week*, 10.

47. "Toxic Cloud Leaks at Carbide Plant in West Virginia," *New York Times*, August 12, 1985.

48. Diamond, "1982 Inspector Says Indian Plant was Below U.S. Safety Standards."

49. "Gas Deaths in India Exceed 1,000, with Thousands Hurt; Gandhi Seeks Compensation," *New York Times*, December 5, 1984.

50. Reinhold, "Disaster in Bhopal."

51. "Like Breathing Fire," *Newsweek*, 30.

52. "The Legal Damage," *India Today*, January 15, 1985, 60–63; Mokhiber, "Paying for Bhopal."

53. "Bhopal: City of Death," *India Today*; Sanjoy Hazarika, "Indian Journalist Warned of a Leak," *New York Times*, December 11, 1984.

54. "Bhopal: City of Death," *India Today*, 23.
55. "Belated Awakening," *India Today*, 62.
56. Reinhold, "Disaster in Bhopal."
57. Matt Miller, "Words Still Speak Louder Than Deeds," *Wall Street Journal*, November 26, 1985.
58. Diamond, "Doing Business in Third World."
59. Newman, "Death in Bhopal: Compensation Seems Not Quite the Point"; "Bhopal: City of Death," *India Today*, 23.
60. "The Legal Damage," *India Today*, 62; Diamond, "The Disaster in Bhopal: Lessons for the Future."
61. Hazarika, "Indian Union Leader Blames Both State and Managers."
62. "Belated Awakening," *India Today*, 63; see also Frost, "Danger Zone: Chemical Plant Safety Still Just Developing."
63. "Gassed in Bhopal," *The Economist*; "India's Bhopal Disaster Raises Important Issues for MNCs, Governments," *Business Asia*, December 14, 1984, 393–94.
64. William K. Stevens, "In Bhopal, Signs of Tragedy Are Everywhere," *New York Times*, December 10, 1984; Stevens, "Workers at Site Described as Unskilled."
65. Stuart Diamond, "Carbide Says Indians Altered Bhopal Design," *New York Times*, December 21, 1985.
66. Robert James Bidinotto, "Bhopal: The Fruit of Industrial Policy," *The Intellectual Activist*, July 19, 1985, 2–5.
67. Gladwin and Walter, "Bhopal and the Multinationals."
68. Bidinotto, "Bhopal: The Fruit of Industrial Policy," 2.
69. "Belated Awakening," *India Today*, 63.
70. See James B. Stewart, "Legal Liability: Why Suits for Damages Such as Bhopal Claims Are Very Rare in India," *Wall Street Journal*, January 23, 1985; "The Legal Damage," *India Today*; Tamar Lewin, "Bhopal Claims: A Vast Burden," *New York Times*, February 2, 1985; and Diamond, "Carbide Says Indians Altered Bhopal Design."
71. "Union Carbide Fights for Its Life," *Business Week*, 60–61; "Liability Insurance: The Added Burden of Bhopal," *Chemical Week*, February 13, 1985, 30–31.
72. Stuart Diamond, "Sweeping Insurance Changes May Increase Business Costs," *New York Times*, June 11, 1985; Carol J. Loomis, "Naked Came the Insurance Buyer," *Fortune*, June 10, 1985, 67–72.
73. "The Biggest Disaster for Insurers is America's Courts," *The Economist*, August 24, 1985; "Where High Risk Companies Run for Coverage," *Business Week*, July 22, 1985, 72.
74. "Coping with the Insurance Shortage," *Chemical Week*, May 15, 1985, 20–57; "Businesses Struggling to Adapt as Insurance Crisis Spreads," *Wall Street Journal*, January 21, 1986, 31.
75. William K. Stevens, "Legions of Lawyers Alighting to Prepare Big Damage Suits," *New York Times*, December 12, 1984.
76. "Text of Declaration at End of 7 Nation Economic Conference," *New York Times*, May 5, 1985.

**Chapter Eleven**

1. "Chemical Safety in Developing Countries: The Lessons of Bhopal," *Chemical and Engineering News*, April 8, 1985, 9.
2. Lynne M. Miller, "Environmental Focus Shifts to Overseas Risks," *National Underwriter*, April 12, 1985, 44; R. A. Finlayson, "Consultants Questioned About Bhopal Disaster," *Business Insurance*, February 18, 1985, 36.
3. Union Carbide Corporation, "Bhopal Methyl Isocyanate Incident Investigation Team Report," Danbury, Conn., March 1985.
4. "Can Union Carbide India Survive The Bhopal Disaster?" *Business World* (Bombay), May 27–June 9, 1985, 46–60.
5. Barry I. Castleman and Prabir Purkayastha, "The Bhopal Disaster as Case Study in Double Standards," in *The Export of Hazard*, ed. Jane Ives (Boston: Routledge and Kegan Paul, 1985); see also Barry I. Castleman, "The Double Standard in Industrial Hazards," *International Journal of Health Services* 13 no. 2 (1983): 5–14.
6. The Indian press was especially thorough and enterprising in its coverage of the details of the disaster. See especially accounts during December 1984 and January 1985 in editions of the *Times of India* by Praful Bidwai, Hindi language accounts of problems rising in Bhopal by journalist Rajkumar Keswani of the *Indian Express* newspaper group, and a comprehensive account of the disaster in *India Today* on December 31, 1984. The key American sources are *Chemical Week*, December 1984; *Chemical and Engineering News*, especially February 11 and April 8, 1985; and the *New York Times'* investigation of the disaster by Stuart Diamond, January 1985. Reports on the disaster by the Delhi Science Forum and Eklavya are important for the perspective of science and public policy activist groups in India, as is "Report of the ICFTU-ICEF Mission to Study the Causes and Effects of the Methyl Isocyanate Gas Leak at the Union Carbide Pesticide Plant in Bhopal, India," International Confederation of Free Trade Unions, July 1985.
7. "Can Union Carbide India Survive?"
8. B. Bowonder, Jeanne X. Kasperson, and Roger E. Kasperson, "Avoiding Future Bhopals," *Environment*, September 1985, 6–13, 31–37.
9. Vishwanath Pratap Singh, "We're Gearing For Takeoff," *India Today*, April 15, 1985, 22–31.
10. K. Nagaraja Rao, Raymond F. Baddour, and Christopher Hill, "Strategic Aspects of Chemical Industry Development in the Rapidly Industrializing Nations," *Technology in Society* 4 (1982): 145–53.
11. See, for example, Nicholas D. Kristof, "Curbs Give Way to Welcome for Multinational Companies," *New York Times*, May 13, 1985; "Here Come the Multinationals of the Third World," *Economist*, July 23, 1983; "Bhopal Should Not Stop Cooperative Development" (letter from J. B. Sumarlin, Minister of Planning, Republic of Indonesia), *New York Times*, March 2, 1985.
12. Tamil Nadu, Chemical Manufacturers Association, "The Bhopal Episode and Its Implications," Madras, India, January 1985.
13. *World Labour Report*, vol. 2 (Geneva: International Labour Organisation, 1985).
14. See, for example, Bill Paul, "How a Drug Company Deals With Disputes Over Its Medicines," *Wall Street Journal*, June 1, 1984.

15. George Ledec and Robert Goodland, "The Role of Environmental Management in Sustainable Economic Development," presented at Annual Meeting of International Association of Impact Assessment, May 24–25, 1984.

16. Richard J. Meislin, "Mexico's Wayward Waste," *New York Times*, March 14, 1985.

17. Dilip Mukerjee, personal communication, January 1985.

18. Bowonder, Kasperson, and Kasperson, "Avoiding Future Bhopals."

19. Jerry S. Purswell et al., *Safety and Health Practices of Multinational Enterprises* (Geneva: International Labour Organisation, 1984); see also Anil Agarwal, Juliet Merrifield, and Rajesh Tandon, *No Place to Run—Local Realities and Global Issues of the Bhopal Disaster* (New Market, Tenn.: Highlander Research and Education Center, 1985).

20. Purswell, *Safety and Health Practices*.

21. "The Chemical Industry and Accident Prevention," *Industry and Environment*, October–December 1983.

22. David H. Ott, "Bhopal and the Law: The Shape of a New International Legal Regime," *Third World Quarterly*, July 1985, 648–60.

23. Ibid.

24. Miller, "Environmental Focus Shifts"; Finlayson, "Consultants Questioned."

# Index

HC59.72
E5M85
1987

ACA 8369

hill

BM